This is an authorized facsimile, made from the master copy of the original book.

Out-of-Print Books on Demand is a publishing service of UMI. The program offers xerographic reprints of more than 100,000 books that are no longer in print.

The primary focus is academic and professional resource materials originally published by university presses, academic societies and trade book publishers worldwide.

U·M·I Out-of-Print
Books on Demand

University Microfilms International
A Bell & Howell Information Company
300 N. Zeeb Road. Ann Arbor, Michigan 48106
800-521-0600 OR 313/761-4700

Printed in 1991 by xerographic process
on acid-free paper

The
Novel
before the
Novel

The
Novel
before the
Novel

Essays and Discussions
about the Beginnings
of Prose Fiction
in the West

Arthur Heiserman

The University of Chicago Press
Chicago & London

THE UNIVERSITY OF CHICAGO PRESS, CHICAGO 60637
THE UNIVERSITY OF CHICAGO PRESS, LTD., LONDON

© 1977 by The University of Chicago
All rights reserved. Published 1977
Paperback Edition 1980
Printed in the United States of America
8 7 6 5 4 3 2   81 80

Library of Congress Cataloging in Publication Data
Heiserman, Arthur Ray, 1929–1975
  The novel before the novel.

  Includes bibliographical references and index.
  1. Classical fiction — History and criticism.
I. Title.
PA3040.H38   809.3   76-8102
ISBN 0-226-32573-3

Contents

Prefatory Note

Arthur Heiserman finished this book on Sunday, November 23, 1975. He died sixteen days later, a month short of his forty-seventh birthday.

The book was to be the first of several devoted to the analysis of early fictions. The author was especially eager to write the volume on medieval fictions, about which he felt he had many new things to say. Perhaps one of his students will be able to graft his notes onto a continuation of this critical history.

Although the author had thought of such a book for a decade or more, the actual work was blocked out in the spring of 1971 after he'd learned that he had a melanoma. For four years he worked assiduously and lived intensely, so intensely that most of us thought the cancer had been checked. The author remained vigorous in every way until the last weeks of his life. In late October 1975 he told me he'd just about finished the book. It had all but a final summary dialogue, which he was simply too tired to write. It would have to end where it did.

As he did not live to read over the final typescript, let alone the galleys, there remain a few dark sentences in the text. Nonetheless, I believe the book is very close to the one he would have seen through the press.

Richard Stern

Preface

The present volume is designed as the first of three books that will attempt to trace certain persistent habits of art in long narratives written in the West between the third century B.C. and the seventeenth century A.D. It is meant, however, to stand on its own. Since I believe that literary history must honor the uniqueness of poetic works, I have devoted my substantive essays to individual novels and relegated discussion of the more general problems aroused by the essays to various dialogues. Friends have advised me to eliminate these discussions from my text altogether. I have in the end rejected this advice but pass it on to the reader.

I must acknowledge most helpful readings from my colleagues, Anne Burnett and James Redfield. Neither of these friends, however, could obliterate all the errors of fact and judgment that must remain in my text. I acknowledge also the patient support of my wife and children over the years consumed by this study.

The
Novel
before the
Novel

❧ I ❧
Erotic
Suffering

This book offers explorations, not exhaustive analyses, of the earliest Western novels, along with discussions sketching what some modern critics might make of the explorations. It aims to discover a few of the aesthetic, psychological, and cultural powers that vivify several long stories written between the third century B.C. and the fourth century A.D. These time limits are somewhat arbitrary. A study of origins ought to begin before the Flood, with Homer; and a history of early narrative art might well work itself through the tenth century, embracing saints' lives and histories and fictions long and short, composed in verse as well as prose. But the origins of literary species pose such special problems of causation that the present inquiry must confine itself almost entirely to full-blown specimens of only one perennial kind of Western art: the extended prose fictions called novels or romances. Moreover it is a history of this kind of art only in an old Greek sense of the term "history": it is a reasoned inquiry into what happened.

The materials that prompt such an inquiry are scant. A few papyrus fragments of long prose fictions survive from the first two centuries before Christ, but only four of these so-called Greek romances are extant: *Chaereas and Callirrhoë*, written by a legal secretary named Chariton about 50 A.D.; Longus' *Daphnis and Chloë* and Achilles Tatius' *Leucippe and Clitophon*, both probably composed in the 160s A.D.; and Heliodorus' *Ethiopian Story*, written in the 230s A.D. Two others come down in epitomes—an extensive summary of the *Ephesian Story* by Xenophon of Ephesus (made shortly before 150 A.D.) and a much shorter one of the *Babyloniaca* by Iamblichus (written around 165 A.D.).[1] Several other narratives, Latin as well as Greek, also demand discussions here: the anonymous *Apollonius of Tyre*, the Clementine *Recognitions*,

3

the *Alexander Romance*, and Apuleius' famous *Metamorphoses*, or *Golden Ass*. Apuleius aside, little or nothing is known about the authors of these complicated novels.

The English term "novel" is of course anachronistic when applied to these old stories, most of which are usually called "romances." How the English language, unlike any other, came to associate *the novel* with realism and *romance* with fantasy need not concern us.[2] But we cannot entirely ignore the fact that "the word Romance is apt to prejudice many against all works under that title; as supposing them to be a mere rhapsody of incredible events; treating of puerile loves, and written in an inflated and unnatural style."[3] And we must point out that the Greek romances work with "novel"—that is, untraditional—stories drawn from the realities of ordinary life, while some of them also deal with the idealizations of love, adventure, and heroism we associate with romance. Since an unacknowledged impression in genre terms can distort inquiry, we might try to resolve this terminological difficulty by adopting the Continental usage, wherein *roman* denotes any long fiction, realistic or fantastic, and *nouvelle* denotes a short one. Or we might contrive our own critical lexicon, based on the fact that adjectives derived from one set of genre terms (romantic, satiric, tragic, comic) can modify nouns derived from another set (drama, epic, lyric, novel). Or we might assume that "romance" is a form laid up in heaven or down in history and define it freshly into existence. But a priori definitions of literary forms, and defiances of common usage, usually do more harm than good. We may therefore cheerfully acknowledge that there must be good reasons why most of the works explored in this inquiry suffer under the pejorative title "romance," provided that we are prepared to discover that they differ radically from one another and that many might as aptly be called comic or pastoral or didactic or romantic novels.

But did the Greeks have a word for the Greek romances? Chariton of Aphrodisia, the author of the earliest extant romantic novel, called his work a story of *erōtika pathēmata*—"a story of erotic sufferings." The term had some currency among the Hellenes. About 30 B.C. Vergil's Greek tutor, an Alexandrian poet named Parthenius, sent to his Roman friend Cornelius Gallus epitomes of several dozen stories he calls *erōtika pathēmata*. They are out-of-the-way *mythoi*, already mishandled, he says, by a few poets, and he hopes that the collection of summaries will provide Gallus with "a storehouse from which to draw material, as may seem best to you, for either epic or elegiac verse."[4] They do indeed suggest the serious treatment appropriate to such verse. In the third epitome, for example, Odysseus slays his bastard son (by Evippe) as a result of Penelope's intrigues and is later slain by another of his bastards (this one by Circe). Most deal with the disasters of love, but not all: in number thirty-three, Heracles, wandering among the Celts, is seduced by Bretannus' daughter Celtine, who produces a son named Celtus, "from whom the Celtic race derived their name." And love's pathetic horrors are not reserved to legendary figures. Number seventeen explains why the historical Periander became such an outrageous tyrant at Corinth. His mother contracted a secret passion for him and offered to procure for him a lovely lady—provided he keep all lights doused. But Periander fell in love with his invisible and silent mistress and one night lit a lamp. Stifling a desire to kill the mother he sees in his bed, he runs mad, "affected in brain and heart," and slays many citizens. Other *erōtika pathēmata* deal with nonhistorical material drawn from "ordinary life"; in number five, for example, a bourgeois father discovers his son and daughter in bed together (they have their mother's secret blessing), stabs the girl, and is slain by his son.

Apparently, the term *erōtika pathēmata* designates a kind of story material suitable for serious treatment in verse or prose, at greater or shorter length. Serious erotic suffering would seem to be most thrillingly manifested in the deeds of horror, perpetrated by well-known figures, which the ancients associated with epic and tragedy; but incest, madness, and murder might also be suffered by the unknown "invented" personages whom the ancients associated with dramatic comedy. And suffering love, even when treated more seriously than it would be in a comedy, need not determine a "tragic" denouement. A Greek romance can blend, in a single story about erotic sufferings (not in a collection of such stories), elements drawn from the old "serious" genres with elements drawn from New Comedy. Its protagonists can be much more admirable, for their fidelity and courage, than the protagonists of comedies and even more admirable, or worthy of emulation, than those of epic and tragedy; but like comic characters, and unlike tragic ones, they are purely fictive, neither legendary nor historical. They suffer the direst threats to their lives and values, threats which the romance, unlike a comedy, can ask us to take seriously; but, as in a comedy, if not in a tragedy, they survive all their perils to live happily ever after. This kind of *erōtika pathēmata*, in which admirable characters survive the perils caused by love, fortune, and their own fidelity, became a most persistent form of Western literary art.

It may be true that romance, or this kind of romance, "is the nearest of all literary forms to the wish-fulfillment dream"[5] and that it deals most directly with our idealizations and fantasies. But our dreams fulfill many kinds of wishes, and it would be hard to say that some kinds are not akin to the forms represented by the *Iliad*, the Book of Genesis, and Aristophanes' *Birds*—works that are more fantastic than any Greek romance. Moreover, the pleasures of wish-fulfilling romance, whatever they may be, can also be yielded by history and biography. Cicero, reflecting the taste of his times, described the biography he hoped might be done of him in terms that neatly sketch out the emotional effects sought by many a romance. The biography would display "the uncertain and varied fortunes of a statesmen who[se] . . . rise to prominence gives scope for surprise, suspense, delight, annoyance, hope, fear; should these fortunes, however, end in some striking consummation, the result is a complete satisfaction of mind which is the most perfect pleasure a reader can enjoy."[6] The striking consummation Cicero had in mind was doubtless not the one that in fact ended his career—decapitation and excision of his golden tongue. But even that pathetic event, if properly treated by an expert writer, could pleasurably gratify our wishes. The writer's conception of his material and his consequent treatment of it are the prime sources of literary power; such at least would have been the assumption of any writer in antiquity. This assumption motivated Parthenius' shipping that "storehouse" of inherited materials to Cornelius Gallus; and presumably Gallus could have "treated" them comically or satirically, for Parthenius' great pupil molded several obscure legends into an epic to show that the Roman Empire was a creation of destiny as well as of men.

Nor do kinds of literary works spring from kinds of literary matter. There is no reason why the stories of Oedipus and Hamlet could not be written as comedies or that of *The Importance of Being Earnest* as a satire or grave romance. This may be obvious, but it deserves illustration here. One candidate for the role of "First Romance in the West" is the *Cyropaedia*, written by Xenophon, the spartanophile admirer of Socrates, about 400 B.C. More particularly, it is the story of Panthea and Abradatas, woven through books 5, 6, and 7 of the *Cyropaedia*, that is clearly romantic. This story is indeed exactly the kind of arcane, serious tale that Parthenius would have called an *erōtikon pathos:* its early date supports its candidacy—though similar stories in Herodotus, and the *Odyssey* itself, would win on this score; and its fame was apparently such that later romances sometimes adopted the name Xenophon—as though nineteenth-century English novelists had habitually signed their works "Richardson." But the story as Xenophon tells it is designed to reveal the virtues of Cyrus; for Cyrus himself, along with his career, is fashioned to show that "to rule men might be a task neither impossible nor even difficult, if one would only go about it in an intelligent manner."[7] That is, Xenophon molds the conventions of the biography, the adventure, and the story of erotic suffering, already ancient in his time, to didactic ends.

In book 5, when Cyrus captures Susa, he wins Panthea, wife of Abradatas, as one of his many lovely prizes, and he asks his young friend Araspas to guard her until he, Cyrus, has time for women. Though Panthea disguises herself as a slave girl, Araspas can immediately identify her because her stature, her "grace," and her tears (which fall "even to her feet") evince her superiority; and this superiority, dramatized when she rends her garments upon hearing that Cyrus is to have her, signals that we are to take her predicament seriously. Already we recognize a convention of romance: the extraordinary and admirable character whose dominant value, marital fidelity, is jeopardized by fate. Xenophon might now have employed another convention: Araspas could here be struck by Eros and fall in love at first sight. But Xenophon chooses to make Araspas a conventional Scorner of Love so that he may return to Cyrus and work through still another convention: the Debate on Love. Many a courtly lover conducts this debate within himself; but Xenophon has Cyrus take part in it (as he could not if his minion were already in love with one of his women) to show how a prudent empire-builder deals with the conventional topics of these debates—Reason and Passion. Cooled by experience, Cyrus argues the right cause of reason and attacks erotic passion with ancient figures of speech: love is a disease, love enslaves even the gods, and so forth. Young Araspas mistakenly insists that love *is* rational—and trivial: "Everyone loves what suits his taste, as he does his clothes or shoes" (5. 1. 11). Later, in book 6, we learn that of course Cyrus is right. Araspas is suddenly brought to his king in chains because he has in the interval fallen so passionately in love with Panthea that he has attempted to rape her. Paternal Cyrus laughs at "the man who had claimed to be superior to the passion of love" (6. 1. 34) and demonstrates his compassionate wisdom by forgiving his squire, who confesses that he has learned "in the school of that crooked sophist Eros" that the soul's bad part leads us to betray our king, while the good part strives to obey him (6. 1. 41). But the psychodynamics inherent in all "courtly love" triangles—especially potent here because the lady has *two* kingly possessors, her husband and her conqueror—hardly interest Xenophon. He uses the situation to enhance our admiration of Cyrus' strategic wit. Since the squire now seems to be his lord's enemy, Cyrus commands him to feign terror, pretend to defect, and return with the enemy's battle plan. When this is accomplished, we appreciate how Cyrus' mercy and intelligence bear political fruit.

But Xenophon has not yet extracted from this story of *erōtika pathēmata* all of its didactic potential. Cyrus rewards Panthea's chastity by permitting her to summon her husband to the camp. Grateful, and urged on by his grateful wife, the man volunteers to lead the van and charges to his death, winning the battle and illustrating how Cyrus' intelligence enables him to rule men. Even the story's final tableau celebrates Cyrus' virtues. In book 7, when he finds Panthea embracing her husband's corpse, Cyrus weeps. But his noble *sententia*—that it is glorious to die a brave victor—fails to console the admirable wife, who stabs herself. This pathetic scene is given a baroque twist when the corpse's hand, shaken by the conqueror, comes off at the wrist; but the conventions of horror soon give way to those of myth: three passing eunuchs who have observed Panthea's suicide stab themselves in frustrated emulation, and the great Cyrus, marveling and weeping, orders the erection of four great stones, one to commemorate the love of Panthea and Abradatas, the other three to memorialize the eunuchs; and these monuments, we are told, stand there to the present day. The intelligence of this wise ruler is crowned by the compassion that can honor passion; it sets an example for those who would rule men and makes the myths by which fame conquers death.

These conventional themes, characters, and predicaments are used in many later romances, tragedies, comedies, epics, and histories, both didactic and nondidactic. But the Greek romances differ radically from Xenophon's work. Few of them are controlled by a moral or political argument, and all of them bring their admirable lovers through terrible perils—separation, captivity, torture, even burial—to a "striking consummation" that saves and reconciles. By means of these conventions and plots they try to arouse fear, hope, surprising joy, and a certain "complete satisfaction of mind" which may result from the gratification of certain fantasized wishes. These very powers have given them a bad name: "romance." In 1497, the Founders' Company of London fined Robert Wells twopence "for romance"—for lying. To the young Nietzsche, the Greek romance represented the final degradation of Greek literary art because it suppressed, by artifice and science, the Dionysian satyr's drunken, joyous whisper, "Man, thou shalt surely die." They are lies. No one triumphs over destiny and death. They are worse than lies. They toy with the fact of mortality, then gratify our puerile wishes for personal immortality by showing victories of "good fortune" over that fact. In them the old heroes, emblems of the human condition, become mere individuals, glorified bourgeois lovers rewarded with happy marriages. For Nietzsche, these artful lies were products of the poisonous Alexandrian spirit, the corrupt Alexandrian theorizing, that destroyed myth by exegesis and promised to "correct the world by knowledge, guide life by science, and actually confine the individual within a limited sphere of soluble problems, from which he can cheerfully say to life: 'I desire you; you are worth knowing.'" The perpetrator of these lies was "Alexandrian man, who is at bottom a librarian and a corrector of proofs." And the power of his lies is manifested in the fact that "our whole modern world is entangled in the web of Alexandrian culture."[8]

Nietzsche himself survived to repudiate many of these views, which perhaps derived in part from the dread that made the idea of his personal immortality, and finally his very sanity, intolerable. Still, his remarkable defense of the regal station of tragedy among the genres argued the abiding powers of "romance," and

Chapter One

an inquiry into these powers might well begin in the Alexandrian era with a little epic sometimes called a romance—the *Argonautica*, written about 250 B.C. by an Alexandrian named Apollonius of Rhodes.

❧ 2 ❧
Resourceless Jason

The austere Tarn said that Apollonius Rhodius was "the precursor of half modern literature."[1] A grave charge if true. Perhaps he meant that no ancient poem is more "important" in the history of romance than the *Argonautica*.

Despite his surname, the "precursor" was an arch-Alexandrian. He was born in the metropolis; at age seventy he was appointed director of the Libraries; and he was buried in the precincts of the Museum. Legend has it that he was driven to Rhodes by the scorn of the scholar-poet Callimachus, arbiter of Alexandrian taste, who would have thought that the first version of the *Argonautica* was too long, too much an imitation of Homer. Callimachus held that a big book is a big folly; to emulate Homeric epic is both blasphemous and silly; the serious modern poet should focus his narrative on a single mythic episode, suffuse it with details from ordinary life, and tell it in language as pure as the water brought by priestesses to Demeter; but epics like the *Argonautica* are like the copious Euphrates—full of garbage. Apollonius supposedly withdrew to Rhodes, fired an epigram or two back at Callimachus in Alexandria, shortened his story to its present 5,835 lines while retaining its Homeric scope and style, won Rhodian citizenship with it, and returned to conquer the metropolis.[2]

Personal rivalries ennobled by literary principles testify to the vigor of a school, and a comparable vigor underlay the remarkable developments in science that occurred during the Hellenistic era, which is conventionally defined as beginning with the death of Alexander in 323 B.C. and ending with the establishment of the Roman Empire by Augustus in 30 B.C. Rivalries among the three (sometimes more) kingdoms into which Alexander's empire had fallen did not prevent the flourishing of many Hellenic cities, old and new, whose mercantile families could possess enormous wealth. Cities from Sicily to India were linked by a single language, which the daughters as well as the sons of citizens were taught to read and write. The older *polis*, which had offered security as well as freedom from the strictures of tribe and clan, was not part of a cosmopolis, a vast life-space that encompassed Greek and barbarian and in which one could find new opportunities for what we call "individualism"—new freedoms and new dangers. The anxieties that can result from such conditions might underlie some of the contradictions of the age. Science comforts reason by measuring the earth and heavens, while magic, offering controls over life, flourishes, as do the mystery cults, which offer controls over death. Myths and legends are explained according to scientific principles, which control the past by redefining it. The literary past is enshrined in great libraries like those at Pergamum and Alexandria, where it is controlled by textual studies, glosses, and cataloging systems like the one invented for Alexandria by Callimachus. The Library is attached to a Temple of the Muses (the Museum), served by subsidized scholars, who satisfy a universal need for authority by defining a canon of official "classics," and for whom the literary past becomes so sacrosanct that it hardly bears imitation. This anxious exactitude is accompanied by a fascination with the depths of time and the most exotic regions of the earth. Callimachus wrote a set of etiologies—myths of origins; Apollonius incessantly converts the exploits of his Argonauts into etiologies, and he sends them not only to Soviet Georgia (Colchis) but up the Danube, Po, and Rhine. A nostalgia for the authentic is reflected in the idylls (sketches) of Theocritus, which offer weary urbanites refuge in the pastoral purities of Sicily. No wonder that the literature of the ear is characterized as both pedantic and innovative, written in a sterile era, when "literature . . . was taking stock of itself,"[3] yet was producing new forms of epic, comedy, and prose fiction, and when Euclid, Archimedes, and Galen could have enjoyed Apollonius' innovative epic precisely for its romantic preciosity, its academic fondling of the antique.

"Alexandrian" is a good enough name for this group of fantasts and calculators. By 200 B.C. Alexandria was the largest city in the world, with perhaps one million inhabitants and 700,000 items in its libraries. The city was itself an Alexandrian phenomenon. In 331 B.C. Alexander had commanded a fishing village to become a metropolis, a "mother city," where the commercial and cultural powers of his infant empire might be nourished, and never has a programmed city been more successful. After his surprising death in 323 B.C., his inheritors in Egypt, Ptolemy Soter (323–283 B.C.) and Ptolemy Philadelphus (283–237 B.C.), established and augmented the Museum and the Library. Had the Library survived, it might be easier to reckon just how philology, linguistics, mathematics, medicine, geometry, and astronomy took abiding shape at Alexandria and why Callimachus could liken Ptolemy to Apollo with genuine enthusiasm. A new father god also took shape there—Serapis, compounded of Zeus, Osiris, and Helios-Re-Apollo. Its principal East-West thoroughfare, one hundred feet wide, was bounded at one end by the Gate of the Sun, at the other by the Gate of the Moon, suggesting that the city harbored everything. And the famous harbor beacon symbolized a radiance calculated to illuminate the world.

Alexandria was still quite young when Apollonius chose to tell one of the oldest and most honored of stories—how heroic Jason led the Argonauts to Colchis and, with the aid of the sorceress Medea, the king's daughter, harnessed the king's bulls, won the Golden Fleece, and returned home with the girl. Homer (*Odyssey* 12. 70) mentions its popularity, and it had been often told. But Apollonius' Jason is curiously unheroic. His most common epithet is *amēchanos*, "resourceless." He is morose, uncertain, and unable to handle the love which he—or the goddesses who support his enterprise—evokes in the passionate Medea. Apollonius draws from his inherited materials a story of erotic suffering; and it is the special quality of suffering, Jason's and Medea's, that gives Apollonius' poem much of its power and therefore demands inquiry here. It also explains why the *Argonautica*, of the surviving epics, seems most like the prose romances written centuries later and why it has been called the poem in which "Greek romance was elevated to the epic," in which "Romance [is] shattered by reality," and in which the "handling of Medea's passion" works "a marriage between romance and reality" that justifies our calling Apollonius "a novelist."[4]

To appreciate Apollonius' accomplishments and failures, we look at the traditional materials he modified. In the Hesiodic *Theogony* (mid-eighth century B.C.), Jason is assigned the seemingly impossible task of fetching the Golden Fleece by his uncle, "overbearing Pelias, that outrageous and presumptuous lover of violence" who had usurped the throne of his brother, Jason's father, Aeson;[5] and Jason marries Medea upon his return home to Iolcus, though there is no mention of his seizing his rightful throne from Pelias. Jason's name means "healer." Does this suggest a reason why he works no vengeance on his wicked uncle? In the post-Homeric Epic Cycle, Medea renews Aeson's youth by cooking him in a golden cauldron; and in another story *she* kills Pelias by giving his daughter inadequate instructions when they try to do the same for their father. Some say that Medea was later cast aside by Jason in Corinth in favor of King Creon's daughter, that she poisoned Creon and fled, leaving her children behind to be poisoned by Creon's friends; others, like Euripides, say that she herself killed her children because Jason betrayed her.

In 462 B.C., thirty-four years before Euripides' *Medea* won third prize at Athens, Pindar wrote an ode (his *Fourth Pythian*) to celebrate the victory won by the king of Cyrene, in Libya, in the Olympian chariot races. Since Cyrene had been founded by descendants of an Argonaut, Pindar relates a version of the Jason story which is the earliest extended account of it now extant. (Other Argonauticas may have been written before Apollonius, but they are lost.) In it we learn that Pelias is doomed to be killed by a man who will appear in Iolcus with one foot bare. Jason arrives one day wearing only one sandal but carrying two spears. His aspect is terrible and beautiful: his hair flames down his back, and he wears a leopard skin. He looks like Helios-Apollo, his patron, who is patron of Cyrene, too, and father of Medea's father and Apollonius' namesake—the god who of course inspires the *Argonautica*. Frightened, Pelias calls Jason a bastard. Jason calmly replies that he has come to claim the rights stolen from his father by Pelias, who here is Jason's cousin. After Jason's father and two brothers have greeted him, Jason tells Pelias that he may keep the property but that he, Jason, must have the "scepter of absolute rule."[6] Pelias claims he has dreamed that the ghost of Phrixus, a kinsman who had ridden the golden ram to Colchis to escape the murderous knife of his stepmother, was calling him to steal the Golden Fleece and thereby to avenge the fact that the Colchians had not buried him (an abomination). Jason agrees to take on this pious task; and in Colchis Aphrodite teaches Jason how to win Medea from allegiance to her family. Medea's ointments preserve Jason from her father's fire-breathing oxen, which he must harness (only the father could do this) and use to plow a field. Jason's success at this enrages the father; but that night Jason slays the last guardian of the Fleece, a monstrous serpent, and sails off with Medea, whom he marries on the island of Lemnos, where women slay men. We learn that Medea will kill Pelias; but now only the founding of Cyrene interests Pindar; that and the praise of its victorious king—who, by the way, was a grandfather of Apollonius' rival, Callimachus, who was a native of Cyrene and a descendant of the founders of that Apollonian city.

Invoking Phoebus Apollo, Apollonius announces his intention: *palaigenōn klea phōtōn mnēsomai*—he will commemorate the luminous fame of ancient heroes who at the command of King Pelias sailed the ship Argo over the Black Sea in quest of the Golden Fleece. As in Pindar's ode, an oracle has warned Pelias that he will be killed by a man with one foot bare; and when he spies Jason, a newcomer in town, he sends him on "a perilous adventure overseas" in the hope that he will "never see home again." But Apollonius does not say why Jason accepts this adventure. He does not mention the rivalry between Pelias and Jason. In Pindar's ode, Jason has "come home / Claiming the ancient honour of / His father"; in Apollonius' poem he means only to attend "a banquet that Pelias was giving in honor of his father Poseidon and all the other gods, except Pelasgian Hera, to whom he paid no homage."[7] Much later (3. 64 ff.), Apollonius reveals that Jason had lost one sandal while helping an old woman cross a river and that this old woman was Mother Hera herself, who was "putting human charity on trial" and is now using Jason to work her revenge on Pelias. Thus Apollonius suppresses Jason's traditional motivation and predicament and substitutes the motives of an angry female god for those of a righteous male inheritor.

It cannot be that the cuts prompted by Callimachan strictures cause these omissions and substitutions: Apollonius immediately expends 200 lines on a conventional catalog of heroic Argonauts. Perhaps the celebratory intentions announced in his first lines made an uncle-nephew rivalry troublesome. But we know that oracles in stories must come true; and when the epic ends, abruptly, with a "heroic, happy breed of men" stepping ashore at home with joy, not vengeance, in their hearts, we must feel a certain frustration, because neither Jason's predicament nor Hera's plan has been worked out. Besides, Apollonius' passive

Jason is neither heroic nor happy enough to warrant much celebration.

Perhaps some of the reasons underlying Apollonius' modifications of his materials can be inferred from the emotions stirred by his tragedy. The dangerous adventure itself arouses our awe, and the catalog of Argonauts recruits us for the journey. Who would not want to join a crew composed of Heracles, the strongest warrior, Orpheus, the finest musician, Mopsus, the best seer, and Polydeuces, the most skillful boxer, among others? Our fear for them is strong: the task seems impossible, "and they must get there first," says a townsman, "and the going will be hard." But their powers are so fantastic that we cannot doubt the outcome, and we can join them only through an entirely fantasized image of our own powers. Jason's powers, however, fall wholly within the human scale and often seem inferior to what we would imagine ours to be. On the one hand, we rejoice with him when, "delighted" and "warlike," he summons strength from Apollo, "the god of his fathers," and the crew elects him leader; on the other hand, we can sympathize with him when, at the crew's feast in honor of Apollo, he sits apart, "his resolution gone." Our fear for him is more genuine than it is for his superhuman crewmates, and it is deepened when Apollonius dwells on the pathos of boys leaving home. Jason's father grieves, "wrapped in bed, like a figure cut in stone." The sufferings of passive, petrified fathers usually go unrecorded; but the anguish of Jason's mother, who has "no hope ... of an unclouded end," is fully expressed when she holds "her son fast as ever in her arms ... like a girl who in her loneliness falls into the arms of her old nurse, her one remaining friend ... fresh from the blows and insults of a stepmother who makes her life a misery." This bizarre simile, which converts the mother into a child and the son into a nurse, is somewhat clarified when the mother wails that she will be left "pining in misery for love of you, my pride and glory in days gone by, my first and last, my only son." Jason is not by tradition an only son. Perhaps Apollonius makes him one only to enhance the pathos of sons leaving mothers and to focus our emotions on a hero not much more invulnerable than ourselves.

But Jason's sufferings are deeper than his traditional heroic character would warrant. At the feast he "retired within himself to brood on all his troubles. He looked like a man in despair."

What are his troubles? We have not been told that he has many rivalries with Pelias to worry about, even though we surely know of them despite Apollonius' suppression of that material. Idas asks our question: "What are these deep thoughts that are keeping you to yourself? Tell us what is the matter with you. Has panic got you in its grip?" Jason does not answer. We are never told why he is so often resourceless. We are never told why he accepted Pelias' command to steal the Fleece. That he accepted shows that he is not a simple coward, and we would be reluctant to follow a cowardly hero anyway. We must supply the answers ourselves. We supply them, and thereby fill out our aesthetic identifications with this curious hero, as we follow him through his feelings and adventures. These feelings and adventures, taken together, form a familiar and remarkably consistent pattern of human suffering. Jason is confronted by the mysterious need to defeat one king, the terrible Aeëtes of Colchis, in order to satisfy the mysterious and unspoken need to reclaim from another king, the violent Pelias, his own filial inheritance. To do this, he must rely on the female sorceries of the girl who is possessed by the king he must defeat. He is, throughout, the tool of Hera, wife of Zeus, and he is at every turn aided by one female deity or another. We may perhaps appreciate his reliance on feminine powers when we see that his true father is mute, that he is an adored only son, and that his paternal god, Apollo, is clearly incarnated in his kingly rival Aeëtes, who is Apollo's son. In this light, it makes no difference that his rivalry with Pelias is left unexpressed: it is fully projected onto his confrontation with Medea's father. No wonder that he sits resourceless at Apollo's feast, that he is mysteriously morose and indecisive throughout, that he drives the girl who loves him to despair, and that even at his one moment of triumph, when he at last holds the sunny Fleece in his arms, he feels "glad as a girl who catches on her silken gown the lovely light of the moon" (4. 167–68)—not an inappropriate simile for a hero who has accommodated, temporarily, the challenge of the masculine sun by adopting the powers of the feminine moon.

This seems to be more a diagnosis than a characterization. It seems to rest on the inane assumption that Jason is a neurotic human being, not a character inseparable from a particular story. In fact, most of the first two books—the first half of the poem—

relates the adventures of the whole crew, and Jason can often be forgotten. Still, it seems to me to be an accurate account of the special qualities of Jason's suffering love and to explain some of the power of Apollonius' poem.

They depart. "Jason wept as he turned his eyes away from the land of his birth. But the rest struck the rough seas with their oars" (1. 535 ff.). Now we are embarked on fantasies of power, stimulated by the active crew, and fantasies of powerlessness, stimulated by the passive Jason. Both yield their pleasures, but the wish to be superhuman now holds sway. Two of the crew, sons of the North Wind, chase harpies through leagues of air. Polydeuces kills a brutish challenger with a single blow. Phineas the prophet, aided by Lady Athena, helps them negotiate the Clashing Rocks. And, everywhere the Argonauts go, their deeds are commemorated by a place-name, a feature of landscape, a custom. "The beach is still called Argo's Aphetas because she [the Argo] took off from there." "To this day the Ionians of Cynicus, when they make their yearly libations, grind the meal for cakes at the public mill." Dozens of episodes in books 1, 2, and 4 recount the sort of charter myths that must have appealed to an Alexandrian taste. They also suffuse our fantasies of power with pleasurable, even megalomaniacal grandeur, and, at the same time, they provide poetic evidence that these awesome fantasies were in fact acted out.

Though he often disappears from view, Jason remains a problem for his comrades and himself, if not for the reader. After the Argonauts are seduced by the aggressive women of Lemnos, who have slaughtered their fathers, husbands, and sons but now regret it, Jason bids farewell to their queen, saying that "relief from toil" and a return home are all he wants; and, should she bear him a son, will she send it to Iolcus to console his parents (1. 900 ff.)? When his men quarrel after inadvertently abandoning Heracles on a savage shore, Jason cannot calm them, but, "paralyzed by a sense of utter helplessness, added no word to either side of the dispute. He sat and ate his heart out, crushed by the calamity" (ll. 1286 ff.). When Phineas describes the terrible Fleece and the enormous serpent that guards it, Jason, "unmanned by his misgivings," asks, "How shall I manage?" Phineas, as though understanding the special terror of pubic fleece and phallic serpent for a boy like this, advises him to rely on the power of Aphrodite. Even after an escape from danger, as when the longboat successfully penetrates the Clashing Rocks, Jason says: "I am obsessed by fears and intolerable anxiety" (2. 622). Jason's fears of course express the thrilling fear we are to feel about the whole adventure and reinforce the dynamic pattern of tension and release from tension that structures the first two books. They also rouse the specific dreads suffered in fantasy, if not in reality, during projects such as his: the guilty desire to castrate and the guilty hope and fear of being castrated by an admirable but outraged king.

The famous third book, which is usually taken to be the only well-made section of the epic, relates how Jason manages "to rob [King Aeëtes] of his own"—his Fleece and his daughter. In his first encounter with Aeëtes, Jason uses, as his mouthpiece, Argus, who asks Aeëtes for the Fleece on the grounds that it was his (Argus') father's—which it was.[8] But Aeëtes is not fooled. He was "filled with rage as he listened to Argus. And now, in a towering passion," he says to Jason, "You scoundrel! It was no fleece that brought you and your confederates from Hellas, but a plot to seize my sceptre and my royal power" (3. 367 ff.). Aeëtes is factually wrong about this, but he represents a psychological displacement common in life and myth. He seems to feel that what the oracle had told Pelias would happen when Jason arrived might now happen to him. Aeëtes is a safer rival than Pelias because Fate, or a familial relationship, does not demand that Jason displace him; but he is a more thrillingly complete rival because he possesses a woman whom Jason may use and steal to defeat him.

Jason stands "speechless ... resourceless in the face of his dilemma" (3. 22 ff.). He is offered a test: if he can harness Aeëtes' two fire-breathing bulls, plow a field with them, sow serpents' teeth into this field, and slay the men spawned by the teeth, he may have the Fleece. It is like a fantasy come true. Faced with these symbolic terrors, poor Jason must say, "Your majesty, right is on your side, and you leave me no escape whatsoever" (3. 486). We must admire him, and fear for him, when he at last says, "I will take up your challenge."

Now Queen Hera takes counsel with Athena to plot ways by which Jason may win over the king. They recruit Aphrodite, who bribes her unruly son Eros to strike Medea with one of those arrows that produce more suffering than joy. Pierced by this arrow, Medea thinks that Jason shines with beauty and grace. He is ideal. But

> her heart smouldered with pain as [Jason] passed from her sight, and her soul crept out of her, as in a dream ... and weeping quietly she voiced her woes: "What is the meaning of this grief? Hero or villain (and why should I care which?), the man is going to his death. Well, let him go! And yet I wish he had been spared. Yes, sovran Lady Hecate, this is my prayer." [3. 443 ff.]

It is Medea's, not Jason's, erotic suffering that has made the *Argonautica* famous. The sentiments, the style, and the structure of the soliloquized love debate exploited by Euripides are here fully incorporated into an epic, and Apollonius' Medea becomes the direct ancestress of Vergil's Dido and thereby of innumerable later suffering heroines.[9] But Medea's suffering is particular as well as conventional. The goddesses' plot to give Jason the feminine ways by which he may meet his destiny creates one of the girls whose love, idealizing such boys, compels them to betray their fathers. "Evil on this side, evil on that," says Medea, feeling that unless she betrays her father she will lose her beloved, "and I must choose between them. In either case my plight is desperate, and there is no escape; this torture will go on" (3. 772 ff.). So it does. Medea's suffering is more immediately accessible to us, more noble and therefore more affecting, than Jason's. But the suffering entailed by her kind of love becomes inextricably bound to the suffering entailed by Jason's kind.

By tradition Medea was a witch. Apollonius converts her into a girl the stages of whose erotic suffering would also become conventional: she worries about the wicked tongues that will wag about her betrayal of her father; she longs for her innocent girlhood; she contemplates suicide; then she dupes her handmaidens into contriving an assignation with Jason at a temple—the temple of her patroness, Hecate, queen of witches. There Hera makes Jason seem radiant with graces—or rather, like the Dog Star that troubles the flocks. That Medea's love derives from overvaluation we know, because we know Jason; and this elicits more pity for her. Inspired by his patron goddesses, Jason charms her, and, "uplifted by his praise . . . she revelled in his need for her" (3. 960 ff.). Jason cites an odd exemplar of betrayal and flight—Ariadne; and when he neglects to mention what every reader knows, that Ariadne was abandoned by her hero, Theseus, our pity for Medea grows. It's true that "Love stole into Jason's heart"—when he saw her weeping for him; and he does propose honorable marriage: at home, where "wives and mothers" will honor her, "there shall be a bridal bed for you which you and I will share"—as though it were her or the bed's affair (3. 1128 ff.). In Pindar's ode Jason marries her on Lemnos; and it is Pindar's resolute Jason himself, not his female deities, who makes Medea forget "To honour those who begot her" and causes her heart to "tremble under the lash of love." In Apollonius' poem Jason refuses to bed the girl until forced by circumstances on Corfu; in the *Argonautica* love is complex, and its sufferings remain incurable.

With meticulous awe Apollonius describes the nocturnal, underworld arts of Medea's witch-goddess Hecate which will save Apollonian Jason from the Apollonian king. The king appears at dawn looking like the sun, "his golden helmet with its four plates bright as the sun's face" (3. 1228–30). To underscore this identification of Aeëtes with Helios-Apollo, Apollonius gives his son Apsyrtus a nickname—Phaethon, who "holds his father's swift horses and well-built chariot." The poet seems bent on emphasizing the fact that Jason's enemy is a god in human form. Anointed with Medea's salve, Jason harnesses the sun-bulls and plows the field; and to complete the sexual conceit, Apollonius adds the old myth of autochthonic generation: Jason sows serpent-seed in the field and then slays its ferocious spawn. What about the serpent who guards the Fleece itself? It is not cut down in Apollonius. That night, as Aeëtes schemes and rages, Medea enchants the serpent, which merely goes limp with sleep. And Jason "snatched the Golden Fleece from the oak," where it "hung bright as a cloud incarnadined by the fiery beams of the rising sun," and Jason is glad as a moonstruck girl. If we now expect a triumphant catharsis of the tensions that have been built by this profound adventure, we are disappointed. The Fleece becomes a new burden. When Jason "slung it on his left shoulder . . . it reached his feet. But now and again he made a bundle of it in his arms. He was

mortally afraid that some god or man might rob him on the way"
(4. 162 ff.). For Hesiod's Jason, success "fulfills the will of Zeus";
Pindar's "trusts in God" and dreads no retaliation for success.

Like a figure in a thrillingly bad dream, Phaethon pursues the
Argo through regions both known and imagined—across the
Black Sea, up the Danube, up the Save, into the Adriatic, where,
goaded by Medea, Jason at last murders him. Jason had been
quite willing to placate his avenging brother-in-law by returning
the stolen girl. Outraged, Medea had asked him, "Has your
splendid success destroyed your memory? . . . I am yours. . . .
You should be ready to stand by me. . . . Why not run off
with me? . . . I hope that Hera, Queen of Heaven, whose favorite
you claim to be, will never let you have [a happy home-
coming] . . . ; I hope the Fleece will vanish like an idle dream" (4.
353 ff.).

Medea is out of love. She has discovered that she made a disas-
trous choice when she "defied convention and . . . conscience"
and followed passive Jason. She cannot return to her furious
father, and Jason's inhibitions make her hysterical (she wants to
burn the Argo). Apollonius himself now apostrophizes the suffering love that is more his subject than the adventures of happy
heroes: "Unconscionable love, bane and tormentor of mankind,
parent of strife, fountain of tears, source of a thousand ills, rise,
mighty Power, and fall on the sons of our enemies with all the force
you used upon Medea" (4. 455). The language of this choric aside
may be conventional, but Apollonius' characters embody some of
the reasons why love can be an irresoluble torment. Unlike
Medea, Jason seems incapable of discovery or change. His astonishingly savage murder of Phaethon, "lopping off the dead
man's extremities" as he at last vents rage on a rival, only rouses
the wrath of another mighty male: "Zeus, King of the gods, took
umbrage at the horrid deed" and now pursues the Argo.[10] But,
aided by Mother Hera and by Circe, they placate the father god
only to be confronted by another party of Aeëtes' avengers at
Corfu. Medea cannot fend them off by saying she's married:
"Alas, no one has touched me; I am still the virgin I was at home"
(4. 1023). Another woman, wife of King Alcinous, takes charge
and decrees that Jason may keep Medea provided he marry her.
Jason is reluctant but agrees, and a bed is prepared with "the
shining Golden Fleece on top of it." The Fleece kindles in the

eyes of attendant nymphs "a sweet desire"; but the lovers, "though they loved and delighted in each other, were haunted by fear" of father Aeëtes, and their troubles do not cease until they cease.

In one postmarital adventure the Argonauts are stranded in tidal lagoons along the Libyan shore, and Jason is once more resourceless. This time the Libyan mother goddess appears: "Why this despair? . . . You must repay your mother for what she suffered all the long time she bore you in her womb" (4. 1328 ff.). This riddle elates Jason, but he cannot understand how he can repay his mother. Peleus explains: the Argo herself is his mother; she has "carried us in her womb; we have often heard her groaning in her pain. Now, we will carry *her*" (4. 1370 ff.). Jason never learns that it was Hera whom he had carried over a stream or that he owes her a debt for having saved him from all the troubles she has caused him; still, he happily helps carry Mother Argo over the sands for nine days and nights.

In another episode, manly Heracles reappears to slay a local serpent; another serpent kills Mopsus the seer; a brazen, sunny giant who blocks a harbor in Crete is killed by Medea, who bewitches his eyes "with the evil in her own . . . and in an ecstasy of rage" curses him to death. As the Argo approaches home, Euphemus has a dream. Euphemus is the ancestor of the founders of Libyan Cyrene. Back in Libya he had been given a clod of earth by Triton, a clod which would lodge against the Aegean island that would one day shelter Cyrene's founders. Euphemus dreamed

that he was holding to his breast the lump of earth . . . and was suckling it with streams of white milk. The clod, small as it was, turned into a woman of virginal appearance; and in an access of passion he lay with her. When the deed was done, he felt remorse—she had been a virgin and he had suckled her himself. But she consoled him, saying in a gentle voice: "My friend, I am of Triton's stock and the Nurse of your children. . . . Give me a home . . . in the sea near Anaphe, and I will reappear in the light of day in time to welcome your descendants." [4. 1731 ff.]

This dream weaves such a complex fantasy of desire, power, and guilt that analysis could hardly do it justice. It seems to be

Apollonius' own invention, and it might have been dreamed by his hero. The dreamer identifies himself with both nourishing mother and incestuous father; his virginal daughter is also his wife; and aided by a fecund gift he resolves his sexual troubles in a myth of origins and power.

Jason's troubles, however, are resolved only by fiat of the poet. Almost immediately after the dream, Apollonius suddenly says: "Farewell, heroic, happy breed of men! Your blessing on this lay of mine. And as the years go by, may people find it a sweeter and sweeter song to sing. Farewell; for I have come to the glorious finish of your labors. . . . The coast of Attica slipped by . . . and with joyful hearts you stepped ashore at Pagasae."

I have slighted the pleasures given by the repeated triumphs of these happy heroes over many fantastic difficulties. In exploring the pattern of the lovers' erotic suffering, I have all but ignored the fantasies of power that envelop their unresolved difficulties. But Apollonius made a comparable error. He launches on a conventional bardic enterprise of commemorating and celebrating heroes, but he finds in his traditional material a story of erotic suffering that makes his protagonists neither heroic nor happy. He tries to make us forget not only the oracle and Hera's vengeful plan but the inevitably tragic consequences of the flawed love which he himself has depicted so profoundly. We are left dissatisfied because the terms of the story, as Apollonius lays them out, have not been fulfilled. Still, Apollonius' aesthetic error, his dwelling on the causes and consequences of unhappy love, led him into a historic success. His suffering bride and troubled hero, surviving many marvelous dangers through many marvelous escapes, are visible in the later prose romances. The manner in which they express erotic suffering was taken up by Vergil and Ovid, and through these poets it became a precious possession of Western writers until the eighteenth century. Treating the materials of *erōtika pathēmata* in epic scope seems to have freed Apollonius' genius. No earlier tragedian—including his mentor Euripides—and few later romancers cut as close to the nerves of tormented love.

There are at least two ways to describe the emotive powers exercised by Apollonius' story over its reader or hearer. The first description follows the dynamic unfolding of the story and calls the emotions by names that would have been familiar to

Apollonius in one form or another. The second tries to isolate the emotive gist of the Jason-Medea portion of the epic and uses terms that might have bewildered or appalled an Alexandrian poet.

Here is the first:

A home-loving young man is commanded by the king of his region to perform a presumably fatal task—to fetch a Golden Fleece from the eastern rim of the world—because the king, advised by an oracle, fears that the young man will kill him. Along with his townsmen and family, we fear for the admirable boy, who is as handsome as his patron, Apollo; but the heroes and demigods who join him remove real doubt that he will succeed. When he bewails his fate and suffers resourceless despair, we pity him; and we feel that under similar circumstances we might feel as he does. At the same time, we are awed by the marvelous triumphs of his companions over the fantastic dangers that confront them, and every episode creates a pleasurable tension that is pleasurably relieved. But a stronger fear builds as we approach Colchis, where our unhappy hero, who does not possess the superhuman prowess of his comrades, will be on his own. We now learn, however, that certain goddesses are protecting him, and we are somewhat relieved when they enlist the magical powers of the king's own daughter. This famous sorceress is, we see, an innocent home-loving girl, though her powers are more awesome than any owned by the young man, for whom we now feel more pity than admiration. When the girl is tormented by a love inflicted on her, and when she struggles with the inflicted necessity of betraying her own father, we pity her more deeply than we do her seducer. But we want her to save the Argonauts and the man she loves, especially because her outlandish, semidivine father, as well as the test that guards the Fleece, seems infinitely more powerful than the young man we have come to know.

Our allegiances are divided: the victory we desire and expect for him will wrench the girl from the home she loves. We are titillated by her dark powers; the defeat of the arrogant king pleases us; and we expect the paradox of our allegiances to be resolved by a triumphant escape to home, honorable marriage, and rulership won by just vengeance worked on the task-making king. This does not happen. The young man is not consoled by victory or love, and the girl discovers that her love is misplaced.

Another series of perils, each escaped in the nick of time, leads up to the murder of the girl's brother; and another marvelous series works out the consequences of this murder. Even after the marriage of the protagonists, our tensions are not relieved, nor are our paradoxical allegiances resolved. The hero neither learns nor changes, and the heroine's recognition that the young man cannot possess her remains an unrelieved pain that results in her hysteria. Though we may continue to enjoy wonderful perils and escapes, we can no longer grant our fear to the protagonists; and our pity for them sinks to a level that shuts out admiration. In the end, no episode or system of episodes purges the strong emotions elicited by the characters and the early predicaments of the story.

This account ignores what every reader would have brought to the *Argonautica*—a knowledge of the traditional outlines of the story. But all traditional materials are malleable, and Apollonius' innovations may explain why his version won him fame in Rhodes and Alexandria. By suppressing the Jason-Pelias rivalry and the tragic aftermath of the Jason-Medea affair, Apollonius made the Argo story a happy one. At the same time, he developed the *erōtika pathēmata* embedded in this story along Euripidean lines and offered his readers some of the pleasures of tormented love. But the contradictions inherent in this paradoxical intention may explain why a poet-critic like Callimachus objected to the copious poem, just as it may explain the poem's mixed reputation in modern times or why it can now be praised for suffusing romance with realism. If the above account describes the "romance" in the *Argonautica*, making it a story of marvelous adventure and love that is not as serious as it pretends to be, the following account may describe the gist of its profound, almost clinical, "realism."

A home-loving young man is challenged to defeat two older men, both kings—one the uncle who possesses the boy's kingdom, the other a king who personifies the boy's family god. The first king's fear that the boy will kill him is aroused by the boy's fateful, exposed foot; and, as exposed limbs can—and do—represent fears of castration, the fact that it is exposed expresses a desire to be castrated as well as a fear of being castrated. Though it is the king who fears being killed, this too, along with the oracle, may be taken as a projection of Jason's desires. In such situations, there is only one psychic center, and the emotional point of view in this story is obviously Jason's. When we later learn that the exposure resulted from Jason's having succored a goddess, the wife of Zeus, to whom Pelias does not pay sufficient homage, we may understand that Jason's guilty fear of being castrated, and his desire to be castrated in just retribution, result from his genuine love of the powerful woman whom the paternal figure shamefully ignores. Hera's plan of vengeance likewise projects Jason's belief that the mother really loves him and not the usurping king. But such beliefs are very troublesome. They align one with the powerful woman in a struggle against the male; they can lead one to rely on feminine powers to combat the male inside and outside oneself or to adopt the feminine ways that placate men and win the love of the father—a love which, after all, remains very desirable.

The second king in fact possesses a woman along with an apparatus of bulls, plows, and serpents; and he also possesses the brutal male power needed to master them all. To pass the test set by this apparatus and power naturally arouses an anxiety which causes a paralyzed resourcelessness because it challenges the boy to confront his most dreadful desires—to castrate the possessing male and take his woman. His anxiety is intensified by the character of the prize itself, the marvelous fleece of the pudendum, which his other fears make as dreadful as it is desirable. What is worse, the king himself incarnates the male deity, Apollo, from whom Jason is supposed to draw strength to overcome the king. This precisely expresses the dilemma of boys who observe that they must use the powers enjoyed by their male models in order to overcome their male models. A common solution to this dilemma is to renounce the love of women, obviate the possibility of castration by accepting psychological castration, and seek the love of men. But the advantage of this solution cannot be fully Jason's. Destiny, or the story, demands that he play out the role of masculine hero. Still, though he castrates the king, he cannot enjoy his triumph. The Fleece and the woman remain burdens because he cannot escape the guilty fear of retribution or respond to the erotic passion of the girl and the divine love of the goddess. His story must end in a contrived joy.

This makes Apollonius' Jason more pathetically flawed and therefore less admirable than a conventional tragic figure. Medea's character and predicament are perhaps more affecting. Since, unlike Jason, she is the victim of a compulsion caused by deities not her own (Hecate and Artemis) but those of her beloved, she is pitiable; and since, unlike Jason, she nobly struggles against her destiny, she is admirable. She must suddenly transfer her dutiful but strong love for her father to a stranger, and this means that Eros causes her to idealize Jason. Jason seems as unworthy of such love as her father; but the result is inevitably the love described as a mild psychosis derived from overvaluation of an object. This love prepares her for the anguished hysteria that results when the idealization evaporates and she is stuck with a man who cannot love and protect her. Her frustrations and guilts turn her from a priestess into a witch, from a lover into a manipulator. Apollonius shows reasons why she could end as the murderess of Pelias, Creon, and her own children.

This second account names the passions suffered by the characters but not those stimulated in the reader. The terms "pity," "fear," "awe," and "admiration" in the first account may be gross, but they are still meaningful; no general terms, however, could adequately designate the emotions stirred by the material described in the second account. Moreover, since the account reads like a case history of paired neurotics written after their deaths, it forbids our emotional response. Still, the description offers a valid answer to the question, "What are the particular qualities of the erotic suffering in this story?" It is valid because it shows that the obvious symbols inherent in the traditional story are given meaning by the consistent behavior of the characters in their predicaments and that the symbols, episodes, speeches, and meaning can all be derived from a single set of well-known causes.

The first account is addressed to the particular art of Apollonius' poem, the second to universal constants of the soul. It is Apollonius' genius that makes both accounts seem appropriate and any real distinction between them artificial. He molds the universals of human suffering to the particulars of his story, and vice versa. His tranformation of his inherited materials, with its condensations, displacements, and determinations, may be likened, in a now-familiar analogy, with ordinary dream work; and the principles that guided, consciously or unconsciously, his innovative transformations must have been the psychological ones suggested in my second account, for such principles, enlivened by the unique structure of the dreamer's psyche, guide his work on the materials available to him in any given dream. This is not to say that a poem is a dream. It is not. But the formal principle that synthesized for Apollonius the various materials latent in the *erōtika pathēmata* of Jason and Medea, and led to the formal failure of the whole poem, must have been personally important for him; and since the same psychodynamic principles are also important, in varying degrees, to us, they help explain the power of his poem.

❧ 3 ❧
Discussion
One

KAPPA: You have soured his sweet song with your insidious psychoanalyzing.

ALPHA: I thought it was blatant.

KAPPA: You have introduced the notion of realism. Very well. I trust you'll forgive me if I translate realism into candor, because I observe you deal almost entirely with translations. Your labor has brought forth the mouse called Oedipus, whose squeak, you will assure us, or have assured us, resounds in every soul, from the dark backward and abysm of time. Sophocles heard it by the Aegean once, and Apollonius heard it in Alexandria and piped it into poor Jason, whence to us. *Credo in complexum Oedipum*. It is the ground-note of the human condition, male and female. It is what every schoolboy knows. It is the realism underlying Apollonius' sweet, happy romance. In fact, it spoils that romance, as it spoils life.

SIGMA: Your candor is anger, Kappa, and it's concealing something. It shows resistance to something threatening.

KAPPA: I won't have that. I won't have self-justifying systems. Of course I grant the Oedipus complex. But I cannot grant that my rejection of an analysis is explained by the analysis I'm rejecting. And I do not reject it entirely. Of course a dwarf Oedipus squats inside us all, fretting, symbolically castrating himself. I remember my surprise, fifteen years ago, when I actually enjoyed working up the *Argonautica*; it was a set text on one of my exams. I enjoyed its style, clever and wet. Perhaps I really enjoyed it because my Oedipus complex was a bit riper then than it is now.

SIGMA: Did you mention the Oedipus complex, Alpha?

KAPPA: It is trendy not to mention the Oedipus complex. Jason, the new Alexandrian hero, unheroic, effeminate, alienated, did not mention that he wanted to displace Pelias, castrate Aeëtes, make love with his mother and/or father. All these dark matters Alpha reads into his text, so you must forgive me if I read Oedipus into your text. In fact, it is precisely what is *not* in the text that is the "realism" of the text, the true sense of the poem. But of course both the poem and the interpretation of the poem are like dreams. The nub of the matter is revealed by what is concealed, or concealed by what is revealed.

ALPHA: I am so trendy that it did not even occur to me to mention the Oedipus complex. "Oedipus complex" is a term like "romance." It conceals more than it reveals when stuck onto a particular work or human being. It's a crutch.

KAPPA: Often used by swollen-footed critics. So I misread you. I thought you were doing an ordinary thing. You were *explaining* Jason by putting him into a category, a pattern of human experience vaster than the pattern of any particular man or piece of work. After all, this is how we gratify our wish to abolish mysteries, isn't it? Poor Jason is no problem when he is seen to be another of the poor Oedipuses suffering through life and literature from that time to this. You were led to do this, I suppose, not only because it's a way the mind ordinarily converts the unknown into the known, but because you were looking for the "power," whatever that is—the power of the poem *now*, for us. We are not third-century-B.C. Alexandrians. We can't know, in actual fact, what moved them in their time. So we fall back on something universal, something without historical content, something that rather mysteriously touches us. No, sorry, I'm wrong. We don't fall back on Oedipus. We *find* him through interpretation of what is and isn't in the text. The explanation is in actual fact an interpretation. And the interpretation results, Alpha, from your question, "What's the power in the poem?" The question makes the interpretation, the interpretation makes the explanation, and I wonder what exactly is explained. Just how does Jason move us? Your Jason may be comprehensible, clinically comprehensible. A doctor reduces his patient to an example of a known syndrome, and he does this partly to prevent himself from being moved by the unique, individual patient himself so that he may treat him; but you were saying that Jason moves us *because* he is clinically comprehensible. I am touched by this paradox. You offer us a Jason diagnosed—and you apologize for this—diagnosed by psychoanalytic categories, yet you say that it is these categories, this generalized Jason, that moves us. In short, I wonder how your interpretation explains the power of the poem.

SIGMA: Now that Kappa has settled down, let me try to sort out the problems we're talking about.

ALPHA: Let me respond to Kappa.

SIGMA: No, I'm sorry, I can't even tell the difference between an interpretation and an explanation.

KAPPA: An interpretation finds sense, meaning, in a work. An explanation discovers the causes that make the work what it is.

ALPHA: Are these causes outside the work?

KAPPA: Outside and inside. Mostly outside, in the poet and his society.

ALPHA: Then the sense is a cause. Your distinction between interpretation and explanation is false. If the writer invents an episode, a speech, shapes a character to portray some leading idea or sense, the idea becomes an intrinsic cause of the work.

KAPPA: Right. The idea is in the poet, and he gets it from his psyche and his vision of the world, and the psyche and the vision are both determined by the structural dynamics of his society. The explanation must therefore go to the world to find effective causes, which is simply to say into the society, the structures and values, as they are determined by the ways people have devised to exploit nature, accumulate goods, and bugger their neighbors. An interpretation is an inference about the particular meaning of a particular work, and critics infer differently according to how *they* are shaped by the world.

SIGMA: And the flesh and the devil.

ALPHA: Inferences from what is said and not said in the text?

KAPPA: Only from what is said. Nothing warrants anyone going outside the text.

ALPHA: Except to find causes of the work.

KAPPA: And the best interpretation is the one that takes into account the maximum quantity of the text. Of course you can't really imagine that a poem causes itself. Nothing causes itself.

SIGMA: Except God.

KAPPA: Exactly. Which is to say, Nature. The trouble with your explanation, Alpha, is that it found no causes except the

Oedipus complex, which you read into the poem, and maybe a vague cultural *Angst* in what you are pleased to call the Hellenistic or Alexandrian period. And the trouble with your interpretation is that it found no meaning in the poem. The *Argonautica* remains meaningless. Worse, you set the poet against his poem. Apollonius says he celebrates a happy breed of heroes. You make him Viennese and neurotic.

ALPHA: I did not find the kind of causes and meanings you wanted me, in all charity, to find. I set out to inquire into only a few, but an interesting and important few, oddities in the poem itself. Jason and Medea suffer in ways unprecedented for heroes outside the theater, and even inside it, but in ways that would become common in later narratives. Just *how* do they suffer, and why do they suffer in this way? Jason is resourceless.

KAPPA: Which makes him, by the by, an almost exact antitype of Odysseus.

ALPHA: Yes, and he suffers in a self-consistent way, through success after success. He is a consistent character set among old heroic types, human and divine. The consistency, the *how* of his suffering, turned out to be of a familiar kind. Oedipal, OK, but entirely different from the suffering of Sophocles' Oedipus, for example, who in fact, or only, acts out what every man has dreamed, as Jocasta says. But the Oedipus complex is not the cause, the *why*, of Jason's suffering, or of Medea's, though Medea's can be seen as an effect of Jason's. The question of *why* is much more complex, of course. Jason was made by Apollonius, who tranformed, distorted, his inherited materials to do so. When I saw that Apollonius had suppressed the Jason-Pelias rivalry, emphasized Hera's role, and so forth, it was clear to me that Apollonius' distortions of his texts had their own consistency. He was making an interpretation of his texts, in your terms, because he was finding a particular meaning in them. It may not be a meaning in your terms. It is not a message; it tells us nothing about what is good and bad in the world or how to behave or what to think. It derives not from a vision of the world but a vision—and I must say that I hate the trendy, pompous word—a vision of an important kind of human suffering. Jason's and Medea's suffering *is* the primary sense of the poem, and it is a primary cause of the poem because it, or Apollonius with it, makes the focal characters and episodes what they are.

KAPPA: And botches his poem.

ALPHA: In a way, he was working at cross-purposes.

SIGMA: Why did he do that?

KAPPA: Let me speak to that.

ALPHA: Just a moment, please. There is at least one more cause related to these. I must assume that Apollonius, like all writers, wanted to move people. I see no evidence that he also wanted to teach them anything.

SIGMA: Freud said that he also wanted fame and the love of women.

ALPHA: Sure, at least the former, and he got it, with fortune to boot. His poem was a success with the Rhodians, Alexandrians, and Romans, though not with Callimachus. To move people is a good cause; and the so-called meaningless sense that was a principle of Apollonius' selection of his material, his condensations and expansions and distortions, that became the synthesizing principle of his version of the Jason-Medea story, must have moved him so that he thought, consciously or unconsciously, that it would move other people.

KAPPA: Wait! Listen! Am I hearing Aristotelian causes—final, formal, efficient, material?

ALPHA: Not exactly. But they add up to the kind of causation of a particular poem that Apollonius would have understood. That a poet should interpret his traditional story, and make it to a certain end, was part of the literary dogma of his "world." Apollonius may have been uncertain about his ends.

SIGMA: Why? A bad poet?

KAPPA: Alpha is telling us that the poem was such a resounding success because it was such an obvious failure. There is in actual fact some sense to that, as in all paradoxes.

SIGMA: Paradoxes, and critics quibbling over terms and methods, seem sterile to me.

KAPPA: Then we have annoyed you mightily. But in poems, critics, and dreams the principle of contradiction does not apply. And as Apollonius, like all poets, made his poem through a kind of dream work, distorting old stories along the lines of his own neurotic psyche, we must look into the depths of his soul to find the true cause of his poem. What a pity we can't stretch him on the table here and start him free associating; *that* would resolve all quibbling over explanations and interpretations.

SIGMA: There can be no objection to the terms and methods that make truths, or seem to make truths. Perhaps these are the same thing. But I still cannot grasp the problematics here. What are we interested in? Here we are in the presence of the beginnings of something interesting, if Alpha is to be believed. We have a precursor. When you have a precursor, you have a concept of development and a problem of causation. You have inevitably the category of the future. Alpha suggests that this problem is uninteresting or insoluble. But Alpha seeks the causes of what is clearly interesting, at least to me—the poem itself. Are these causes interesting?

KAPPA: Happy is he who knows the causes of things, said Cicero.

SIGMA: Very well, we are following the pleasure principle. And following it, Alpha psychologizes everything. He psychologizes the culture, he psychologizes the poem, he psychologizes the poetic process.

ALPHA: Because people have psyches, and because the making and enjoying of art are psychological processes.

KAPPA: But can he psychologize his prime cause, Apollonius?

ALPHA: I could do that, but it would give me little pleasure. And if I could do it to my satisfaction, I could also psychologize the dynamics of literary tradition, if that would give me pleasure. I hope we can agree that there is nothing wrong with pleasure. If we can't, we might be driven to find meanings in poems whose only meaning is the pleasure they give. We might want to sanction inquiry, and art itself, by offering it up on the altar of ourselves, of our private moral views of history and life. We might want to vulgarize the blooming, buzzing creation of man and God and Nature by recruiting it, through interpretation, into the service of our narcissistic self-righteousness. But I trust we will not do these things.

KAPPA: Nor will we rest with the trivial disguised in elitist hedonism. Let Alpha put Apollonius on the couch.

ALPHA: Sure. All we can know about Apollonius comes from his odd epic and from his rivalry with Callimachus. The poem shows he understood men like Jason and that he chose to tell the story of the Argonauts, founders of Cyrene. Why not this choice? But why? Callimachus ran the literary show at

Alexandria, he was probably Apollonius' teacher, and he was a
patriotic descendant of the royal house of Cyrene. He wrote a
civic hymn in honor of the town's patron, Apollo, in which he
accused Apollonius of envying him, and he says that envy
should be kicked with scorn. Apollonius ends his poem with the
dream that prefigures the founding of Cyrene, and he expands
the story's adventures in Libya, where Cyrene was to be. He has
a snake kill Mopsus there, for example; and his earlier dig at
Mopsus, as being one of the inglorious seers who cannot understand love, is taken to be a dig at Callimachus. He also has
Triton, not Apollo, give that clod of earth to the Argonauts,
though the Argonauts were praying for help to Apollo when
Triton surprisingly appears. Apollonius consistently under-
plays the role of his namesake, Apollo, in his story, though he
invokes him at the outset. No, he emphasizes the power of
Apollo in Jason's antagonist, Aeëtes. OK. Power makes for
rivalry, and Callimachus had power. It's not unlikely that
Apollonius had strong feelings about his poetic overlord. Is it
possible that Apollonius in the *Argonautica* was challenging Callimachus on his native grounds? The grounds being Libya and
Apollo and the Argonaut story itself, celebrated at Cyrene by
Pindar. Is it possible that he saw Callimachus as Jason sees
Aeëtes, as a kind of Apollo, an enviable version of himself
whom he fears, admires, and wants to surpass? He even wrote
the kind of epic that Callimachus said shouldn't or couldn't be
written.

KAPPA: This kind of mythic, biographical psychocriticism gives
me the absolute bloody horrors.

ALPHA: It doesn't explain very much even if you believe it.

KAPPA: The *Argonautica* is almost exactly the length of three Attic
tragedies plus the satyr play—the length Aristotle said epics
ought to have. Following Father Aristotle and not challenging
Uncle Callimachus, that's what Apollonius was up to.

SIGMA: But it explains everything. Jason is a latent homosexual
because Apollonius was one. Aeëtes is Callimachus, Apollo is
the paternal power all four fight over, the Golden Fleece is the
directorship of the Library, and Medea is the deep blue sea. By
suppressing the deep Jason-Pelias rivalry, which was probably
too threatening for him to face, and by making his hero a
coward who couldn't enjoy success or sex, Apollonius wrote a

flawed poem and therefore succeeded, as all victims of castration anxiety want to succeed; but they then find somewhere along the line that nothing succeeds like failure.

ALPHA: But Apollonius did conquer the mother city. And Rhodes as well, another place dedicated to Helios-Apollo.

SIGMA: I congratulate you. You've carried this line of causal analysis as far—and maybe then some—as a sensible man would want to carry it.

KAPPA: I entirely agree with you. I may now confess that I agree, too, with your explanations, Alpha, as far as they go; though your interpretation, or noninterpretation, leaves something to be desired. There is in my humble view only one thing wrong with your explanation. It doesn't explain why this odd little epic appeared in the mid-third century B.C. One cannot ignore history when one writes history. I hardly know where to begin. What is new in the *Argonautica?* It is not dark erotic suffering. Euripides had all that. It is an anxiety-ridden hero who wants only to get back home again. And who can blame him? He is no Odysseus or Heracles. He's an ordinary citizen, a bourgeois like you and me. His fears are as realistic as those of Odysseus, but he can't take joy in success until he achieves the final, real success—getting home again safe and sound—because he's a citizen caught in an old-time heroic task. His fears cast doubt on the potency of the old heroism. His alienation from the Argonauts also casts doubts on the ideals of heroic triumph, on loyalties to an adventurous, vengeful band. His only real loyalty, and therefore security, is at home with mum and dad. This is why Apollonius suppressed, as you say, the home-based rivalry. Unlike Odysseus, Jason need not reestablish his kingship by slaying rivals at home because he is not a king and could never be one. But, at the same time, you have all those fossilized heroes overcoming the fantasized perils of the world. They don't fit into Jason's world, nor Jason into theirs. Here are the contradictions that explain the ambivalences in Apollonius' poem. The happy heroes bespeak the nostalgia for the past, the bourgeois longing for potent, aristocratic dominance over everything, that is characteristic of Alexandrian poetry, just as those shepherds in Theocritus, singing their bloody hearts out, reveal a typical romanticizing of the peasantry. In the bizarre geography of the trip home you see a bourgeois exuberance for space, expansion, conquest over everything, fate, barbaric forces, the owners of magic and golden fleeces—the lot. All this is in contradiction with bourgeois doubt and anxiety about whether the world can be exploited without the old heroic powers. Jason feels resourceless because he's terrified by a task imposed on him by history: to exploit nature, to get the gold and the fleece, to wrest power from the traditional owners of things and of superhuman force. And he knows that all the ideals, all the heroes of the past, can't really help him.

ALPHA: You're telling an old story. Who was it that pointed out that the quest for the Golden Fleece reflects the expansion of Greek trade into the trans-Euxine?

KAPPA: Of course it's not as simple as that. And the Golden Fleece is not as simple as pubic hair, either.

ALPHA: I wouldn't have thought so either, but the poem itself, or Jason's character, gives those things a symbolic meaning. In another story, or another *Argonautica*, maybe an *Argonautica* like the one you're describing, they might have different meanings or no meaning at all.

KAPPA: The *Argonautica* I'm describing is the one written by a subsidized scholar-bureaucrat in Alexandria about 250 B.C. His values, his ambitions, much of his psyche, *must* have been determined by his culture. What else could have determined these things? Now, what were the concrete realities? Seventy years earlier the world had become Greek, in a sense. Vast Hellenic polities, kingdoms, had opened the world to trade, and in the eastern Mediterranean basin you had a rather complicated mercantile system, very affluent, dependent on money, literacy, risk-taking, even venture capital. This was developing a proto-bourgeois class, wealthy merchant families and syndicates exploiting the hinterlands of the cities and trading everywhere they could. This explains, by the by, some of the epiphenomena you described. To make money by trade you have to calculate tonnage, miles, and time. You have to make lists and catalogs. Geography, geometry, astronomy, textual criticism, all that, reflect social realities that demand that people think in abstract terms. The museums and libraries, not only at Alexandria, are the countinghouses of culture. They are also symptoms of an acquisitive spirit, a desire to own things for yourself. You can see the Ptolemies try to stake a claim on Greek culture, buy it, and store it. The same thing happened at Pergamum. They are also symptoms of the loss of a genuine, intuitive sense of art and the past. You feel nostalgia for a mythic past, so you make naive poetry. You wax archaic, sweetly artificial. And the state buys and keeps poets to watch over its stored culture, and this sets the poets against one another; they become rivals for patronage and power like everyone who doesn't really own anything, and this explains the Apollonius-Callimachus rivalry. Apollonius converts an old family-clan rivalry into a myth of enterprise, but his Jason bloody well doesn't like it, he's like the hero of epic as Hegel saw the hero, a man struggling against a new social form, a new class dominance, as Apollonius himself struggled to preserve the old epic form. At the same time, he's like the hero as Marx saw him, a man *ahead* of his time, accelerating history. He's a complicated figure. No wonder he's anxious, resourceless. And that's what makes the book interesting.

ALPHA: And it can move us today because, as Marx said, though the concrete historical realities have changed, the Greek epic returns us to the infancy of the race, and we enjoy returning to infancy.

SIGMA: And if everyone's childhood—your own excluded, Kappa—was a little troubled by sexual guilt, then another part of Jason's appeal is explained. I'm amazed at the number of reasons why we should enjoy the *Argonautica*.

KAPPA: You can also enjoy its language, which Alpha entirely ignores. The art of the thing.

ALPHA: Can we enjoy its art? Hegel said that art springs from intuition, and intuition ended with antiquity. Now that religion is dead and we have advanced to the era of philosophy, we can enjoy art only philosophically, as Kappa has illustrated.

KAPPA: That's very nearly nonsense, you know.

SIGMA: Perhaps you had better let Alpha explain to you why you enjoyed the *Argonautica* even before you understood it philosophically.

ALPHA: I'm still trying to figure out just where Kappa found his historical allegory in the text. It seems to me even more fanciful than the psychological allegory you made, Sigma. Did Apollonius write his critique of Hellenistic contradictions unconsciously, or was he an Alexandrian Bert Brecht? I don't quarrel with your characterization of that society. And of course the values and aspirations of people are in large part determined by what's going on. And the values, especially, are vital in art. And so on. But the values in the *Argonautica* are not unusual. Loyalty, courage, cleverness, even the conscience that tells a girl she shouldn't betray her father and run off with a stranger. Conflicts over these matters move us, as do perils encountered and escaped.

KAPPA: I take Apollonius at his word. He wants to celebrate the luminous fame of the old happy heroes. I take Jason for what he is, afraid, and Medea for what she is, unhappy in love. These things move us. Alexandrians would have been more moved, perhaps subliminally, by seeing, or rather hearing—you often forget that Apollonius' art was an *oral* art—hearing about an unheroic hero trapped in a mythic heroic enterprise and getting away scot-free. It is, in a way, like a complex dream, for them. I know, too, that things like *Oedipus* and *Hamlet* are supposed to move us in other ways, and maybe they do. I can't see this happening in the *Argonautica*.

SIGMA: Just what is the psychology of being moved, subliminally, by an imitation of Oedipal or cultural conflicts? Or have we had enough for one afternoon? I see we have. Alpha, shouldn't I bring Psi along next time to correct your psychologism?

ALPHA: Sure. That's a good idea.

❧ 4 ❧
Bits and
Epitomes

We may now turn to the surviving fragments of some lost novels. What explains the appearance of long prose fictions in the first century B.C.? From what literary genres sprang the unprecedented genre that is none of them? Some say that the romances are primarily developments of civic or tribal legends, others that they are allegorical celebrations of the mystery cults, especially that of Isis. Some would contend that they are elaborations of vulgar novellas, others that the form originated in the mind of an unknown genius who evoked it from drama and historiography.[1] This diversity of answers reflects a diversity of opinions, often undefined, and this diversity in turn reflects a difficulty in the questions themselves. Since it is generally agreed that the Greek novels are romances, questions about the origins of the novel are usually mixed with the question, What is the origin of the romance? It would be prudent, I think, to divide these questions, because not all novels are romances and not all romances are novels. And having divided them, one would do well to recognize that both questions rest on a questionable assumption—that the novel and/or the romance is a formal entity; and, having adopted this assumption, one would have to define the entity whose origins one is seeking before actually seeking its origins, and one would have to observe how one's definition determined one's answers to questions of origin. Since I am not prepared to adopt the assumption or define the phenomenon, I cannot ask questions about origins. I can, however, adopt the assumption that the narratives which many learned and sensitive people have subsumed under one or another name must share important elements—conventions of character, episode, action, technique, and so forth—which must appear even in the fossils of the presumed genre.

Chapter Four

Among the papyri unearthed nearly a century ago at Oxyrhynchus, a small town some three hundred miles south of Alexandria, are bits of literary works that embody some of the conventions of intact romances so neatly that one suspects that an Alexandrian scholar buried them there to intrigue his archeological heirs. The oldest is the "Alexandrian Erotic Fragment,"[2] a *paraklausithyron*, or lament sung by a lover at the beloved's closed door, written on the back of a contract dated 173 B.C. Horace (*Odes* 1. 3) and Romeo provide later examples of the scene. But in this one the lamenter is a girl, and she addresses herself as well as her beloved in a prosody that is neither epic nor elegiac but a kind of rhythmic prose. These oddities suggest that the fragment is not part of a prose fiction but of a sung mime, one of the playlets performed by itinerant actors in cities throughout the Hellenic world. Even so, its ideas and rhetoric are those of the soliloquized debate of the soul conventional in the prose romances. Love is an enslaver, and the beloved is a betrayer, the girl says. Moreover, it is "a love of one and one alone" that "makes for madness," because this kind of love leads to a choice that binds the soul forever. Here, in a vulgar declamation, is expressed the intensely personal love that binds two souls unto and beyond death; and it is this concept of love that becomes a root convention of the Greek prose romances.

Three fragments of the "Ninus Romance," all of them written in straight prose, survive from the first century before Christ.[3] In one fragment, Ninus, the legendary founder of Nineveh, orders his forces to attack the mad Armenians. In another he urges a lady to allow her daughter to marry him, while, nearby, the daughter weeps wordlessly in an attempt to persuade Ninus' mother to permit the marriage. Ninus rests his case on his chastity: though he is seventeen, he has never "snatched a secret enjoyment"; but now he has been "worsted by the god of love" and has become the girl's "prisoner." Meanwhile, the girl "would open her lips and look up as if about to speak but could finally utter nothing. She heaved with broken sobs, her cheeks reddened with shame (*aidōs*) at what she must say," and like Medea she sways "with an inward disturbance between her varying emotions." When Ninus' mother says, "This I like better than ... words," one is reminded of the woman whose sins Christ would later forgive because she "loved much." Speechless sincerity bespeaks a love sanctioned by suffering, and this too becomes a vital convention of romance. Moreover, the love that imprisons seems to lead only to marriage, as it had for Medea; but here, as in the later prose romances, marriage involves parental permission, as well as the premarital chastity that not even Jason could claim. To us these values are still rather admirable if somewhat archaic; only the names of the characters are surprising. The bride is Semiramis, the ferocious foundress of Babylon, who was a figure of the terrible goddess Ishtar. Her mother is Derceia—that is, the even more terrible goddess Derceto. Readers of the "Ninus Romance" were as accustomed as we are to seeing the Olympians portrayed as bitches and martinets, but here a more bloody pantheon of witches and tyrants speaks and behaves like dutiful Victorians. The "Ninus" romancer has transformed legendary demigods into the chaste, suffering scions of powerful Hellenic families. The literary archeologist cannot be surprised when the third "Ninus" fragment fits like a molar into an already reconstructed jaw. It describes a violent storm and shipwreck, a scene that has become a hallmark of Greek romance,[4] though tempests, like legendary lovers and campaigns, fit as well into epics, tragedies, elegies, and histories.

Another prose fragment, which may antedate the "Alexandrian Erotic Fragment," displays the conventional Scorner of Love—a young man who claims that Eros does not exist, that the notion of an ageless boy flying about the world transfixing souls with arrows is absurd.[5] Given the conventions, we know what will happen to him. Still another fragment bears another hallmark of romance—magic. It is not the grand magic of Medea but that of an ordinary countryside witch who, though she claims that she can walk on water and move the stars, possesses no drug that can control Eros, because "the earth, being in awe of the god, does not produce one."[6] Witches, like tempests and pirates, were familiar in everyday life: professional sorceresses were usually available to the lovelorn, impotent, or vengeful inhabitants of Hellenic towns. But it was literary convention that told people how to talk about the power of Eros over scorn and magic. And of course all of these conventions of the erotic sufferer, of chastity, of love rhetoric and battle rhetoric, can be found anywhere at almost any time—in Sanskrit, in Chinese, in Coptic. In fact, two other conventions closely associated with Greek romance—the episode of resurrection from death and the figures of Joseph and Potiphar's Wife—appear in Egyptian stories of the thirteenth century B.C. As the scriptural Joseph was rejecting that lady, stories about powerful young men rejecting the amorous wives of their overlords were being told in Egypt.[7]

These papyri from a single provincial town in lower Egypt suggest a widespread literacy and readership for prose fictions as well as an interest in literary criticism. "Make and send me copies of books 6 and 7 of Hypoicrates' *Characters in a Comedy*," reads a letter of the second century B.C. "Harpocration says they are in Pollion's bookshop.... He also has epitomes of Thersagoras' work *On the Myths of Tragedy*." And a postscript in another hand corrects Harpocration: the epitomes are actually "to be found in the bookshop of Demetrius."[8] For the ordinary reader or theatergoer, such treatises (now lost) and precious old epics like the *Argonautica* may have been somewhat abstruse. His—or more likely her—tastes for the awesome and amusing might have been gratified by the impassioned troubles of legendary figures like Ninus and Semiramis, characters as worthy as those in the "myths of tragedy," yet made to seem not entirely unlike those in mime or the New Comedy—admirable characters who survive exotic perils and erotic suffering while bolstered by familiar ideals of chastity and marriage.

One such story has come down to us in an ample epitome— Xenophon of Ephesus' *Ephesiaca*. So dense is the epitome, which was made in the early part of the second century A.D., that one cannot assess the aesthetic value of the original; but this very fact makes it especially valuable for anyone investigating the conventions of old novels. It is a test tube crammed with marvelous incidents, paradoxical peripeties, thrilling catharses, and erotic suffering.

In Ephesus the citizens honored sixteen-year-old Habrocomes "as though he were a god, and indeed some of them ... bowed down when they saw him and offered him a prayer."[9] But unlike Apollo-like Jason, this boy is a Scorner: "He even denied that Eros was a god; nay, he dismissed him as a cipher and banished him utterly." When he insults the god's statue, "Eros waxed wroth; jealous is that divinity ... and [he] marched against Habrocomes." During a procession honoring Ephesian Artemis, Habrocomes sees fourteen-year-old Anthia, a priestess of the virginal

Great Mother, and her eyes "were lively, shining sometimes like a girl's, sometimes severe, as of a chaste goddess." Anthia wears her patroness' fawnskin cloak, carries her bow and javelin, and the crowd "bowed down to her as to Artemis.... Some of the spectators suggested that she was the very goddess, others declared that she was a replica fashioned by the goddess. But all did obeisance to her." Glimpsing Anthia, Habrocomes falls in love; and "with her whole being [Anthia] caught the beauty of Habrocomes, which flowed into her wide-open eyes."

Already in the first one hundred words we have more conventions than can conveniently be described. But since many of them persist in the initial episodes of later narratives (note the "Renaissance Platonism" of the eye play), we must attempt a list.

    I. ELEMENTS OF CHARACTER
        A. A hero
            1. Young
            2. Godlike
            3. A citizen
            4. A chaste scorner of love
        B. A heroine
            1. Young
            2. Godlike
            3. A citizen's daughter
            4. Sacerdotally chaste
        C. Eros
            1. Jealous
            2. Powerful
        D. Artemis
            1. Chaste
            2. Powerful
        E. A crowd
            1. Adoring
            2. Holding diverse opinions
    II. ELEMENTS OF SITUATION
        A. A city
            1. Real and well known
            2. Site of a famous cult
        B. A religious procession
        C. Love at first sight

III. ELEMENTS OF VALUE
  A. Ethical
     1. Chastity
     2. Piety
     3. Vengeful jealousy
     4. Capacity to love wholly
  B. Natural
     1. Beauty and dress evince character
     2. Love links psyches
     3. Youth is volatile
  C. Religious
     1. The gods move psyches
     2. Psyches evince deities
     3. The gods may be cruel or beneficent
IV. ELEMENTS OF TECHNIQUE
  A. Narrative
     1. Thought and feeling dramatized in indirect discourse
     2. Psyches fully known and reported
  B. Verbal
     1. Plain periods
     2. Tropes

Such a list is meaningless, as inert as the elements themselves, unless we appreciate the judgmental feelings and expectations which this particular cluster of conventions, set in an initiating episode, is presumably designed to arouse in us. We admire the lovers' chastity and beauty, in which they are superior to us; but their youthful ignorance makes them somewhat inferior. They are godlike but possess no supernatural powers; like us, they are pious citizens of a familiar city. Their falling victim to love may give us some satisfaction, because they are better than we are; but we remain sympathetic, because they are admirable and we are wiser in the ways of love than they are. We know that they will suffer, that their suffering will be serious, and that they must—being apparently flawless—survive.

Such an episode is like an incomplete utterance that demands development if it is to acquire full emotional meaning. But perhaps we are to infer other meanings from it. For example, does the characters' likeness to certain gods refer us to a semantic system, composed of the "meanings" conventionally assigned to these gods, which is extrinsic to the work itself? Perhaps we are to read rhetorical propositions about the overwhelming powers of Artemis and Eros into this episode about Anthia and Habrocomes. Perhaps the characters and their experiences are elements in an argument designed to teach us something about the gods.[10] If so, the whole story, or at least its crucial episodes, should make the argument clear.

Anthia and Habrocomes suffer "agitation... deep anguish. ... Habrocomes pulled his hair and ripped his clothes," saying, "Now another seems fairer than myself, and I acknowledge that Eros is a god"; while Anthia, though she does not express her suffering in the language of defeated narcissism, stamps on her soul the image of Habrocomes. Mystified, their parents summon comically incompetent doctors (perhaps from the conventions of mime), who announce that the malady is caused by underworld daimons, whereupon the parents consult the oracle. We readers now enjoy a knowledge of true causes superior to that of everyone in the story save the lovers, and this, too, links us to the protagonists. Experienced in the conventions, we already know what the oracle will tell the wondering parents: that the lovers will "undergo toils protracted"—pirates, captivity, fire, "a bridal chamber [that] will serve as a tomb"—after which "their lot grants a fortune that is better." In the light of our superior knowledge, only the victims of love's fate fully deserve our admiration and sympathy; and our superiority is doubtless even more pleasurable when it assures us that we are more mature than these flawless darlings, whose capacity for erotic suffering and survival is doubtless superior to our own.

As mature voyeurs, we may enjoy their wedding night, with its panting, shame, and "thoughts... transmitted through their lips from the soul of one to the soul of the other." Then they are put out to sea by their parents. Why? To obey the oracle (and, of course, to make the story). But this motive, this alliance with a fate determined by love, is even more mysterious than the motive and fate obeyed by Jason. Jason's obedience and resourcelessness could be explained in terms simpler than those that would be needed to explain the more various sufferings of these lovers. In any case, we admire their vows: "I solemnly invoke to witness ... our great Diana of the Ephesians," says Anthia to Habrocomes, "and that divinity who has so well implanted in us passionate love for each other, that if I am separated from you even for any short shrift of time, I shall not live." Anthia does not keep this vow, but the love that motivates it will govern her as it governs the values of the story. The chastity of Diana/Artemis has allied itself with the passion of Eros to produce the madness of loving one person alone, and this madness becomes the dominant ethical and religious ideal of this and later stories. It is a malady that conquers misfortune and death. The ensuing action works through sequences of perils that are erotic in character— seduction, separation, enslavement, rape, and death itself. Being paragons, the characters cannot undergo any genuine enrichment or erosion of soul as they suffer these intense perils. The tale must therefore be one of action more than of character, one "that appeals to the feelings by strange escapes from danger . . . paradoxical deliverances from desperate unhappiness."[11]

Though the characters remain static, many incidents appeal to the fantasies and dreads that must underlie the idealization of erotic love and the pursuit of erotic suffering. On the open sea Habrocomes dreams that an enormous woman dressed in scarlet burns their ship, though precisely what this imago may signify we cannot say because the characters are so shallow and the story so bare. The pirates who now capture the ship are captained by a homosexual, Corymbus, whose name might suggest the Corybantes, the self-castrating devotees of the mother goddess Cybele. In fact, we might infer that the scarlet woman was Cybele and that the story here adumbrates a rivalry between her and Artemis. But Corymbus is no villain. The desire he promptly feels for Habrocomes is not made to seem contemptible in itself, and he woos our hero through a courtly go-between, Euxines. When Euxines fails, and Habrocomes exclaims that to submit would make him "a harlot and not a man," we understand that the attempted seduction, like the imago and the identifications of the protagonists with deities, is meant primarily to enhance the emotive powers of the story itself, not to argue a case for certain gods. What some of these emotive powers may be is suggested by homosexual temptation itself—nobly resisted. Others are suggested when Euxines, filling out a neat package of perils, woos Anthia, and the lovers, lost in an erotic wilderness, cry in unison for "Father! . . . Mother! . . . Home!" Erotic love has meant for them a fated departure from home and childhood, and now another home beckons: "Let us die, Habrocomes," says Anthia;

"we shall possess each other after death, and none shall trouble us." In this story, as in others, death is an attractive refuge for erotic love. It is in fact a condition of life where vows of fidelity may be kept free of all temptation.

The frustrated pirates sell Anthia and Habrocomes, along with their devoted slaves, Rhoda and Leucon, into slavery, whereupon Habrocomes faces a heterosexual threat. When their master's daughter, Manto, falls in love with him, even Anthia advises him to submit, announcing that she will merely kill herself. But Habrocomes responds, "They may have power over my body, but my soul I keep free"; and Manto, having written him the love letter which we know by convention will doom her, fills out her conventional role by accusing him of having attempted what she has attempted. Imprisoned, and tortured in pleasing detail, Habrocomes disappears from view for a while and is thus separated from Anthia until the consummation of the action.

Manto now sends Anthia to a nearby goatherd with orders that he rape her, but the paternal old rustic is so moved by the girl's radiant innocence that he spares her. Then Manto learns that her new husband, Moeris, is enamored of her rival in a different way, and she orders the goatherd to kill her. "O pernicious beauty," cries Anthia—an apostrophe that rings through many romances —"thanks to you, Habrocomes is dead . . . and I am about to die here." But the price of beauty is not always death. In another act of pastoral virtue, the goatherd sells her to passing pirates, who are forthwith shipwrecked near Tarsus and captured by brigands led by another homosexual—Hippothous. These duplications of earlier perils do not signal that the author's invention has run its course. Hippothous' band suspends Anthia naked from a tree as a target, to sacrifice her to their patron, Ares; and this sadomasochistic thrill is quickly succeeded by still another kind of temptation: the police who save her (Hippothous alone escaping) are led by a very desirable match, the rich and unmarried Perilaus, who falls in love with her and proposes honorable union. Anthia must fall back on a claim ("I know not on what pretext," says the author) that she must observe thirty more days of virginity before marriage. Leaving us suspended (he hopes) in this narrative web, the author returns us to Habrocomes.

Habrocomes dreams that his father releases him from prison and that he (Habrocomes) is a galloping horse; in fact it is Manto's benevolent father who releases him (having found that incriminating love letter), and Habrocomes walks up the Phoenician coast, seeking Anthia. Whom should he meet in the forest but the melancholy brigand Hippothous, who, after a ten-day journey with his chaste friend, suddenly breaks into tears. He explains these tears with a "history of his life": he is a brigand, he says, because years earlier his love for a boy had been thwarted "by a jealous god," and the boy had died in his arms. The nobility of his erotic suffering warrants his inclusion in this serious plot; and indeed it will be he, motivated by homosexual love, who will engineer the resolution of the action. Now he sparks another marvelous discovery and reversal: as Habrocomes speaks of Anthia, Hippothous remembers a blond, soft-eyed Ephesian girl— "Anthia!" shouts Habrocomes. And they set off in the wrong direction to find her.

Meanwhile, Anthia escapes Perilaus by persuading a doctor to poison her; but the doctor substitutes an opiate, and she is entombed alive. When she wakes, she laments her revival; and when grave-robbers break in, she cries, "Touch me not! I am consecrated to two deities—Love and Death!" So she seems to be; and so, too, are most of the remaining episodes of the story. No other romance draws so plainly on relationships between Eros and Thanatos. After the awed ghouls have taken her to Alexandria for sale, Habrocomes, finding her tomb empty at Tarsus, cries, "Wretch that I am, I am deprived even of your remains, my only solace. Now I am altogether determined to die; but first I must endure until I find your body; and, when I have embraced it, I shall bury myself with it." Such scenes of death and lament and resurrection may seem to play on the experiences of initiates in the mystery cults, which promised salvation from death, but they more obviously play on a desire to embrace safe death. In either case, they make for an exciting story. Anthia does in fact use a cult to escape her next perilous temptation. She lies to the barbaric Indian who has purchased her at Alexandria, saying that since, "at her birth her father had consecrated her to Isis," she must remain chaste for another year; and it is the lie, not Isis, that works.

Habrocomes is sold by pirates to an old soldier who treats him like a son and whose amorous wife urges the boy to kill the paternal master and marry her. When Habrocomes rejects this profound temptation, the woman does the murderous deed, accuses Habrocomes of it, and he is crucified on the bank of the Nile. But he prays to the river, which rises; the cross collapses and carries him downstream, where a marveling prefect sends him to a pyre which the river, responding to another prayer, quenches. All the gods of Egypt seem to be conspiring to save the lovers from death and temptation. We are not told that they are moved by the sufferers' chaste fidelity, but we may infer this, since Anthia prays in the great shrine of Isis at Memphis: "O greatest of goddesses, until now I have remained chaste because I was believed to be thine, and I have preserved my marriage to Habrocomes unsullied. . . . Either then deliver me, the unfortunate . . . and return me to Habrocomes in life, or, if it is inexorably fated that we die apart from each other, accomplish this: let me remain chaste to him that is dead." The powers of the gods, and the heroic virtues (including cunning), have been brought into the service of the eros of marriage, and the eros of marriage into the service of many erotic fantasies, and these into the service of a thrilling story.

Habrocomes drifts to Sicily, where he encounters an ideal of marital life. Once again he is sheltered "as a child" by an old man, this one a fisherman. Years earlier the fisherman and his wife had been driven from Sparta by parental disapproval, a mundane form of the jealous Eros that had driven our lovers from Ephesus. But their love, too, had survived this obstacle, and death itself. In fact, the fisherman's wife lies embalmed in the next room, and the old husband says that he daily covers her with kisses and eats and sleeps with her. "Now I clearly see that age does not end true love!" shouts Habrocomes, delighted with this discovery.

Meanwhile, Anthia has once more fallen captive to Hippothous, who has returned to brigandage and acquired her frustrated Indian's caravan but does not recognize his friend's beloved. This time he confines her to a cave; and when her guard attempts rape, she kills him, in punishment for which she is buried alive in a pit with two mastiffs. Another official rescues and falls in love with her, but he, awed by her refusals, leaves her untouched and sells her to a brothel-keeper of Tarentum, a city not far from Tauromenium, where Hippothous has at last settled down with a dowager, not far from where Habrocomes lives peacefully with his fatherly necrophiliac. At this point, as our principals are drawing together, Habrocomes learns that his and Anthia's parents have died, either by suicide or grief. It hardly matters which. The death of parents can of itself release true love in children. Habrocomes decides, on the strength of this news, to look round Italy for Anthia.

Anthia has permitted herself to be exposed to potential custom- ers at the brothel; but when the customers come inside, she falls into fits—or pretends to. The explanation she gives her keeper for this unprofitable behavior makes the difference between con- scious pretense and compulsive hysteria unimportant. Once, when she was a child, she says, she was separated from her parents during one of those processions in honor of virginal Ar- temis. She found herself beside the tomb of a recently buried man whose spirit attempted to rape her. Though she struggled, the erotic ghost did not release her until daybreak, giving her a blow that caused her fits. Anthia is doubtless lying again. But this lie is so remarkably appropriate to a devotee of Artemis, for whom jealous Eros has dictated frustration of love, and to one who is once more separated from her parents and confronted with the prospect of erotic plenitude that we must congratulate "Xenophon" for his insightful invention.

Hippothous, now a rich widower and accompanied by a beauti- ful Sicilian boy, recognizes Anthia in the Tarentine slave market, where her sympathetic keeper is selling her. He buys her freedom and sails with her toward Ephesus, whither the unknowing and unhappy Habrocomes is also sailing. The culminating recogni- tions and reversals are now at hand; and since they must relieve the tensions accumulated by the whole action, they are prolonged. The two parties, obeying the logic of geography, stop off at Rhodes, where the lovers' loving slaves, Rhoda and Leucon, now freed, have also disembarked. The famous quadrennial festival devoted to Rhodian Helios is now in progress. The grieving freedmen set up a stele commemorating their presumably dead master and mistress, and, seeing it, Habrocomes recognizes his former slaves. Anthia offers the sun god her hair, and this familiar act of melancholy self-mutilation is rewarded when Rhoda and Leucon discover her golden tresses beside a telltale inscription. They inform Habrocomes, who runs through the streets to the shrine of Isis, where presumably Anthia would be at her prayers. The lovers fall into each other's arms. The mixed, contrary emo- tions felt by the gathered townspeople convey, as usual, what we are to feel: "pleasure, pain, fear, memory of the past, apprehension of the future, all mixing in their souls." This paradoxical mix of emotions is a conventional *topos* used by all Greek romancers to describe the catharsis that results from recognition and reversal of fortune. But cathartic "relief from tension" is accompanied by a positive sense of gratitude. "O great goddess," say the lovers to Isis, "above all the world you are dear to us, for it is by you that we are reunited." What about Artemis and Helios? Don't they deserve some thanks? Has the romancer or his epitomizer converted an Ephesian legend honoring Artemis into an argument in favor of Isis and/or Rhodian Helios? Theologically, the story is a mishmash, but this romance is not a theological allegory. The gods serve the story, not vice versa. Whether we are Rhodians or Ephesians or Hellenic Egyptians, our pleasure is enriched by a vague sense that some deity has all along been working to reward human virtue and is now presiding over the purge of tensions that we are at last permitted to enjoy.

That night, everyone, including Hippothous and his boy, goes to bed. In bed, Anthia recounts her adventures before asking Habrocomes whether he too has remained faithful. He has. They all sail to Ephesus, where, after a somewhat perfunctory thanksgiving to Artemis, the lovers build a magnificent tomb for their parents. And Hippothous raises a great monument to his dead beloved on Lesbos, then returns to Ephesus with his new love-boy, and lives happily ever after with Anthia and Habrocomes.

I have epitomized this epitome at such length in order to present the material conventions of a notoriously convention-ridden genre. A list of the elements that appear in at least one other Greek prose romance might go like this:

I. ELEMENTS OF CHARACTER
   Lovers: young, beautiful, faithful, clever,
      unknown in myth
   Parents: rich, doting
   Slaves: faithful, protective
   Onlookers: awestruck
   Doctors: incompetent
   Pirates/brigands: awestruck, amorous, sym-
      pathetic, cruel
   Another woman: amorous, awestruck,
      just, unmarried

Homosexual friend: loyal, outlawed, sympathetic

Barbarians: awestruck, amorous, superstitious, rich

Brothel-keeper: sympathetic

Rustics: awestruck, sympathetic, old

The author: awestruck, sometimes ignorant of causes

II. ELEMENTS OF SITUATION OR EVENT

Love at first sight; shrines and festivals; marriage; oracles and dreams; captivity, enslavement, imprisonment; attempted rape, seduction, marriage, prostitution; escape by chance, lying, miracle; separation of lovers; attempted execution, sacrifice; live burial; shelter by rustics, fishermen; recognition and reunion; death of parents; homecoming

III. ELEMENTS OF VALUE

Marital fidelity; veracity of oracles and dreams; power, amorality and morality of Fortune; benevolent but obscure power of cult gods; Eros as irresistible, cruel, and salvific; desirability of death; piety; family loyalty; superstitiousness of barbarians; goodness of lower orders; honor among brigands, rapacity of brigands; genuineness of homosexual love

IV. ELEMENTS OF STYLE

Military, medical, and scientific conceits; allusions to dramas and epics; laments, debates of the soul in soliloquy; apostrophes to fate, the gods, the beloved, beauty; similes, balanced antitheses

Such a list is like a primitive glossary. Adopting a conceit drawn from linguistics, we might say that the principles—syntactic, morphemic, phonetic—that vivify these lexical items, and give meaning to whole aesthetic utterances, are left out of the list. But this conceit also suggests that the conventional elements are not in themselves empty of meaning. A live burial, for example, or an attempted seduction, arouses fundamental dreads and desires which constitute the semantic content of the conventional episode; while the principles that govern the place, the shape, and the effects of the episode in a whole action give it aesthetic significance. Again, each of the stock characters listed above must be defined in terms that suggest the moral judgments and emotions that give meaning to poetic works. But a variation in only one term can have profound aesthetic consequences. For example, Habrocomes and Anthia, unlike Jason and Medea, are unknown in myth. Both sets of lovers are so extraordinarily beautiful, godlike, and fundamentally virtuous that we know they will triumph over any extraordinary obstacle, and the supernatural powers enjoyed by Medea and Jason in fact add nothing essential to our hopes and fears for them. But the mythic reputations of Jason and Medea are so awesome that Apollonius may rely on them to elicit our admiration, whereas Xenophon, depriving himself of myth, must insist on his protagonists' godlike qualities, replacing mythic reputation with moral flawlessness, in order to win our awe. The conventional heroic stature of Jason permits Apollonius to modify his conventional character. He may introduce an ordinary resourcelessness that has its own appeal while retaining, he hopes, the appeal of the imperiled triumphing hero. Xenophon, on the other hand, must keep his protagonists flawless, pitiable victims of Eros and fate or must, at best, reduce the murderous frustrations of a Medea to the noble lying of an Anthia. I say "at best" because a flawed or mistaken hero has a potential for the suffering and discoveries that we associate with an art profounder than that of the *Ephesiaca*. Apollonius failed to exploit successfully his modification of conventions, partly because it conflicted with his desire to retain the conventional goal of celebrating triumphant heroes. But Xenophon certainly exploited his conventions fully—perhaps, to a fault. Had someone offered romancers, or epitomizers, a prize for the story that included the maximum number of wonderful incidents illustrating "the uncertain and varied fortunes" that give "scope for surprise, suspense, delight, annoyance, hope, and fear" in the minimum number of words, the author or epitomizer of the *Ephesiaca* would have won hands down. And it is these effects, along with that of the "striking consummation" that affords the "complete satisfaction of mind which is the most perfect pleasure a reader can enjoy," that he was obviously aiming at. His conventions helped him do this; and, freed of myth, he could project erotic dreads and desires into incidents involving the brigands, whoremongers, seducers, and idealistic lovers of the ordinary world.

It may be that "romance" is nothing more than a set of conventions similar to those plainly visible in the *Ephesiaca*, always treated seriously but varying slightly to reflect the social and religious values that change from age to age. Even so, the conventions are inert matter until vivified by the narrative arts that give them aesthetic meaning. These arts are themselves conventions and may be likened to principles of syntax—principles that are rules within the whole grammar of extended narratives. For example, the episodes of the *Ephesiaca* are arranged in large units or phases that could not be rearranged. The first phase, or act, of the whole action generates pitying admiration for the lovers and fear that their love will not be consummated; the second phase generates fear that they will be separated; the third, fear that they will never find each other again; the fourth, a growing hope that they will be reunited; the fifth, a grateful joy in their salvation. The "meanings" generated by this syntax of the whole action are the emotions aroused and relieved in the characters and in us, the readers. A comparable syntax governs the arrangement of incidents within the episodes. Dread, hope, admiration, disdain, joy, piety—nearly every episode generates such feelings through a syntactic ordering of conventional materials that brings one of the principals to a crisis—a threat to his life, values, or task—which is relieved by an escape that produces still another threat, and so on.

As an example of the syntax that works within episodes, consider Anthia's difficulties with the attractive Perilaus, who has rescued her from her antecedent peril and wants to marry her. First, the author tells us that, during Anthia's thirty-day grace period (acquired by a lie), an old Ephesian doctor is shipwrecked nearby. Suddenly it is the wedding day, and this crisis generates four scenes. In the first, Anthia's turmoil is dramatized in a soliloquized speech that makes us pity her plight and admire her resolve: Habrocomes is braver than she, she says, because he has chosen death before dishonor. Our knowledge that he is not dead may support our hope that they will one day be reunited, but here it also intensifies our fear that Anthia may kill herself in ignorant emulation of him. In keeping with the convention, Anthia's soul debate results in a decision, the decision we fear: she will join him in a tomb that will be their "bridal chamber," thus fulfilling one article of the oracle which we and she know must somehow come true. Thus, the episode and the incidents within it are linked to the whole action, a sign of a well-made plot.

In the second scene, Anthia asks the old doctor to poison her. This intensifies our fears; but our tensions are quickly relieved when the author tells us that the doctor decides to give her a sleeping potion instead. The third scene brings us to the wedding feast. As the guests arrive, Anthia delivers another soliloquized soul debate, a speech ordered by its own syntactic conventions: "What shall you do, Anthia? Will you violate the oath given to your spouse, Habrocomes, who has perished for you? . . . No, I am not weak on this point. . . . It is resolved: drink the poison, I must have no other spouse than Habrocomes; even dead, I belong to him alone." Our admiration and hope now subsume our fear that the potion may not work properly. And when, at the wedding table, Anthia drinks the drug, saying, "Soul of Habrocomes . . . now I keep the promises I made to you. . . . Receive me joyously and make me in the house of the dead find happiness with you," we are awed by the notion that death may be transmuted into life by love; and our awe is pleasurable because we do not expect that this admirable girl will die. In the fourth scene, we join Perilaus, who is lamenting silently over her apparent corpse as it is swiftly entombed; we are relieved by her escape, slightly apprehensive that she will not be rescued, and expect that those who will rescue her will confront her with still another thrilling threat.

The syntax of such episodes, and the emotional meanings generated by it, do not differ from the syntax and meaning of the whole action. Apparently inescapable peril is brought to a climax, moral if mistaken decisions are made, and the peril is escaped through chance, probable good fortune, miracle, or moral decision. In the episode, as in the whole action, authorial telling is pleasantly paced with monologue and dialogue. The syntax itself raises hope with one hand and dread with the other; and it is partly this two-handedness that enraged Nietzsche, disgusts us literati, and enthralls the ordinary reader.

Persistent material conventions and simple syntax give these stories the formulaic quality we associate with popular art. So too do some other principles that might be called morphemic rather than syntactic. The first is that of Duplication: attempted seduction by an attractive widower gives way to attempted seduction by a rich barbarian; the homosexual pirate chief is matched by a homosexual brigand; and the Nile must save the hero twice. By a second principle, Parallelism, one lament is matched by another, a shepherd is balanced by a fisherman, and so on. In accordance with a third principle, Interlacement (or "Meanwhile"), reports of the heroine's adventures are interwoven with reports of her spouse's, and the hero is left in mid-peril as we learn how the interrupted predicament of the heroine is resolved. None of these principles is peculiar to romance, though some critics would make them characteristic of medieval romance, claiming that they evince the romancers' celebration of the patterns of courtly life.

It was perhaps the formulaic character of these material and technical conventions that aroused the parodic scorn of Petronius, Nero's arbiter of elegance, who in the 60s A.D. wrote his *Satyricon libri*, only fragments of which survive. His very title ("Books of Satyr-Business") makes a pun on unchaste satyrs, the Roman literary genre *satura*, and the titles of Greek works like the *Argonautica* and the *Ephesiaca*. In lieu of flawless young heterosexuals suffering serious perils at the hands of Eros and Fortune, Petronius offers a pair of foolish young homosexuals suffering through scrapes caused by the old phallic god Priapus. In the romances, lovers preserve their sexual ideals through thick and thin; but nothing preserves the chastity of Petronius' boys—except Priapus, who inflicts impotence on one of them. Just as separated lovers in the romances endure shipwreck, capture, witchcraft, and brigands, so too do Petronius' frantic heroes. Petronius misses hardly a trick of the Greek prose romance, and he turns them all to the ridiculous. His work is doubtless more than a satire of these novels and of Roman philhellenism,[12] but it does show that they were popular enough for him to scorn them even in 60 A.D., a date earlier than that of the earliest surviving romance.

Eight centuries later, however, a most perceptive scholar and critic took them seriously enough. Photius, the remarkable patriarch of Constantinople, saw fit to discuss three Greek prose romances and to summarize two of them in his *Bibliotheca*—a collection of some 280 epitomes he made to guide the reading of his younger brother. Hellenic culture had flowed to Photius without breaks apparent to him; and his remarks reflect what much earlier Hellenes might have thought the materials, techniques, and effects of narrative romance were.

Read the *dramatikon* written by Iamblichus, says Photius.[13] By *dramatikon* he means a narrative dramatized in scenes in which both the author and his characters speak. Iamblichus' *Babyloniaca* in sixteen books is a *dramatikon* characterized by its material: it is an *erotas hypokrinomenon*—a narrative of love intrigues. As for its *lexis*, or style, "it is soft and flowing... characterized less by intensity than by what may be called titillation and nerveless-ness." A fourth aspect of such a work is its *synthēkē*, its arrange-ment or structure. This evokes another judgment: "Iamblichus is so distinguished by excellence of... arrangement... of the nar-rative that it is to be regretted that he did not devote his skill and energies to more serious subjects instead of puerile fictions."

A material, manner, style, and structure—these make a narra-tive romance. And Photius compares the *Babyloniaca* with only two other works, the stories of love intrigues written by Heliodorus and Achilles Tatius. Heliodorus' *Aethiopica* (c. 240 A.D.) is the best of these because, he says, it presents the spectacle of chastity strictly observed, which shows that he is "more serious and restrained" than Achilles Tatius (c. 160 A.D.), whose story of love adventures is indecent and scandalous. "Seriousness" or "worthiness" is thus another quality of such stories, though it is a variable one. And finally, all these narratives achieve comparable effects, primarily by means of *diaskeuē*, what I have called narra-tive method or syntax. Heliodorus achieves superior effects partly because his *diaskeuē* is "diversified by actual, expected, or unex-pected incidents that appeal to the feelings by strange escapes from danger...; peripeties occur which are either unexpected or even unhoped for, so that there are marvelous (*paradoxoi*) deliver-ances from desperate unhappiness" which provide a *katharsis*.

The learned Byzantine, using a critical vocabulary derived in part from Aristotle, has given a cogent account of some of the material, efficient, formal, and final "causes" of these prose ro-mances. It would be hard to do a better job of this, though we may wonder why he bothered to epitomize Iamblichus' "puerile fiction." We may be grateful, because the *Babyloniaca* survives in no other form; but his epitome of it—and my epitome of his epitome—contains almost more astounding or absurd paradoxes than a reader can bear.

Garmus, king of Babylon, desires Sinonis, wife of Rhodanes. He binds her in golden chains and condemns her husband to the cross. They escape. Two royal eunuchs—having been further mutilated (noses and ears) for permitting the escape—set off after them in a pursuit that will continue to the end (book 16). The married lovers flee to a meadow where there is a hidden treasure and where a ghostly goat, enamored of Sinonis, chases them away just before the eunuchs arrive. They hide in a cave open at two ends, one end being concealed by thick bushes. Discovered, they escape via the unbushy opening, perhaps enacting a common infantile fantasy of birth. Then they are stung by poisonous bees. These bees (one is reminded of Demeter and Egyptian Neith, to whom bees were sacred) drug the lovers but kill the pursuing soldiers. Having fallen, apparently dead, by the roadside, the lovers wake and flee on donkeys (beasts profane to Isis) to the house of a recently murdered man whose brother accuses them of the murder (the brother had done it) before he poisons himself. While sheltered by a cannibalistic brigand, the lovers are once more discovered by soldiers, who kill the brigand and set fire to the house, from which the lovers flee, climbing over donkey carcasses, shouting "We are ghosts!" Joining the funeral procession of a girl who is not—as a passing Chaldean informs them—really dead, the lovers hide in her empty tomb, and, surfeited by her funereal food, fall into a sleep that causes the soldiers to mistake them for corpses. Reviving for what must be the third or fourth time, the lovers are arrested by the king's magistrate, Soraechus, and decide to poison themselves; but Soraechus, moved by pity, substitutes a sleeping potion and loads them into a cart for Babylon. Waking, Rhodanes shouts so loudly that·Sinonis, startled, stabs her breast; but the wound isn't serious, and, when they explain their plight to compassionate Soraechus, he takes them to a shrine of Aphrodite.

This shrine stands on an island between the Tigris and the Euphrates. Its priestess has three sons, named Tigris, Euphrates, and Mesopotamia, the last of whom was so ugly that his mother transformed him into a beautiful woman, for whom three suitors have slain one another. Tigris has died after eating a beetle-infested rose (a flower sacred to Isis). Rhodanes looks so much like the dead Tigris that the mother-priestess mistakes him for her dead son when he arrives at the shrine, and she mistakes Sinonis for Kore, daughter of Demeter. Bemused, the lovers do not correct her.

A eunuch arrives and arrests Soraechus, but the lovers free him. He also arrests Euphrates, thinking he is Rhodanes, and Mesopotamia, thinking that he/she is Sinonis. The geographical siblings do not protest; and the freed lovers, along with their friend, Soraechus, hide in the house of a farmer whose beautiful daughter is mourning her dead husband. When this girl tells the lovers that the eunuch is hovering nearby, Rhodanes politely kisses her goodbye. This kiss so enrages Sinonis that she tries to kill their benefactress; but Soraechus prevents this and takes Sinonis to the house of a man who tries to seduce her. She kills this man and runs with the sword to kill the kissed daughter; but she is arrested and sent off to the amorous King Garmus, whereupon Rhodanes almost kills himself. Overjoyed, the king orders that all his prisoners be released in celebration, forgetting that Sinonis is one of his prisoners. When he learns that she has again slipped from his clutches, he has her guards buried alive, along with their wives and children.

Meanwhile, Rhodanes' dog has discovered the partially de-voured corpses of a girl and her slave-lover-murderer. Thinking that the female corpse is Sinonis, Soraechus hangs himself; and Rhodanes is stabbing himself when the farmer's daughter rushes in, shouting, "This girl is not Sinonis!" Both men live. When Sinonis herself happens by and sees the farmer's daughter ban-daging Rhodanes' wounds, she once more tries to kill her. Prevented by Rhodanes, she runs off, shouting, "I invite you to Garmus' wedding"—an irony that (who knows?) may not have been unique in this astounding tale of death, love, and resurrection.

At last Rhodanes and Soraechus are captured and taken, along with Euphrates and Mesopotamia (who, all along, have been im-personating the lovers), before King Garmus. But the king, seeing that Mesopotamia is not, in fact, Sinonis, orders her decapitation. The executioner, however, has already fallen in love with the beautiful transvestite and sends her to Egypt, whose queen has long been in love with her, apparently in her female form. When Garmus learns that Mesopotamia is now possessed by Egypt, he threatens war.

Meanwhile, Euphrates has been freed by *his* executioner, who is in fact his father, the priest of Aphrodite. And Soraechus is also freed in the nick of time: he is being crucified in that mysterious meadow to which the lovers had originally fled, but a band of marauding nomads arrives to chase away his executioners. Pretending to be a magician, he shows the superstitious barbarians a hidden treasure (Rhodanes had told him about it), and they elect him their king and defeat Garmus—but that, as Iamblichus and/or Photius says, happened later. (Photius may have rearranged the order of Iamblichus' episodes, as he did those of Heliodorus.) Rhodanes is also being crucified; and as Garmus dances around his cross, news comes that Sinonis has married the king of Syria. Feeling abandoned, Rhodanes of course wants his crucifixion to proceed, but Garmus persuades him to lead an army against the Syrians, planning to betray him later. This plan goes awry. Rhodanes recovers his bride and himself becomes king of Babylon, as a swallow had predicted he would. Thus end the sixteen books.

In a digression, Iamblichus remarks that he is a Babylonian writing in the reign of Marcus Aurelius about the year 165. He says he's a magus, adept in all "types of enchantment"—by locusts, lions, hail, snakes, and mice, the last method being the most ancient, because from "mouse" (*mys*) comes "mystery" (*mystērion*). I am inclined to agree that he must have been an adept magus and to lament the loss of his mysterious work. It seems to have been one of the most richly fantastic of fictions or one of the richest parodies of such things. Or it may have been the ancient romance most clearly generated by an extrinsic argument—a sort of second-century *Faerie Queene*, an epitome of which might seem as silly as the one above. That is, it may have mocked or celebrated the cults of Demeter, Isis, Aphrodite, and other gods. It may also, and at the same time, have been a political allegory. But had it been, we would expect that Photius, an adept exegete and allegorist, would have said so, especially as he was himself setting off on an embassy to Babylon after dictating his 280 epitomes.

In any case, Iamblichus seems to have exploited almost obsessively one powerful convention of ancient romance—the episode of apparent death and marvelous resurrection. This convention has its own persistent history. So do all the material and technical conventions I have mentioned, and one could trace them through novels, poems, plays, and histories ancient and modern. But commonplaces have no meaningful history apart from the particular works in which they exist, and I now turn to the surviving handful of extant prose fictions.

❧ 5 ❧
Discussion
Two

KAPPA: "Flesh-eaters," quite literally, made of limestone, because lime accelerates the decay; these were carved in Asia Minor, mostly, and then shipped to Rome. Look back here. You can see how the trade accommodated itself to Roman custom. This long side is left uncarved because your Roman always put his sarcophagus against a wall, for some reason. This is second-century, called "Germanicus."

SIGMA: Was Germanicus buried in this?

KAPPA: "Buried" is not quite accurate, is it? Only the millions who couldn't afford tombs and immortal things like these masterpieces were buried. A bust of Germanicus stood above it in the earl of Arundel's town house. Oracles could make promises about tombs being bridal chambers only to lovers of the highest class. The point is, these fat little chaps, here, playing with bits of armor, are *erōtes*. Doesn't look like second-century armor to me.

ALPHA: Workshops usually work with old patterns.

KAPPA: Right. And these two fellows dancing at the corners are also cupids, and these two holding the medallion.

PSI: Eros dances on the sarcophagi.

SIGMA: That's not a portrait of the deceased, I hope.

KAPPA: No, no, no; it's Medusa scaring off infernal demons. Now, on this one over here the cupids hold a blank medallion. The workshop left it blank so that a portrait could be carved on it at Rome; but money was apparently not forthcoming. Now, this winged little fellow embracing the draped girl must be Eros himself, and the girl is Psyche.

PSI: Very affectionate. Eros needs no clothing, Psyche does.

KAPPA: In actual fact, male nudity was the convention, female nudity the rarity. It's all a matter of mere convention, as Alpha would say.

Discussion Two

ALPHA: Only stale conventions are mere conventions.

SIGMA: The *erōtes* on this one have loincloths.

KAPPA: A stylistic variation.

PSI: They wear loincloths because they are guarding something?

KAPPA: Only the corners. The point about this little one—made for a child, of course—the point is the design covering the whole thing. These long S-shaped flutings, very deeply incised, are imitations of the grooves cut in stone wine-pressing vats. The grapes' juices could flow out through them, you see. In fact, the sarcophagus is a wine vat. Wine frees the soul from the body, and so does death, if you're a believer. The drunk and the dead are both ecstatic.

PSI: And to make the point already made by Alpha and Xenophon, Eros on a wine-vat sarcophagus shows that wine and death both seem to release erotic energies.

KAPPA: One must not oversimplify these ideas. Come over here. This is magnificent. The whole panel shows a procession of Dionysus, and, as it's second-century, it's not surprising that Dionysus himself does not appear. But everyone is drunk. Look at this centaur strumming a lyre, this one with the bacchante on his rump, she's twirling like a dervish out of her mind, and these people banging timbrels, baby satyrs underfoot, and this snake rising from the basket to frighten the boy, that's clearly comic, and look at the expression on the face of this chap pouring out wine. Joy on a sarcophagus, freedom from the woes of this life. Full of life, I grant you, but "erotic" is too simple, too shallow.

PSI: For the Greeks, you would say, life was heaven and heaven was hell?

KAPPA: I'm not sure that there was anything that can be called "the Greeks." There were all sorts of Greeks, and these things were made for Romans. Would you step over here, please? There is nothing erotic about this superb lid. Here is the Wooden Horse, on wheels. These are the Trojans being murdered at their victory feast. Note Priam caught at the altar here, that gush of blood remarkably well articulated. Then we have this flashback narrative *technique!* This is Achilles dragging the corpse of noble Hector. What a powerful contrast to the romances!

PSI: But this is altogether a different kind of story. To be buried under the Fall of Troy is not at all romantic.

KAPPA: Right, but that's not quite my point. The sack of Troy is not essentially different from an ecstatic procession. Why? Both show energy, *energy*, life! All men die, true; but some, like the heroes at Troy, can turn defeat into victory by heroic cunning, and others by initiation into an ecstatic mystery cult. You have only comedy and tragedy on the sarcophagi, never romance; and this, I think, was what Nietzsche was driving at. In the romances everybody talks about dying, but nobody has the guts to do it. Or to live, for that matter.

ALPHA: It's the sarcophagus that makes the romance.

PSI: I don't follow that.

ALPHA: I have two points to make. The first is strictly aesthetic. The master of a sarcophagus workshop in, say, Pergamum must have had several designs in his repertory. Perhaps he got them from the Pergamene friezes, or from anywhere. These designs were his conventions. But the Fall of Troy or a bacchic procession meant one thing carved on a temple, another on a building in the marketplace, still another on a sarcophagus. It is the context, the specific function, that gives specific meaning to traditional material. The same is true of literary commonplaces. The same battle speech, the same lament, can mean one thing in a comedy and another in a romance. Isn't that Heracles killing the Calydonian boar on that lid over there?

KAPPA: It is. Heracles became immortal because he triumphed almost to the end over the outrageous tasks given to him.

ALPHA: Still, we wouldn't think that Heracles or the Fall of Troy would be appropriate images for coffin lids if they weren't on coffin lids. On coffin lids they suggest the possible triumph of man over the most outrageous task set by destiny, which is death. I mean to say, the sarcophagus gives meaning to Heracles more than Heracles gives meaning to the sarcophagus. The *Ephesiaca* gives meaning to those death-and-resurrection scenes more than the other way round.

PSI: Would you say, then, that Thanatos gives meaning to the Eros of the romances?

ALPHA: No. Maybe the other way round.

PSI: Yes, it is always the other way round. Love triumphs over death because, in the unconscious, death can be a form of being loved. These romances show this with marvelous insight.

ALPHA: My point had to do with the relation between convention and form in art. My second point is this. These elitist artifacts here, like the elitist romances, express a universal wish—an idealized wish that has nothing to do with social classes or elites. The wish is for victory over fear. The form of the wish is a story. The ritual of the drunken procession is the enactment of a story. The wine vat is an instrument in the ritual of the vintage, the Fall of Troy and the Labors of Heracles and the affair of Cupid and Psyche are all ritualized, that is conventionalized, stories, and these sarcophagi are instruments in the ritualized event of death embossed with stories. The story is the crucial element. It underlies ritual and the perception of life and death. The dying man, if he has the opportunity, even as we're told as he's going down for the third time, and his mourners, whether they are happy or sad, must see death as a scene, an event in a life which must be seen, given human memory and form-making, as part of a story of a life. The stories carved on these coffins ask the mourners and the dead man and us to understand, or rather feel, the individual death in terms of a universal, or mythic, story. And the story must always deal with particulars—Troy, Heracles, Achilles. But the story is always a confirmation of the universal wish to triumph over death. The romances take part of their appeal from this universal wish. But they are demythologized—forgive my ugly past participles—particularized stories. That may be one reason why they so often allude to Fate, the gods, and cults with their ready-made myths. They must draw strength, aesthetic power, from these cultural forces. In any case, they are in some ways like the sarcophagi. Both kinds of artifacts tell stories about the triumph of virtuous life over chaotic death.

KAPPA: Now you are getting at the concrete realities.

SIGMA: The limestone realities.

KAPPA: The limestone realities of these stories. I was surprised, though I shouldn't have been, at your underplaying the role of the mysteries in the *Ephesiaca*, et cetera. You apparently want to turn stories into mere pleasure machines.

SIGMA: Pleasure utterances.

KAPPA: Pleasure utterances. I grant that they may not be arguments about the gods saving people from death and rape. But when I look at this lid or read a Greek romance, can't I learn something about the powers of the gods while being pleased by the story?

ALPHA: So you can. So can I. But if you're the writer, you have to decide, or feel, whether you're going to make your story to show their power or to convert people to their cult, or write your story essentially in its own terms and bring on the Mothers or the Nile from time to time in prayers and miracles to show how serious it all is, to make it more thrilling. If you were going to preach a mystery cult, you'd have an initiation and show its good effects, and salvation would be more than going back home and living happily ever after in marriage.

KAPPA: But salvation in most of the cults was precisely that: being adopted into the family of the god. That's what initiation was. You died and were born again, this time as the child of the goddess. In the mysteries of Demeter you apparently drank milk, a thing only babies drank in Hellas. Or perhaps you were in some mysteries married to the god. We know remarkably little about these initiations, but in some way you were adopted into the family of a deity after passing through terrible perils—death itself; and this was a great comfort. Apuleius, for example, said that he was led into death and was born again during his initiation into the Isis cult. Reading a romance must have been like an experience—a cheap, trouble-free experience—of initiation. My point is, without the mystery cults there could have been no romances. The underlying reality of the romances is the cults; and under the cults is a terrible anxiety of alienation, a fear of being cut off from home, from civic cults like that of Artemis at Ephesus. Adrift on the seas of the big world, full of tempests and pirates. The universal cults gave you another home, wherever you were, since Isis was everywhere; and so too did ideals of personal fidelity. You could be loyal to your vows to a spouse no matter where he or she was. Your soul wasn't your family's or your family's god's; it was your own, your spouse's, and your private god's, who lived everywhere. Christianity capitalized on all this. And under all this, all this individualism, this idealization of marital sex and personal religion, is the struggle of a class to root itself morally, theologically, in the large fearsome world it wants to exploit. These romances don't show a wish to conquer death so much as they show a wish to prove that the bourgeois values of marriage and home can conquer the world, just as Dionysus, and Heracles and the Greeks at Troy, conquered their worlds. Come along upstairs where we keep our mother goddesses.

SIGMA: Kappa is leading us up to a deified social reality.

ALPHA: But Psi isn't giving us much guidance. He seems to be of the old school.

SIGMA: And by profession a listener, a questioner, and a player with mythic concepts. He can hardly be mundane and clinical with types like us, but he does love literature in a grandiose way.

ALPHA: How do you love it?

SIGMA: I am often moved by poetry, and I am always amused by literary criticism. Trying to make true interpretations in the teeth of the fact that no single interpretation is verifiable. On the other hand, all the interpretations I've heard seem true enough to me.

ALPHA: You're getting only a small sample of possible true interpretations. Can't you scare up a Frenchman or someone who knows Northrop Frye?

SIGMA: Sufficient unto the day.

KAPPA: Now, we have very few Great Mothers here, but this is a rare one. This crude stele is mid-second-century-A.D. African—Tunisian, actually—and this lady standing in the door of the little temple is the deceased, and this lady up here above the temple is Tanit herself, the Carthaginian mother goddess. And these figures floating beneath her sky are Aphrodite and Bacchus. These beasts on the temple tympanum must be goats, and these things in the sky are pomegranates and grapes.

SIGMA: At least they didn't believe in pie in the sky.

PSI: Now, what did this woman do to deserve immortality at the hands of her mother, Tanit?

KAPPA: I don't know. We know very little about Tanit. But she is one of a type. Mothers like Cybele and Astarte castrated·their lovers or sons or fathers and gave them immortality, rebirth, in exchange. But they were far too crude for most Hellenes, who preferred Artemis the virgin, lover and mother of nobody, whose priestesses were once temple prostitutes; or, better still, the greatest Mother of all, Isis, whose priests shaved their heads and married only to beget little priests. Isis was chaste but never castrated anybody. In fact, she once wandered over the world picking up the pieces of her husband-brother Osiris, dismembered by Typhon, that lascivious ass.

ALPHA: There was one piece she didn't find.

PSI: The one she wanted most for herself but could not have? Yes? Then, by not finding it, she also castrated her man.

KAPPA: But that was an old story. Isis was full of compassion. And she never treated anybody as Cybele treated her son, Attis. Cybele pursued Attis over the world, because he wanted to marry a girl, until he finally fell exhausted, cut off his penis, threw it at Mom's feet, and shouted, "For you!"—and then died. Even Cybele regretted this and turned him into a pine tree.

PSI: Such romances were never carved on coffins?

KAPPA: In the Hellenistic period, certainly in the Roman period, everything is idealized, and most of the Mothers were seen to be really one, who Isis claimed to be. And these stories are not in fact romances.

PSI: No, the romances I have read for this discussion are written under the motto Lead Us into Temptation and Lead Us Out Again, but the myths and rituals tell us only how to be led out. And I am struck by the passivity of the lovers, which is almost megalomaniacal. Eros comes to torment them from outside, the gods come from outside to save them. Salvation is always in the cards.

ALPHA: The gods don't save them, the story saves them. And the story must save them because they are so admirable, because we could not bear a story that destroyed such paragons. And the story saves them repeatedly in a certain way—by surprising, paradoxical, reversals of fortune. What's remarkable is how seldom the gods intervene. And the more marvelous the paradoxical reversals, the better; because it is this kind of reversal that is the most exciting, the most likely to produce a catharsis of tension.

KAPPA: *Katharsis* was the word used to describe the purging, the experience of the initiate in a mystery cult. Even your Aristotelian word is religious in content.

ALPHA: Granted. The fact remains that these stories are driven by a literary theory, not a religious one. The salvation is not religious but rather, as you say, social, bourgeois.

KAPPA: You simply can't separate the two, really. They all—cults and romances—come from the same piece of cloth. And you know it was the daimon, the guardian spirit, of the initiate that was adopted by or married to the goddess. And your goddess was also your daimon. As I recall, when Anthia says goodbye to Habrocomes in prison, she says that the same daimon which rules both their lives will keep them faithful to each other. And Menander uses the same term for what we call "character" in a play. Now this suggests that Anthia's character, or daimon, is both her own and Artemis' or Isis'. In short, Xenophon's readers would have understood that Artemis and her chastity live in Anthia and Habrocomes.

ALPHA: OK, and that proves that Anthia does not "stand for" Artemis in the story. She's a good girl, typical of those who worship Artemis. And, on the other hand, I wonder what this says about the new individualism you see in the romances.

KAPPA: In a way, these characters are less individual than the old heroes. They are flat precisely because the stories are fables of bourgeois anxiety and conquest fantasies. To understand them, you first have to understand the group whose feelings and ideals they express. Identifying the group, that's the first step for a critic. This lady here went back home to mother, the matriarch of a family as large, but no larger, than the world her class could imagine; but it's a family that doesn't include everybody, only those who can pay the fees. So here she is in the homey hereafter, snug as Anthia in Ephesus. She would have liked Xenophon much better than I do.

PSI: This is doubtless true. But you drive out erotic content with social content.

KAPPA: I do not. Sex, aggression, family structure, all that lot are shaped by the social realities of life. A formalist like Alpha would say it's brute matter formed by the demands of the form going at the time. I'm saying something simple and obvious. If you want to understand the origins of the novel, you have to understand the group that made and consumed it.

SIGMA: That seems to settle the matter. But I am playing with three words here. Paradox, meaning a marvel, and daimon, and katharsis. Each of them appears repeatedly in these novels, right? Right. And each of them has a religious, an aesthetic, and a psychological meaning. This long-dead lady here, reading Xenophon's novel, would not have sorted these meanings out. She knew all about the obvious affinities among art and ritual and myth. In her own life-story the climactic episode was her daimon's being marvelously purged by Tanit; so Anthia's salvation was not unlike her own. It's not paradoxical to me that none of the three terms has a specific social meaning if I agree with Kappa that society is the matrix of everything aesthetic, religious, and psychological. So I am embarrassed. I must agree with all of you.

ALPHA: Even that groups write novels?

SIGMA: Novelists write novels. They have psyches, they are conditioned by their society, and they obey the rules of narrative art. And granted, the rules don't change much from society to society. But these are abstractions.

ALPHA: A novelist is not an abstraction. He is an individual. And his novel is not an abstraction, it is a particular telling of a story. The story can be abstracted in an epitome; but the way it is told is always unique, and this *way* makes the novel what it is.

PSI: And is the novel of Xenophon not a way of telling an old story, a very old story that does not change much, alas, from society to society? It is a story of paradoxes in the soul, and this too is obvious; though it puts me, if you will forgive me, in some disagreements here, because underlying the aesthetics and the religion and the society are paradoxes of soul. But in Xenophon's book, only a few paradoxes. This unceasing danger and escape belong to a simple dynamics, to deny and to achieve erotic gratification at one and the same moment, to escape into and to escape from death simultaneously, that is, to enjoy safely the torment in eros and the eros in death. There is even an obsession here on a sadomasochistic pattern. Rape, brothels, crucifixions, archery targets, necrophilia. Even marriage is seen in this light at the beginning, Eros himself being a tormenter and the fate he dictates being cruel. This suggests an unwillingness to find gratification through normal channels, and here is a well-known source of erotic suffering.

KAPPA: And as you will surely now say, here is the Freudian principle of society: that society demands that gratification be postponed.

PSI: Of course. Civilization depends on this principle; and if these stories seem to pander to society, if they show that pleasure finally does come to those who wait, we may understand the disdain of Nietzsche and others. But I speak here of a somewhat different principle, a paradox: that denial of satisfaction results in satisfaction. And I speak of the characters in Xenophon's story because it seems to me that one must begin with the characters in a story; we are moved by persons more than by the story itself or by the social class. And one must adopt the point of view of the characters, as the story makes one adopt it, as one must adopt the point of view of a patient and, at the same time, see that what he dreads is in himself and not, perhaps, in reality. Now, what is the reality here? The parents approve of the love of these lovely children. There is no social barrier to their happiness. Why don't they marry and love freely? Only a mysterious fate bars this. Happiness is somehow unacceptable. And the poor parents are mysteriously involved in this unacceptability. They are made to become accomplices of denial. They send their children away to obey the oracle, and only after the death of the parents can the children find happy marriage. This shows that we are reading about the fantasies of the two main characters, perhaps of the author too; and it is these fantasies that we readers adopt temporarily.

Sigma: Just how does that work?

Psi: We hardly have time to discuss the etiology of paranoia, dread of homosexuality, sadomasochism.

Sigma: I meant, how do we adopt such fantasies?

Psi: That may be an even more complicated subject. Fantasies are catching, like the common cold. I could not diagnose these characters; and besides, the story cures them more fully than people can be cured. That too is a fantasy. I mean to say that it is as though they imagine that Fate and the parents who obey Fate are behaving as though they disapproved of their erotic desires, whereas the parents, at least, do not really disapprove. The death of the parents signals the completion of this fate that dictates erotic suffering; and news of their death comes after the hero has discovered, with the fisherman and his embalmed wife, that parental love goes on after parental death. This relieves his anxieties. It's as though he wished their death, or feared they would have to die before he himself could love as they love—as he wants them to love, in fact. Now he sees that love survives death, a message often repeated in the story; so he needn't worry about his fears or wishes for their death, so he may sail for home, find his bride, and build his monuments.

Kappa: And this explains the book.

Psi: I speak of only one episode, but a revealing one. All the other dangers invented by the writer fall into a clear pattern, a pattern of obsessional hysteria. Anthia even tells us of a trauma. It is a lie, perhaps, but a true one. When she tells the brothel-keeper that she falls into fits because she was once raped by a ghost, we must remember that it is very common for hysterics to imagine that they were once raped by a relative. And she was raped because she was separated from her parents during a religious procession, just as she fell in love with Habrocomes during such a procession—thus separating herself, she fears, from her parents. Her troubles throughout the story may be seen as projections of a single fear: forms of rape; but under such fears lies the wish for erotic possession, for being possessed, by the man she loves but cannot possess, a ghost in her by now. And the necessary masochistic pain. Well, the hysterical fits, the lies, these work very well for her, as usual. But the parents being dead, she too may abandon guilt and fantasy and find her husband, whom her hysteria has also served. This is our catharsis. The daimon of Diana the Virgin is at last reconciled with the daimon of Eros the Tormentor in marriage after they are purged by death. It is a healthful book, in the end.

Kappa: It is a boring book. I understand that you can reduce trifles like it to a few simple psychological concepts, but you can't really inflate it to a fantasy of cathartic health.

Psi: It is a trifle, and the deepest voices speak most plainly in trifles. And the clock tells me that I have an appointment, which I regret, because I fear you will talk on without me.

Sigma: We will. We are not as healthy as you are.

Psi: On that score I must again disagree.

❧ 6 ❧
Aphrodisian Chastity

It seems that *Chaereas and Callirrhoë*—if it was in fact written about 50 A.D.—might be the oldest extant romantic novel.[1] Chaucer's *Troilus*, Chrétien's *Erec*, Apuleius' *Metamorphoses*, and, for all I know, Homer's *Odyssey* have already blushed under this dubious accolade; and I do not mean to celebrate an old Greek book by thrusting an English genre label upon it. But nothing quite like *Callirrhoë* survives from an earlier period of Western literature; and following our inclination to comprehend such a phenomenon by fitting it into familiar categories, we would call it a novel because it is an extensive prose fiction of ordinary moral life that conforms to a recognizable canon of realism, and a romance because its admirable protagonists suffer the most serious threats to their lives and values but survive them all. Its author, a certain Chariton of Aphrodisia, a small city in the province of Caria in Asia Minor, says it is a story of *erōtika pathēmata*, an accurate label. In any case, I am not here concerned to argue that *Callirrhoë* is the precursor of such entities as the novel, or to speculate about its cultural origins, or to point out its obvious likenesses to later narratives. I do want to discuss the habits of narrative art that Chariton exploits in his book and to explore a few of the ways by which he makes erotic suffering pleasurable for his readers—us, and the leisured, literate members (perhaps mostly ladies) of the bourgeois households that had for centuries flourished in the great Hellenistic cities of the eastern Mediterranean basin.

It is possible that Chariton develops his novel from a story explaining the origins of the two famous tyrants of Syracuse named Dionysius. According to Diodorus and Plutarch, Dionysius the Elder rose to power partly on the strength of his marriage (in 405 B.C.) to a nameless daughter of Hermocrates, the general who had led the army that destroyed the great force Athens sent against Syracuse in 414. Diodorus says that this anonymous girl was beaten viciously by her new husband's political enemies, and Plutarch adds that she killed herself as a result, whereupon Dionysius married two women on the same day, one of whom (a foreigner from Locris) gave birth to Dionysius II.[2] Chariton's heroine, Callirhoë, is a daughter of the great Hermocrates. Being as beautiful as Aphrodite, she is much courted; but one day at a festival she falls in love with Achilles-like Chaereas, the son of her father's political rival. They marry. But Chaereas, duped by jealous friends and suitors, imagines that his bride is a wanton and kicks her in the stomach. Callirhoë apparently dies, is entombed, rescued by grave-robbers, and sold to a magnifico of Miletus, a principal city of Caria, not far from Chariton's Aphrodisia. This powerful, attractive widower is named Dionysius, and Callirhoë marries him to give her child (father by Chaereas) an honest name. Grief-stricken, Chaereas tracks her to Miletus but is himself sold into slavery. Callirhoë, meanwhile, attracts the adoring love of ever more powerful men—first the Persian governor of Caria, then the Great King, Artaxerxes himself. She unceasingly laments the Aphrodisian power in her that causes these erotic triumphs, and she never sacrifices her ideals of marital—if bigamous—chastity to her devotees; but her sufferings are prolonged until Chaereas, heroically aiding the Egyptians in a revolt against the Persians, is at last forgiven by Aphrodite, Callirhoë's patroness, for having imagined that his bride was unchaste and is permitted to rescue her from a harem. Reunited with her first husband, Callirhoë secretly consigns her nameless son to her second (who imagines that he's the father), and the couple returns to a joyous Syracuse.

Legend may have given Chariton his initiating episode and a few of the names and events that seem to set his story in a distinct if murky historical period (for example, the Egyptians did rebel against Artaxerxes, but in 460 B.C.)—and such settings, as Tasso and Hawthorne later remarked, can invest romance with a needful verisimilitude. But Chariton is not interested in the lineage of tyrants born four hundred years before his time. Every episode in his story is focused on Callirhoë.

Taken together, the episodes compose a single action: from the time she is kicked to the time she is reunited with Chaereas,

Callirrhoë's fortunes steadily rise in the world; but this rise is seen by the heroine, and therefore partly by the reader, in a certain moral light that makes the rise seem to be its opposite—a decline in which her desire to be faithful to her first husband is put into greater and greater jeopardy. This moral action, or plot, adumbrates a paradox familiar in ordinary life: a fantasy of erotic power (I am beautiful as Aphrodite! Even the King would adore me!) is in conflict with, and therefore sanctioned by, a fantasy of moral power (I am one who would be faithful to husband and child unto death!). This paradox constitutes the character of Callirrhoë, and she—or it—is the single cause of what happens in the story. In her soul is enthroned her daimon, Aphrodite; and Aphrodite is at once her divine enemy and her divine protectress, the source of her worldly success and her moral suffering.[3] Chariton's plot resolves all the paradoxes from which it springs by reconciling our desire to be Aphrodisian with our desire to be good; and it is this pleasant reconciliation that guides Chariton's adaptation or invention of his material.

Paradoxes, and the word "paradox," abound in the novel;[4] and since the concept may have something to do with the notion of "fantasy," with which English usage associates literary romance, it deserves comment here. The paradox—that which is against or beside reason—fascinated the dialecticians and rhetoricians of Chariton's time. The universe itself was a paradoxical harmony of contraries. To define, grapple with, reconcile, or scorn great opposites (One/Many, Passion/Reason, etc.) was one of the principal acts of a philosopher; and Cicero showed how rhetoricians could use the paradoxes of the Stoics—maxims contrary to general opinion (e.g., that the possession of virtue is sufficient for happiness)—as commonplaces to argue any side of a case.[5] The romances also used the paradox as a commonplace of their art, but in a somewhat different sense of the term—the vulgar sense of "marvel" or "miracle." That is, an astonishing reversal of fortune, an event contrary to expectation, a recognition or discovery that evoked strong contrary emotions like joy and fear—these were all "paradoxes." When art made a paradoxical peripety or recognition seem probable, the reader might also enjoy a wonderful reconciliation of opposite opinions—that fortune is mindless and that there is a design in life after all; and this latter, sublime inference could be an aesthetic equivalent of the speculation that resolved contraries within a philosophical system. But since the main job of poets was thought to be the arousal and consummation of powerful emotions, the dramatic paradox, the marvels generated by the plot, naturally became the stock-in-trade of narrative art. It is important to note, however, that the dramatic paradox was not a "fantastic" event; the marvels of early romance were necessarily seen to be possible, even probable, incidents whose "realism" was established by the literary conventions of the time. Only when they were made to seem realistically probable could the paradoxes be taken seriously enough to appeal to the fantasies of readers. Chariton, for example, eschews myth, adopts a romantic historicism, and wants us to imagine that the dramatic and psychological paradoxes he so thoroughly exploits were actually, seriously suffered by citizens of the world he knew.

He also adopts a narrative method that may be especially appropriate to the aesthetic exploitation of the paradoxes of this life. This is the method of the intrigue. Callirrhoë's rise/decline does not proceed through a sequence of perils encountered and escaped but through a system of intrigues of the kind conventional in New Comedy. In fact, every episode develops one or another intrigue that works against what Callirrhoë feels is her best interest or an intrigue that she works in her own behalf. There may be a profoundly affective relationship between the psychodynamic process of the intrigue, of which the projecting intriguer can feel himself to be the special victim, and the almost megalomaniacal fantasy of erotic power systematically resisted by moral fears. If so, Chariton's narrative method taps this affective power and in itself expresses the fantasies enacted by his heroine. We cannot explore such profundities here but must confine ourselves to the more obvious emotional consequences of the intrigue—how it recruits our sympathies for the heroine, elicits our fears for her, and permits us to enjoy the triumphs which from her point of view, and ours, are disasters.

The action of the novel mounts in seven phases, each phase turning on an intrigue.[6] In the first phase, the rejected suitors of Aphrodisian Callirrhoë draw her new husband Chaereas out of town and make it seem that she has presided over an orgy during his absence. To our relief, this intrigue fails. Callirrhoë may look exactly like Aphrodite, but she would never behave like her. Then one of the boys who misses Achilles-like Chaereas at the gymnasium tells him that he is Callirrhoë's lover and, using a slave girl in the darkness, convinces the husband that this is so. Next morning, enraged Chaereas kicks his bride in the stomach, and she seems to die. Although pity and fear for Callirrhoë may be the strongest emotions in us, the erotic content of these intrigues (and perhaps of the kick) does derive naturally from the strange fact that this chaste girl's patroness is unchaste Aphrodite: could such plots be directed against a bride whose daimon was Artemis?[7] We are outraged at the intriguers and angry with Chaereas. Still, he himself is a victim, and—most importantly —we know that the plot must eventually reunite these lovers because they are fundamentally admirable; we are therefore eager to forgive the kicker—after he has suffered for his deed. To help us here, at the outset, the author describes Chaereas' remorse at considerable length and in a trial has him vote "paradoxically" for his own condemnation. Moreover, Callirrhoë herself, when she wakes in her tomb, castigates Fate, not Chaereas: "O dreadful Fate . . . I have been buried alive though I did no wrong." But *we* know that she is a victim of a plausible intrigue, not of Fate or an oracle, and that this intrigue succeeded partly because of her Aphrodisian beauty. Our pity is enriched by the paradox of her predicament: it is her desirable beauty that causes her suffering. Since even her husband is one of her tormentors, our sympathies are focused primarily on her, and with her they will remain.

The *second* phase turns on the intrigues of Theron—the tomb-robber who saves Callirrhoë only to sell her to the highest bidder. Her salvation is itself paradoxical—"Callirrhoë and her fortunes met with a new and more dreadful sort of resurrection"—and is meant to stimulate a paradoxical mix of relief and fear. To underscore the paradox, and to arouse awe, Chariton alludes to the awesome experiences of the mystery cults, in which one was paradoxically born through dying. Hearing crowbars prying at her tomb, Callirrhoë asks, "What does this noise mean? Has some divinity come to seek me in my misery, as is common in the experience of the dying?" Paradoxically, the noise is made not by Isis or Demeter, seeking the daimon of an initiate, but by a brigand, seeking loot. And Callirrhoë's new life will be guided, not by a chaste mother goddess, but by the patroness of those erotic triumphs which cause girls like Callirrhoë to suffer.

Awestruck, Theron decides to sell the matchless girl. They sail toward Athens, but Theron "did not care for the peculiar officiousness of that town" (anti-Athenian sentiments often crop up in Chariton's story), and he sails on to Miletus. There the "realism" of this novel demands a lengthy intrigue, by which the freeborn status of Callirrhoë is concealed from the purchaser, and Theron's illegal shenanigans at the same time increase our fear for the heroine.

The *third* long phase proceeds through several intrigues and counterintrigues that culminate in the marriage of Callirrhoë to Dionysius, the most powerful Greek in Ionia (which in the story is under the hegemony of Persia). As Callirrhoë comes ashore at one of Dionysius' country estates, the conventional crowd of onlookers mistakes her for Aphrodite, "the foam-born," who indeed sometimes appears in this region. In fact, Callirrhoë is secured in a nearby shrine of Aphrodite, and this, along with the crowd's mistaking her for her patroness, only deepens her sadness: "Behold, yet another tomb more lonely than the first," she says of the shrine. Her epiphany as Aphrodite has, however, pleased Dionysius' steward, who uses the girl to win favor from his master. This man, to whom she must now be erotically enslaved, is handsome, remarkably well educated, and in melancholic mourning for his wife—which shows his capacity for love. In fact, no man in this part of the Hellenic world would make a more desirable husband. Therefore, we paradoxically want the steward's plot both to succeed and to fail. The steward draws the despondent Dionysius to the rural shrine in which Callirrhoë has lamented, "How unfortunate I am! Here too is the goddess Aphrodite, the cause of all my woes," and where she prays that she may never please any man but Chaereas. "Aphrodite refused this prayer," Chariton tells us, "for she is the mother of Love, and she was laying plans for still another marriage, though she had no intention of keeping that unbroken, either."

So the master intriguer of Callirrhoë's *pathos erōtikon* is the goddess of love. And the reader is meant to ask himself, Is Aphrodite intriguing for or against the girl? Or, paradoxically, both? Can the girl's divine enemy give her what she desires—chastity, fidelity? What female reader wouldn't envy a heroine whose beauty makes her an image of Aphrodite and admire her moral resistance to the consequences of this beauty? And every reader, female or male, must respond to the fulfillment of contrary wishes—the wish for enormous erotic power and the wish to conform to the social ideals of marriage.

When Dionysius sees Callirrhoë in the temple, he believes that she is in fact Aphrodite and strikes his steward for claiming that she's a mortal. But, convinced that she's human, he takes to his bed with a lovesickness in which "you could observe a struggle between reason and desire"; and this convinces us that he is worthy of Callirrhoë. Dionysius contrives his own intrigue to win the girl, and he is aided by Fortune, "against whom alone human reason has no power." Like Eros, Fortune loves "opposition," or paradoxes, "so on this occasion she too brought about a situation that was astonishing, and even incredible [paradoxical]"— Callirrhoë discovers that she is pregnant.

This paradox, which will force Callirrhoë to "compromise her honor" by marrying desirable Dionysius, occasions a remarkable soliloquy that dramatizes a soul intriguing with itself. Agonizing over the possibility of abortion, Callirrhoë presses a portrait of Chaereas against her abdomen: "Behold, we are three—husband, wife, and child. Let us plan together what is best for all." She wants "to die as the wife of Chaereas alone. This is dearer to me than parents, homeland, and child—not to have experience of another husband. But you, my child, what do you choose for yourself? Death by drugs before seeing the sun? . . . Or rather to live and have two fathers, one the leader of Sicily, the other of Ionia?" What an embarrassment of riches—two husbands! rulers of great cities that bracket the Hellenic world! We not only forgive her inevitable decision to marry Dionysius; we enjoy erotic triumph sanctioned by moral suffering.

The *fourth* phase of the action turns on more obvious paradoxes and intrigues. We revert to Syracuse and the day of Callirrhoë's dreadful resurrection. Astonished by her empty tomb, the Syracusans send ships captained by Chaereas to find her; and "Fortune, without whose aid no work is ever complete," causes Chaereas to find Theron's ship adrift on the sea, all the crew save Theron dead of thirst. Why does Chariton thus strain our credulity in order to reintroduce Theron? Because only he can direct Chaereas to Miletus (it would be even more improbable for Chaereas to run across her accidentally there) and because Theron's trial and punishment offer opportunities for more paradoxes and intrigues. Poor Theron (there are no real villains in this story) schemes to conceal his personal knowledge of Callirrhoë's fate, but he provides enough information to fill the Syracusan assembly with a paradoxical mix of emotions: "They were all filled with both joy and grief—joy because Callirrhoë was still alive, grief because she had been sold into slavery." This little packet of contrary emotions, itself a convention of the ancient romances, is here enriched with the reader's special knowledge, which is pleasurably superior to that of everyone in the world (save Callirrhoë): *we* know that Callirrhoë is not a slave but the bride of a potentate. And what will happen when husband number one meets husband number two? Paradoxically, the prospect of rescue is a prospect of disaster, and we are more knowledgeable on this score than Callirrhoë. Meanwhile, even Theron's crucifixion (he's now recognized to be a pirate) occasions a paradox: he "gazed from the cross out upon that sea over which he had carried captive the daughter of Hermocrates, whom not even the Athenians had been able to capture." The pleasures of paradox, with which Chariton seems almost obsessed, are not unrelated to the pleasures of superior knowledge which the plot, or the controlled release of information, constantly grants the reader. When Callirrhoë is praying to Aphrodite to "be reconciled with me" and asks "one boon: Save my fatherless child!," we know that the father is at hand. When Chaereas is captured by barbarians (recruited by the intrigues of Dionysius' steward) and sold into slavery, we are both saddened and relieved; and when Callirrhoë is assured that he has been slain, our sorrow for her is relieved by knowledge of the facts. From the outset we have known that the master intriguer, Aphrodite and/or Chariton, can only bring such morally admirable protagonists to a final happiness; and, secure in this belief, we can take particular pleasure in the sufferings of people who are more beautiful, brave, and magnificently unhappy than we are. At the same time, their superiority to us compels us to take their sufferings seriously. Perhaps these paradoxical mixtures of superiorities and inferiorities make for that paradoxical mix of "identification" and "aesthetic distance" that helps us enjoy the imitation of pain.

The *fifth* phase turns on an intrigue by Mithridates, the Persian governor in the province, to win Callirrhoë from Dionysius. He has been smitten by the girl while attending the elaborate funeral she has arranged for Chaereas, who we know is in fact a slave of this Mithridates. When Mithridates learns his slave's identity (Chaereas is being crucified when this happens, and his eleventh-hour reprieve causes him grief, which ennobles him in our eyes), he permits him to summon Callirrhoë from Dionysius, hoping to take her for himself. But Chaereas' letter is intercepted by Dionysius, who believes that it must be a forgery, and Callirrhoë's second husband determines to prove this in the court of the Great King himself.

The *sixth* phase centers on a trial in which great men argue and scheme to win Callirrhoë. Since trials by convention often produce the resolving recognitions and reversals, we may now expect a cathartic scene. But Chariton's plot seems designed to lead Callirrhoë into deeper and deeper erotic perils and greater and greater erotic triumphs. Her beauty radiates in Babylon like "a great light . . . suddenly seen on a dark night." The barbarian ladies fall down before her, and the Great King becomes hopelessly enamored. Like Dionysius, the king is consumed by melancholy adoration, not lust. And once more Callirrhoë's triumph torments her: "O treacherous beauty," she cries, "given me by nature only to be overwhelmed by scandal!"

Chariton, who was an attorney's clerk, contrives an expert trial scene that displays four of the important sources upon which he drew to arouse and enhance our passions. These are rhetoric itself, the mystery cults, drama, and the paradox. Dionysius, as Greek rhetor, uses the Attic style to persuade the court that Mithridates has designs on his wife; and Mithridates, a barbarian, responds in the Asiatic style—the two together providing textbook examples of forensic rhetoric. But Mithridates concludes with a marvelous *coup de théâtre* which draws upon the experience of the mystery cults as well as upon the powers of the drama. "Dread powers who rule Heaven and Hell," he prays in the courtroom, "come to the aid of this virtuous man! Grant to me Chaereas at least for this trial. Appear, noble spirit! Thy Callirrhoë is calling thee!" Lo and behold, the living Chaereas appears in the best-staged forensic resurrection to be found in any old romance. And the alliances among ritual, drama, and paradox are clearly noted by the poet, who has rather self-consciously used them all: "What dramatist ever produced so incredible [paradoxical] a situation on the stage?" he asks us. "Indeed, you might have thought you were in a theater, filled with a multitude of conflicting passions... tears, joy, astonishment, pity, disbelief, prayer." A rivalry between playwright and romancer may also be adumbrated here: their art pursued the same goals, of course; though one wonders whether Chariton is emulating the effects of comedy, tragedy, arena spectacular, mime, or some combination of them all. Perhaps he hoped to produce such special effects most powerfully in his peculiar mixed narrative, which seems to combine the admirable characters and serious suffering of tragedy with the mundane setting and inevitable salvations of comedy.

Chaereas is not permitted to take possession of Callirrhoë on the spot. He has not yet demonstrated the prowess, or suffered all the agonies, that will make him worthy of her; and Callirrhoë has not yet suffered fully the Great King's love, which is conveyed to her through a wily eunuch. "Farewell, father, and you too, mother, and Syracuse, my native land," she nobly cries. "O treacherous beauty, you are the cause of all my woes... pirates, the sea, the tomb, slavery, the courtroom, and hardest to bear of all is the king's love." Such speeches have for a long time seemed to mark the degenerate branch of romance we call melodrama. But even though we make allowance for changes in the conventions by which emotions are made to seem genuine, we cannot believe that the king's love is hardest to bear, partly because he is presented to us as being just, virile, and worried about his adulterous passion. Our disbelief is supposed to be submerged in our pleasurable belief that virtue like Callirrhoë's resists *all* temptation; and perhaps it is, because we also believe that the cause of all our heroine's woes is a treacherous beauty for which she is not responsible but one which we would be most pleased to possess. We enjoy, I think, the suffering entailed by a beauty we envy; but we cannot accuse ourselves of these unworthy feelings because we at the same time admire, and would emulate, the woman who denies herself the erotic satisfactions offered by her beauty—in this case, union with the most powerful man in the world. Like Callirrhoë, we have it both ways—the pleasures of Aphrodite and the pleasures of chastity.

In the *seventh* and final phase of the action, Chaereas falls victim to still another intrigue (he believes Dionysius' lying slave, who tells him that the king has given Callirrhoë to Dionysius) and joins the Egyptians in their rebellion against their Persian overlords.

This second separation of the married lovers fulfills one aspect of the generative fantasy of the novel—it thrillingly abandons Callirrhoë to the king—as it frustrates the other—her chaste desire to rejoin her husband. The rebellion also gives Chaereas the opportunity to reveal at last his true Greek valor and thereby to earn the bride he abused. By bravery and intrigue he captures impenetrable Tyre with three hundred Greek mercenaries—a number which, Chariton reminds us in one of his pro-Greek asides, invokes the Spartan three hundred who smote the Persians at Thermopylae. Meanwhile, Callirrhoë, secured with the Persian harem on a nearby island, once more complains against the erotic goddess enthroned in the center of her chaste being: Aphrodite, she says, "though my wretched beauty aroused thine indignation, still it has been the cause of my ruin." Aphrodite's well-known indignation with girls who look too much like her is perhaps not unlike the envy aroused in mortals by such extraordinary beauty. But this beauty can also arouse love and pity when it ruins its innocent possessor, and its possessor must feel a certain anger with those who imagine that she enjoys the wanton fruits of her erotic power. Chaereas had once imagined this, and he still stands in need of forgiveness. But Callirrhoë has never complained of that kick. It is Aphrodite, her daimon, who feels Callirrhoë's anger and grants her forgiveness. When Chaereas captures the harem island and in "a situation at once paradoxical and melancholy," is unaware of the fact that he now possesses Callirrhoë, we are told that Aphrodite, "though she had previously been terribly angered at Chaereas' uncalled-for jealousy, was now becoming reconciled with him. And since Chaereas had now nobly redeemed himself in the eyes of Love by his wanderings from west to east amid countless sufferings, Aphrodite felt pity for him and . . . was willing once more to unite" the lovers. The heroine's feelings are clearly projected onto her goddess, as indeed they are projected, so to speak, into the action of the novel. Chaste Aphrodisians would be particularly sensitive to accusations of debauchery and particularly needful of a return to sanctified marriage. So the boy has suffered enough. The lovers meet. "Simultaneously they shrieked, 'Chaereas!' 'Callirrhoë!' As they rushed into each other's arms, they fainted and fell to the floor."

Chariton had begun his final book by saying, "I think that [it] will be the most pleasant of all to my readers, and in fact will serve as an antidote [*katharsion*] of the former ones." It would seem that the recognition and reconciliation of the lovers might be catharsis enough, but a residue of anger apparently remains to be discharged, even after the couple have manifested themselves in a final *coup de théâtre* at Syracuse. (They sail into the Great Harbor unannounced, then an arras is pulled back to reveal Chaereas in the uniform of a general and Callirrhoë reclining on a golden couch in Tyrian purple, looking like one of the goddesses she always knew herself to be.) Callirrhoë's truly reviving, cathartic embrace seems to have been reserved for her father, Hermocrates, who, leaping aboard the ship and "embracing his daughter, . . . cried, 'My child, are you really alive or am I deceived in this too?' 'Yes, father, I am—really so, now that I have seen you alive.'" We must remember that Callirrhoë has worked a silent vengeance on her two husbands: in a loving letter to "her dear Dionysius" she has committed her and Chaereas' son to him, and she never tells Chaereas that he had begotten a son in the womb he had kicked. This leaves the true father sonless and the false father richer by a son—to make a final paradox that Chariton himself does not commit. As for reconciliation with mother Aphrodite (Callirrhoë's mortal mother is not mentioned), it is somewhat tight-lipped: "My thanks to you, Aphrodite. Once more thou has shown me Chaereas here in Syracuse where as a girl I saw him at thy wish. I offer thee no reproaches, mistress, for what I have suffered; such was my fate. I beg thee, never again part me from Chaereas, and grant us both a happy life, and death together."

We could not ask for a more pleasant and thorough antidote for a story about a chaste girl whose fate was unchaste Aphrodite's wish.

Chariton's latest critic castigates the "fantastic exaggerations . . . complicated plots and bombastic speeches . . . pirates and robbers; countless swoonings and excessive sentimentality" of Greek romance.[8] My exposition of *Callirrhoë* perhaps shows that it does not entirely deserve such scorn. Chariton's invention seems to have been guided by a single conception—the story of a woman whose fated Aphrodisian beauty conflicts with her ethos, her characteristic desire to be faithful to societal and familial ideals. Such a conception could have led Chariton to the writing of a tragedy—as indeed many *erōtika pathēmata* (including, perhaps, the germ of the story, which he inherited) were "tragic." It could even have produced a comic narrative had Chariton made Callirrhoë and her men less worthy of our admiration and so had caused their sufferings to seem more serious to them than they could be to us. But Chariton chose a third way and made a story of an admirable, even flawless, woman whose sufferings are morally noble and whose triumph over them all is made inevitable by her virtuous denials of the potentially wanton consequences of her fated "treacherous beauty." In this sense he made a noteworthy contribution to the richest staple of Western narrative and dramatic art—the stories of admirable characters who survive the most serious threats to their lives and values. If this staple includes such various works as the *Odyssey*, the *Aeneid*, *Parsifal*, *Pamela*, *Moll Flanders*, *Pride and Prejudice*, and *A Portrait of the Artist as a Young Man*, as well as most popular fiction and drama, it would hardly do to cram them all into a single genre-hole labeled "romance"; but then all genres are crammed with works each unique in its characteristics and each classifiable in various ways. My point here is that Chariton apparently composed one of the first extended prose fictions of a type which success on all literary levels has made seem puerile and inane—and that he did so self-consciously. His almost obsessive play with the paradox and the intrigue, his arch comments about drama, recognition, reversal, and catharsis, all suggest that his art derives as much from theories of narrative art as from naive imitations of histories, biographies, travelers' tales, epics, plays, or rhetorical declamations.

If by adopting this third way Chariton made something we would call a "romance," he also contributed to the literary form which, as Northrop Frye has pointed out, "is closest to the wish-fulfillment dream."[9] One can certainly say that in *Callirrhoë* is worked out a kind of kernel fantasy—a standard fantasy entertained by most people, I suppose, probably most often in the so-called latency period of development. By "kernel fantasy" I do not mean what Norman Holland means by "core" or "central" fantasy—the very deep infantile experiences of mankind from which literary works rise and to which they appeal.[10] The "fantasy" at the heart of *Callirrhoë* is simply the fancy of a girl who imagines that she has been, is, or might be as beautiful as the most ideal beauty, worries about the moral consequences of such beauty, and imagines that she enjoys all the erotic triumphs she desires as well as all the satisfactions of chastity. The character of the heroine, the development and resolution of her predicaments, and the sentiments felt and expressed by all the characters seem to burgeon from this one "fantasy," which therefore describes the author's conception of his material, the soul of his protagonist, and the plot or "soul of the work." The approaches of aesthetic formalism and of psychoanalytic criticism converge when one describes a "synthetic principle" in terms of a "kernel fantasy." What these approaches circumvent, however, is a precise exploration of the effects such an aesthetically unifying kernel fantasy might have on readers—especially, in this case, on readers who are not female and not Hellenes of the first century A.D.

Well, we can only acknowledge here that we're all citizens of Aphrodite's town and conclude with a few comments on the emotional effects of narratives that manipulate, as does *Callirrhoë*, marvels (paradoxes), intrigues, and the delicate economy of feelings of superiority and inferiority entertained by readers. None of these factors is special to romance, though the combination of them represented by *Callirrhoë* may be typical of a large group of romances.

We must remember that older authors sought wonderful effects in every genre—biography, epic, history, comedy, satire; and their principal tools for this, aside from pathetic speeches and affecting styles, were the reversal, the recognition, and the intrigue, all of which could produce the pleasures of paradox—the "surprise, suspense, and delight" (in Cicero's words) of events that happen contrary to expectation, marvels that are unheard-of, that are incredible but are, all the same, credible because the causal action makes them so. By these means they could draw upon even more fundamental sources of aesthetic pleasure, two sources that are designated by one Greek verb, *thaumazein*. *Thaumazein* can mean both "to feel wonder" and "to feel surprise." Aristotle had used this word to sketch a psychology of literary effects and paradoxes in treatises that doubtless reflected taste more than determined it.[11] "To feel wonder" is to experience a desire to understand that is, like hunger, at once pleasurable and painful. Narratives stimulate this desire by imitating people in predicaments that neither they nor we fully understand and then progressively satisfy it by cumulative revelations. Recognitions and reversals of fortune are the most moving factors of a plot because they rouse and satisfy our natural desire "to feel wonder," and they do this in a special sense of the word—they "surprise" us. The "complete satisfaction of mind" yielded by a "striking consummation" (Cicero again) in an action must involve both the wonder we have felt at what we did not fully understand, the wonder we now feel at understanding, and the delighted surprise we feel at the way the plot has satisfied our desire to understand in an unexpected but credible—that is, paradoxical—way.

For staid Aristotles, of course, the multiplication of paradoxes by many ancient, medieval, and modern romancers is a shoddy titillation of our desire to feel wonder and to be surprised; and when reversals and recognitions are not credible, they produce a pornography of the reason. But Aristotle was as much unread in Chariton's time as in most others (though Chariton and other romancers knew his lexicon of literary analysis); and Chariton eschewed the miraculous, relying on intrigues to produce results that paradoxically conform with and frustrate what we desire for the heroine. Moreover, intrigues are inherently probable. We give easy credence to a line of action springing from a character's self-interest and capacity to scheme; and when these intrigues culminate in reversals contrary to our expectations, when the best-laid plans go awry or clash with other schemes, and when they all result in the happiness of the principals, who have themselves been victims of the apparently successful intrigues, we may feel wonder, surprise, and the delight that signals a release of tensions artfully built up in us. In the stories we call romances, the triumphant victims suffer seriously, and their triumph gives us sometimes the additional high pleasure of inferring that virtue is rewarded or that life might possibly be organized by a beneficent god after all; but in *Callirrhoë* only a few events result from strokes of fortune, jealous Aphrodite causes nothing to happen that is not dictated by the plot, the whole action, with its many incidents and its final resolution, is motivated by ordinary human desire, and we are not invited to speculate about higher meanings.

Aside from their contribution to the pleasures of paradox, intrigues also of course generate sympathy for their objects. Callirrhoë's innocence and admirable ideals already elicit our serious sympathy, and since her superior beauty causes so many intrigues to be fomented against what she and we feel is her best moral interest, we forgive her the beauty that is the cause of all this woe. More subtle, perhaps, is the way Chariton's intrigues, and those of many later romances, manipulate the reader's knowledge of the heroine's plight—her dangers and her prospects. On the basis of what he knows about her predicaments, the reader feels hope, fear, annoyance, wonder, surprise, and so forth. Every story, of any sort, makes a controlled release of information to the reader; this is a vital aspect of what we call narrative technique. But the effects of any particular story can be partly calculated from assessments of what the reader knows in relation to what the principal characters know. For example, if the reader knows more than the most knowledgeable character in the story, his hopes and anxieties will be of a quality very different from the ones he enjoys if he knows less than a character (as he usually does in the classic detective story). Chariton releases information to us in such a way that we often know more than Callirrhoë about the true circumstances of her predicaments—for example, that Dionysius is a good man, that Chaereas is alive but enslaved, and so on. As a result, we ourselves never fear for Callirrhoë as she fears for herself; and our knowledge of her potential salvation works in pleasurable tension with our knowledge of her genuine distress. If we knew only what she knows, or less, our participation in her suffering would be painful; nor would we be incessantly pulling for her, as we do when we, unlike the sufferer, see the possibility of rescue at hand. Moreover, we are superior to her in knowledge as she is superior to us in virtue, and this in itself makes it more feasible for us to "identify" ourselves with a paragon of beauty and morals. It is true that romance deals with idealizations, with enormities of virtue and vice; so do tragedy and satire; and it is true that the flawless heroes of romance (Galahad, James Bond) elicit emulation in a way that heroes of tragedy do not; but writers also manage, often, to give readers a pleasurable dose of superior knowledge to balance the superiority of their paragons.

But knowledge is feeling. The reader wants some intrigues to fail, some to succeed, even though he knows that all intrigues will end in the happiness of Callirrhoë. In fact, his feelings are, throughout, ambivalent, because all intrigues, good and bad, lead paradoxically to contrary desirable results. Some intrigues lead Callirrhoë toward a desirably higher status, but they are bad because they require bigamy and adultery. The good intrigues lead her toward a desirable domestic life with her first husband—

the man who kicked her. The reader's feelings are therefore balanced between a sense of what the heroine deserves and what she wants. What she deserves is the admiring love of the most attractive men in the world; what she wants is a return to a man who hardly deserves her. What she gets is both. The plot reconciles the discrepancies between what the reader feels the heroine deserves, what he knows she desires, and what in fact she gets. In this sense, the plot is like a daydream. That is, a plot that depicts a rise in fortune that is castigated as a decline, and a decline that leads marvelously to a rise, is not unlike an ordinary daydream that seems to reconcile reality, just deserts, and contrary desires. But if we were to take this familiar analogy seriously here, we would have to show not only that the characters and episodes and resolution of the plot all rise from a single matrix of paradoxical desires, which we have done, but how Chariton's art arouses a similar daydream in us readers, even touches upon our masochistic fantasies of rape and enslavement, on our rebellion against the Aphrodisian sources of erotic triumph, on our anger with taming husbands and the ideals of marriage. This we cannot do. Anyone in Aphrodisia who pays homage to Aphrodite yet wants to preserve social ideals might be moved by the story of Callirrhoë's erotic suffering and extend congratulations to the clerk who tells us only that he is secretary to a lawyer of Aphrodisia named Athenagoras; and though the sophist Philostratus later added that Chariton was a "nobody" whose work would soon perish,[12] that is all we know about Chariton.

It was of course an utterly unknown genius who wrote the unknown first romance, and it was therefore he who was the "origin" of the form romance. Such is the conclusion drawn by Ben E. Perry after a lifetime's contemplation of the mystery—the appearance of long prose fictions in the late Hellenistic period. True, "the new form romance was made for the sole purpose of exploiting drama on its own account"; that is, it filled a gap left by the disappearance of worthy drama in its time, and to do this it adapted the "substance" of that drama to the manner of historiography. But a romance, Perry insisted, is neither a drama nor a history. It is

> an extended narrative published apart by itself which relates—primarily or wholly for the sake of entertainment or spiritual edification, and for its own sake as a story, rather than for the purpose of instruction in history, science or

philosophical theory—the adventures or experiences of one or more individuals in their private capacities and from the viewpoint of their private interests and emotions.[13]

Since romance is an entity unlike any other, Perry cannot find its true origin in any other literary form. The origin must therefore have been a single human being, the man who first committed what no self-respecting literary man in antiquity would have dared write—the bastard prose medley of drama, epic, and history that is romance.

Perry is doubtless correct: a definable species, whether natural or artificial, must have had its Adam or Homer. And given her own definition of romance, Sophie Trenkner must also be correct when she observes that romance originates in "two basic tendencies of the human imagination," one being "an artistic impulse to observe life and portray it mockingly," the other being an impulse to idealize life which "produced romantic tales as projections of the fears and dreams of mankind." These two spiritual causes explain the two distinct species of romantic fiction in antiquity—that represented by Petronius, for example, and that represented by Chariton. The genus romance is composed materially of "conventional adventures by land and sea," and structurally it "consists merely of an accumulation of episodes each forming a narrative unity and linked together only by having the same hero."[14] These definitions support her contention that the primary material origin of romance lies in the enormous fund of brief popular stories possessed by Mediterranean peoples—legends, erotic tales, anecdotes about thieves, chaste lovers, fabulous voyagers, and so forth.

Exegesis and a neo-Jungian approach help Merkelbach find that all the romances (save those by Chariton and Iamblichus) were originally designed to celebrate the salvific powers of Isis-Osiris, and he therefore argues that all derive from the liturgies of mystery cults.[15] The ritualized death of the initiate, his recognition by and union with the god, become in the romances the separation of lovers, their wanderings and several resurrections, and finally their recognition and reunion with each other—all accomplished under the aegis of the goddess. If one could agree that the romances are pieces of rhetoric designed to inspire devotion in the reader, one might also agree that they originated in the cults.

But most etiologists of romance have concentrated on the material rather than the formal origins of the genre. Works like the *Cyropaedia* and the *Alexander Romance* obviously begin in what we call history, while the very titles of works like the *Babyloniaca* and the *Ephesiaca* suggest origins in what we call local legends. Bruno Lavagnini argued that the genre itself springs from local legends, which became popular *novellas*, which became, when crossed with New Comedy and satire, romances.[16] Others have cited the influence of fantastic travelers' tales, others that of the schools of rhetoric where pupils were apparently required to argue hard cases that read like miniature romances.[17] Paradoxically, all etiologies of romance must be correct. Even Merkelbach's theory might win nods from Aristotle and Miss Trenkner if he said that romance grew from the view of life, the yearning for rescue and salvation, that underlay the mystery cults, just as tragedy grew from the view that underlay the dithyrambs and comedy from the view that produced the old phallic songs. Also, if there is such a thing as romance, there must have been a first romancer. And the influence of legend, history, rhetoric, and drama on Chariton's story, for example, is obvious. The theories differ primarily because they derive from differing conceptions of literary form, of literary tradition, and of the things we call romances. I myself cannot offer a theory of origins because, not having examined all the things called romances, I cannot as yet ask the question "What is romance?," much less answer it.

❧7❧
Discussion
Three

PSI: But you have neglected a most interesting scene.

ALPHA: Which one?

PSI: Callirrhoë stands in the temple of Aphrodite. She is the image of Aphrodite. But she is also Artemis because the author says she is now vested as virginal Artemis, or Athena. And she is holding her child. She is a madonna. The author says this is an unprecedented scene. No painter or sculptor has ever depicted an Artemis holding a child in her arms, he says. Here is a tableau of all you have found in this remarkable little book. The reconciliation of sacred adversaries in the psyche of the heroine and the assertion of family life in the temple—in the very teeth—of the twin desires most inimical to family life: the desire for erotic plenitude and the desire to renounce eros altogether.

ALPHA: Yes. No. A story is not a static tableau. It is temporal and dynamic. This scene is meaningful only in the syntax of intrigues that lead up to and away from it.

SIGMA: I noticed that you abandoned your linguistic analogies. What happened to lexical items, syntaxes, grammars?

ALPHA: They don't seem to help much.

SIGMA: I disagree. Your quasi-linguistic terms could help you dig into two of the deep questions you raised—the origin of a literary form and the psychodynamics of literary pleasures.

ALPHA: Well, I refused to ask the first question, and I fudged the second.

PSI: Fudged?

KAPPA: American idiom. In fact, he whipped it up into a homemade bombe. Look, let me dispose of the first unasked question straightaway. Homer was the origin of romance, and romance was the origin of Homer. No? None of your fancy paradoxes? Homer was the origin of romance beacuse he wrote

94

the *Odyssey*. Romance was the origin of Homer because Homer was born in a romance. Proof is the story of his origins: a young woman of Ios was seduced by a god, ran away in shame, was captured by pirates and sold to the king of Lydia, who fell in love with her and adopted her child, whose name was Homer. And if this is too mythic to be romantic, I cite another version, in which the god is only Homer's uncle and the king is a schoolmaster.

SIGMA: Does this satisfy everyone?

ALPHA: Perfectly adequate explanations. But I prefer the second version.

PSI: These stories say only that the true name of Homer is Oedipus and that the origin of romance is the Family Romance. These generalities do not explain particulars.

KAPPA: Then let me cite a particular true story. It shows that the origin of romance lies in ordinary life. Plutarch tells of an executed rebel who didn't actually die, and his wife discovers this when she visits his tomb. She joins him there, sets up a cozy household, pots of jam, et cetera, lives with him there for years, and bears him children. Here is a tableau of pure love in the bridal and domestic tomb. Tacitus also says it actually happened, though in actual fact Plutarch tells it to show that women's love can be as enduring as men's—apparently a hard case to argue in the second century.

SIGMA: Well, if legend and life explain literature, I expect we may as well go home.

ALPHA: I'm ready.

PSI: But are we trying to explain literature?

SIGMA: That is an excellent question. None of us would know an explanation of literature if we saw one. And if one bit me, I'd drive a wooden stake through its heart.

KAPPA: Leaving aside your romantic valuation of ignorance, I must agree it's an excellent question because it reminds me of something absolutely vital. Alpha has been coy about defining, as he puts it, what he keeps calling "romance," and quite properly so. He might as well call them novels.

ALPHA: I agree.

KAPPA: But you haven't got your terms in order. You assume that you're dealing with something grand and mighty called "literature," as though *Callirrhoë* could be ranked with the *Aeneid* or even the *Argonautica*, worthy of the don's hire and the schoolboy's labor. Then you show that the stories are based on certain formulas. Never mind whether these are formulas of the psyche or of literary convention or both, and never mind mere technical variations between intrigues and episodic structures—in actual fact these romances are formulaic stories. What does this suggest? It suggests that we are dealing here with popular literature, literature written for ordinary people, not students of Milton and Joyce. They are novels written primarily for women and girls in leisured bourgeois families. Unless Alpha is willing to confess this dreadful fact...

ALPHA: I'm willing to confess it.

KAPPA: Good. Unless it is confessed, we will miss what is absolutely vital, to wit, that so-called romance is but one kind of popular literature, one set of formulas for penny dreadfuls, and we shall miss what is absolutely interesting, to wit, that we are speaking here about the beginnings of circulating-library fiction—Wilkie Collins, James Bond, science fiction, *The Bengal Lancers*—and it is meaningful only because it bespeaks its culture.

SIGMA: Well, Alpha, I trust your honest confession has been good for you.

ALPHA: It wasn't entirely honest. We are speaking here about the beginnings of prose fiction, which happens also to be prose fiction of a certain sort. It may well have been popular, it may be the Hellenic version of Victorian triple-deckers, but it is not science fiction, adventures of spies, cowboys, and gangsters. It is the sort that became the staple of fiction and drama from that day to this: stirring stories of love, trouble, and triumph, never mind whether they are written by Homer, Shakespeare, or Henry James, and never mind whether you sat through one on television last night, enjoying an elitist reaction to it. All kinds of literature, high and low, work with formulas, and the same kinds work with the same sets of formulas. A few works innovate, a few find profundities and complexities. We are thankful for this. But it won't do to undervalue books like Chariton's because its formulas became so persistent, so powerful, that they now seem hopelessly out of fashion—melodramatic and sentimental. A beautiful virtuous girl beset by seducers! her virtue finally rewarded!

SIGMA: It's the rewarding of virtue that we mistrust.

ALPHA: Right. That's because we're romantics of the realistic persuasion. But realism is itself a matter of fashion. Already *A Farewell to Arms* seems unrealistic, whereas fifteen years ago it still seemed hard-bitten. And sometimes virtue *is* rewarded.

SIGMA: I can see that we've descended into the mists of evaluation. I also see that you're no longer coy. Can't you now "define," to use Kappa's word, what you call "romance"?

ALPHA: No. I can only put it this way. First, these things are made of Greek words. And if they were stylized as verse instead of prose, they would be somewhat different from what they are, but perhaps not essentially so. The *Argonautica* shows this.

KAPPA: I don't follow you.

ALPHA: I know. I mean that whether you write a story in verse or prose is mostly determined by the current notion of what is appropriate for verse or prose and by what people think verse is as opposed to prose; but the essential character of a thing is not determined by this conventional distinction. The history of drama shows this. And second, leaving the *Argonautica* aside now, the words relate events that might possibly have happened in the past. If we believed that they had in fact happened, or if we believed that they could not possibly have happened, the effect of the story would be somewhat different from what it is. Third, these events are experienced by characters more beautiful, rich, courageous, and wicked than you or I. But these people suffer, decide, and speak more or less as we would like to. That is, we admire and emulate them. That is, we take them seriously. The important distinction here is that they are not flawed, like heroes of tragedy and comedy. If they were characters like Oedipus and Hamlet, we would not emulate them, though we might admire them. We might want to imitate James Bond, but who wants to emulate the hero of a tragedy or a comedy? Fourth, the events are awesome to the same extent as the characters are, but the events, the action, is more important than the characters. They are predicaments, intrigues, escapes that we are meant to take seriously because they threaten the lives and values of characters we are meant to take seriously. Fifth, these threats are mostly erotic, in the widest sense of the word; and if they weren't erotic, the effects of the works would be somewhat different from what they are.

Sixth—forgive all these fingers in the air—the events are disposed into scenes, episodes, acts, and intrigues in such a way that the threats are brought to climaxes, and all the climaxes lead to a final triumph over misfortune, illicit sex, and death. And seventh, the final triumph brings characters and readers to a sense of serious, grateful joy that leaves no residue of mystery, save perhaps a wondering at the powers that align themselves with virtue. And eighth, if any of these factors were different from what they are, the works themselves would be different.

SIGMA: You have two fingers left. Are they for kernel fantasies and syntaxes?

ALPHA: No. But I would need *n* number of fingers to point at the facts, namely, at each of the works, each of which is unique.

SIGMA: Still, you've been pinned down. You've said that these "unique" things have certain characteristics in common. Don't look unhappy. No one wants to go back to Philosophy 101. No one wants to talk about the One and the Many, Chickens and Eggs, Nominalists and Realists.

PSI: But these are fascinating problems.

SIGMA: Of course they are. But is there a Realist in the room, who would want to defend the proposition that there is a One, Essential Romanceness, of which all romances are examples? Or a Nominalist, who would contend that all the likenesses among these unique things are mere figments of Alpha's analytical mind?

PSI: I did not experience an American course in Philosophy 101.

SIGMA: Then we are ready for Philosophy 102, where I may offer an answer to the question of literary genres. What is tragedy? What is the novel? What is romance? I make a simple application of Wittgenstein's notion of classes based on family resemblances. But this drives me to the blackboard. Sorry. Let this top line of arabic numbers represent unique literary works, and the bottom line of letters certain characteristics:

1	2	3	4	5	6
ABCDEF	*ABCEF*	*ABDEF*	*ACDE*	*BDEF*	*BCDEF*

And so on. Now, let's say that *A* is prose, *B* is pretended historicity, *C* is admirable characters, *D* is awesome events, *E* is eroticism, *F* is a final triumph. None of the works is exactly like any of the others, but all share enough characteristics—at least four out of six—to warrant our giving them a common name. Let's say this name is "romance." If you omit C, you have a comic romance. If you omit D, you have a serious romantic novel like *Clarissa*. If you omit A, you have a romance or novel in verse, and if you omit B, you have a serious fantasy.

ALPHA: And if you omit E, you have the Pentateuch. Though I'm not sure you'd have to omit E for that. You have to add G—"not intended for instruction." You've left out the author's conception of his work, and you've left out the "final cause"—the intended effect.

SIGMA: All right. And so did you. Or is it "grateful joy"?

ALPHA: I don't know. It might be "thrills and chills." I've been suggesting that the final cause of each work is its own. In *Callirrhoë*, it's the arousal and satisfaction of a certain paradoxical fantasy. And the *Argonautica* fails because its final-cause is blunted because the author wanted to write a romantic commemoration but used characters as flawed as those in a tragedy.

SIGMA: All right. My point is that you can gather together whatever characteristics you wish under the class names you wish to use, but you needn't assert that all members of your class are identical. My bigger point is . . .

ALPHA: But terms like "comedy" differ from terms like "novel," because you can have comic novels, romantic novels, tragic novels, satiric novels; or satiric plays, romantic plays . . .

SIGMA: OK, all right, it makes no difference. My larger point is that every writer, when he sits down to write, finds himself in the presence of both lines. That's an ungainly image. He comes into the presence of individual literary works that move him and of types of literary works that appeal to him. He doesn't try to make classes. He feels family resemblances. He would like to join a family, maybe. He wants to write a book as good as 1 and 4 and 7, none of which is exactly the same as the others but all of which seem equally moving, and in the same way, to him. He is like a child learning a language. From adults. His learning is partly conscious, partly not. And his language is partly that of literature itself and partly the specific literary language that appeals to him. Literature is a language with several distinct dialects.

PSI: Like the Romance languages.

SIGMA: That analogy will do.

KAPPA: Not all analogies will do. Literature is not a language. It uses languages. It works with ordinary speech.

SIGMA: Analogies are needed in some fields, aren't they? And they do well when they do well. Give me a moment to work on the question of the origin of romance, or of the rise of the novel—it makes no difference—now that Alpha and Wittgenstein have defined these things for us. How does anyone learn a language? I borrow a formula from Chomsky here:

$$L = \text{Language}$$
$$LA = \text{Learning Ability}$$
$$K = \text{Knowledge}$$
$$U = \text{an utterance}$$

The formula is simple:

$$L \rightarrow LA \rightarrow K \rightarrow U.$$

By "Language" Chomsky means all the rules, the grammar, of, say, French. "Learning Ability" in the child must be so complex that I hardly know what can be meant by it. It must include an innate theory that discriminates phonetic classes, a theory that discriminates among semantic concepts and signs, a megagrammar that includes all possible grammars, a method of interpreting grammars, a method of evaluating grammars that can find the right one, French, that fits the babble heard by the fledgling Parisian. "Knowledge" may be active or passive. It can result in an utterance or not. Now, by simple analogy,

$$LL = \text{Literature-Language}$$
$$LA = \text{Literature Ability}$$
$$C = \text{Creativity}$$
$$W = \text{a literary work}$$

and the same simplistic formula would apply:

$$LL \rightarrow LA \rightarrow (K + C) \rightarrow W.$$

LL would be all the rules by which literary works, fancy and popular, are composed. It is the input data that babbles to the infant reader, poet, and critic in innumerable unique works. LA must be possessed by just about everybody, but C is an activating principle possessed mysteriously by only a few, the poets. It's easy to see how C distinguishes the poet from the scholar, but *LA* is very tough. It must include a capacity to discriminate styles and structures, a method of interpreting or feeling various meanings in literary works, and a method of evaluating the appropriateness of all these things to one another in any given work.

KAPPA: The analogy doesn't hold. What are the rules of literature?

SIGMA: I don't know. I also don't know the grammar of English in the sense of "know" that you imply, but I learned to speak it pretty well in about thirty months. I'll never learn to talk novels or lyrics in any language, but I know some of the rules that make them like and different from each other, just as I know some of the rules of Greek and Latin. Let me extend the analogy, bad as it is. Every work is unique, like every utterance. But a literary work is a privileged utterance because it is preserved and at once joins the input fund of *LL*. So this formula should be a ring:

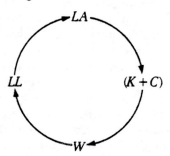

Back here at *LL*. Literature-Language might be composed of a potentially infinite number of complete sentences or works; but if there are rules in it, there must be a finite number of kernel sentences in the whole of it if *LL* has a grammar. Each of these kernels can generate n number of unique utterances. And these kernels may be what Aristotelians call "forms," like tragedy and comedy and satire.

ALPHA: Your closed ring closes out literary change. Some of those *W*s are innovative. New forms go in and out of *LL*, but new kernel sentences don't go in and out of ordinary language.

SIGMA: Granted. Linguistic and semantic change isn't the same as literary change. But the closed ring doesn't close out change. It only shows how innovations keep perking in the literary tradition. And aren't these basic forms, which don't change essentially? Is the sixteenth-century revenge tragedy a kernel form or a mutation of an old kernel? Isn't the novel only a comic or romantic epic in prose?

KAPPA: This is becoming just a bit ridiculous. In a moment you'll have to grant that these kernels are seething in *LA*, that they're innate in man, and that they are kernel fantasies in the human psyche.

PSI: This is a point that may be worth granting. But I do not like the word "fantasy" in this usage. Perhaps the Greek romances, for example, are expressions of a common psychodynamic pattern that is also uttered in plays and poems throughout the centuries.

SIGMA: But they are also uttered according to the rules of the literature grammar. For example, the rules of writing plays differ from the rules of writing novels.

PSI: Of course. So in your Creativity factor there must be a something that makes Shakespeare write plays but not novels.

KAPPA: That something was economic conditions.

PSI: Perhaps. And the Creativity factor makes Henry James unable to write plays, and Sartre able to write both.

KAPPA: Too many mysterious somethings clog this tidy ring. I've even forgotten what it's supposed to explain.

SIGMA: The generation of a new literary genre. Let me enrich confusion with two other terms—surface structure and deep structure. Sentences that look the same on their surfaces may actually have different deep structures, and sentences that look different may have similar deep structures. For example, "The psychiatrist questioned Alpha" derives from the same deep structure as "Alpha was questioned by the psychiatrist," though the surface syntax is different. And "Kappa persuaded the psychiatrist to examine Alpha" has the same surface structure as "Kappa wanted the psychiatrist to examine Alpha," but their deep structures are different.

PSI: I can't follow this.

SIGMA: The surface structure of a play like *Lysistrata* is very different from the surface structure of a novel like *Catch-22*, but their deep structures may be similar or even the same, insofar as both are written to attack war or irrational policies. But the surface structure of *Catch-22* is very similar to other novels, for example *For Whom the Bell Tolls*, which is a tragedy set in wartime. Or think of the deep differences and surface likenesses between Hemingway's *Killers* and Lardner's *Haircut*. It's a simple point. If I were a literary critic or scholar, which I certainly am not, I would call the deep structures "forms" and the surface structures "genres." If I were a literary historian, I'd say that forms are "synchronic" and genres are "diachronic."

KAPPA: And what would that mean?

SIGMA: That would mean that forms can be seen as static. They originate in, and express, human experience itself, or a fundamental conception of human experience. And they develop so slowly after their first appearance that they might almost be said to have an etiology but no history. What has a history is the surface structure, the genres, because these are made of conventions and are subject to fashion. The "novel," for example, is a surface structure, a cluster of conventions that has lasted for well over two centuries, only a century less than its Greek prototype. *Callirrhoë*, as Alpha says, is not the oldest intact novel but the oldest intact romantic novel. And all of this means simply that, in the formula, we do this:

$$SS = \text{Surface Structure}$$
$$DS = \text{Deep Structure}$$
$$R^1 = \text{the first prose romance}$$

When the first romancer comes upon the scene, he confronts this situation:

$$W^n - R^1 \rightarrow LA + R \rightarrow K + (C + R).$$

That is, the first romance is not in the whole extant body of literary works, W^n, but the kernel of Romance, R, must be in the Literature Ability of his contemporaries and in his own Creative capacity. Where else would it be?

ALPHA: Well, you're making Romance an It. You're "entitizing" it.

KAPPA: He has to, because he's making these absolutely amazing formulas with capital letters.

SIGMA: OK, granted. Have pity on him who is trapped in language. Now, what does our infant romancer do? He works out his Deep Structure, DS, which is Romance, R, through one or more Surface Structures, SSs—plays, histories, epics, elegies—to make an unprecedented piece of fiction, R^1—the first romance:

$$K + (C + R) \rightarrow (SS^1 - DS^1) + (SS^2 - DS^1)$$
$$+ (SS^3 - DS^2) \rightarrow R^1.$$

So

$$R^1 = DSR + (SS^1 + SS^2 + SS^3).$$

KAPPA: What are you paradigmatizing?

SIGMA: Nothing. The first romancer consulted his Knowledge, which did not contain Romance, and his Creativity, which did contain it, and made one first romance by subtracting a number of Deep Structures from a number of Surface Structures and using the Surface Structures to express the new Deep Structure, Romance. Then we have W^n plus R^1, and poets imitate R^1:

$$(W^n + R^1) \rightarrow K \rightarrow \langle C + R \rangle \rightarrow R^n.$$

After this happens, people think that the amalgam of surface structures *is R* and begin to define the form in terms of these conventions.

KAPPA: Pardon me, Sigma. May I have the chalk? Your game is missing one or more players. What about Culture, K'? Socioeconomic Conditions, E? and Consequent Literary Conditions, A? In fact, culture *is* economic conditions plus literary conditions plus the whole body of "works." That is,

$$K' = (E + A) + W^n;$$

and so,

$$K' \rightarrow (K + C) \rightarrow R^1.$$

PSI: But where does R itself come from? Is it suspended in the cultural air?

KAPPA: Where else could it be? But there *is* no R, and no DSR. They do not exist. Sorry. But I'll grant you the human psyche, so that

$$(K' + \Psi) \rightarrow (DS^n + SS^n) \rightarrow \text{Poet} \rightarrow R^1.$$

This would explain why a certain literary genre can appear in some historical conditions and not in others.

Psi: But must we not return to this mysterious Ψ? And to the equally mysterious Literature Ability?

Kappa: The blackboard is filled, and thank heaven there is no eraser in the room.

Psi: I shall not need it. I regretted it when Alpha's concept of kernel fantasy was cast into the outer whiteness, or realm of color. Doesn't the idea of "kernel fantasy" help explain the emotional appeal of literary works? Don't the poet and his reader meet in places in the soul that cannot be mapped along the lines of "Literature Ability"? Or of course, they meet in the poem itself. And are not the writing and reading of poems psychological processes? Therefore, quite properly, Alpha began to inquire into the psychic factors *in the poem* that link poet and reader. Perhaps one or another kernel fantasy makes this precious connection that gives so much pleasure and instruction to man. And so might intrigues and paradoxes, though I fear that Aristotle's psychology hardly explains their powers. And one cannot ignore one vital factor in these particular romances—their erotic content, so simply expressed, almost without disguise. Surely this helps explain Kappa's insistence that they belong to popular culture. In some ways they are like the dreams of children.

Alpha: And the conventions are so outdated that they seem simpler than they are.

Psi: Of course. But the threadbare surface structures reveal most clearly what we are *supposed* to admire and emulate in the characters. Ego psychology and phenomena of identification will lead us to...

Sigma: You missed Alpha's psychologizing about Jason and Medea. We were told how people identify themselves with symptoms, suffering, ego ideals, all that.

Psi: I regret this. And did you also speak of phenomena of voyeurism?

Sigma: Not that I recall.

Psi: These also involve processes of identification. I was reminded of these phenomena as Alpha spoke of intrigues and the controlled release of information in a narrative. Of course these are techniques that have no special relationship with romances, save that the romances are erotic in content. Now, does a kind of voyeurism help explain the effectiveness of certain narrative techniques?

KAPPA: I now understand my problem with these romances. I'm not a voyeur.

PSI: Of course you are not. Voyeursim is a malfunction of certain ordinary dynamics. But as such it shows us something, perhaps, about "aesthetic distance" and "point of view" and the "observer" and even "identification." The old notion that there are three basic types of voyeurism may serve us well enough here. In the first type, a person literally observes himself as though he were someone else observing himself. He might observe his own sexual organs with extraordinary interest or experience an extraordinary fear of seeing them. In either case, it is as though he were another party who wonders, doubts, adores, rejects his subject, which is himself. In a second type, the person feels compelled to observe the nakedness of others, but from a safe distance, an aesthetic distance, so that he will not in fact become involved with an object that is indeed so attractive that he must often turn away before the nakedness is fully revealed lest he see, for example, that a woman does not in fact possess a penis, which he hopes and fears that she may not. In both types the person creates an observer in himself who is and is not himself and thereby frees himself to make certain safe identifications; he also prevents himself from meeting certain dreadful demands of reality. A third type involves projective mechanisms as well as identification. Exhibitionism. The man compelled to expose himself, normally to strangers, or who finds himself drawn to the profession of acting in fact identifies himself with the extrinsic observer. He needs another to confirm his own existence or his own sex. Another must admire or fear his sex, which is otherwise in doubt. Or the exhibitionist can achieve sexual gratification only by identifying himself with a passive observer of his own sexual acts. Whatever feelings the exhibitionist has but cannot assimilate are projected onto the observer and enjoyed through him. All these are of course relatively normal processes. If we were not excited by the nakedness of others or did not admire our own, we would not find mates or feel worthy of them. If we were not interested in uncovering hidden truths, we would have no scholars, critics, scientists, spies.

SIGMA: Psychiatrists.

PSI: Indeed! Or readers and audiences, or anyone who takes delight in making intrigues.

KAPPA: Or in doing Soho.

PSI: Exactly. All art must provide voyeuristic gratifications, but the excitement of observing the actions and thoughts of persons who do not exist is special precisely because they do *not* exist. We may freely introject them into the images that incessantly flow through our conscious and preconscious functions and freely permit them to take over these functions temporarily. The very fact that fiction is a patent lie and forbids active participation appeals to the passivity inherent in voyeuristic processes. But my point has to do with the *unfolding* of a story, with the gradual denuding of the truth about the characters and their destiny. Alpha has corrected me on this score. He is quite right. Stories are *dynamic*, in time, from the reader's point of view. I am now relating the technique of narrative unfolding to a basic psychodynamic force. That is, some narrative techniques must focus, or liberate, the dynamics of observing and projecting more powerfully than others. The tantalizing development in a story of deeper and deeper motives, the conflict of opposing motives and actions in the intrigues of a story, the growth of danger, intensify what Alpha has called paradoxes and tensions. Our tensions become literally—no, metaphorically—intriguing! And when we know that these tensions are leading us inevitably but slowly to a catharsis, a purgation, our pleasure is only heightened. No wonder Freud likened this to erotic foreplay and the catharsis to orgasm. But it is the special excitement of the voyeur, the nonparticipating observer, aroused by a controlled release of information and image. And when the technique provides us with intrigues, when we are taken behind the scenes as we watch each scene, our excited passivity becomes that of the old gods. Our narcissistic fantasies of power, of control over the past and future, and of Olympian superiority to the present, must gratify our ego intensely even as it is taken over by experiences not our own. Our fantasies are stirred, shaped, and fulfilled, and we have the pleasurable sense of what Aristotle called "learning" and of what Plato, I believe more accurately, called "recognition"—the sense of discovering something we had already known, but known unconsciously. And this is true. Our preconscious memories—images and words—come to us afresh, with surprise, stimulated by imaginary beings and therefore freed of personal pain, of the annoying resistances. Art makes a truce between forbidden material, the desire to know this material, and the inhibitions to that desire. And techniques, complicated unfoldings of unreal experiences, must especially give us also the pleasure of wonder, surprise, and the reconciliation of opposed forces in ourselves as well as in the plot. But now I have perhaps passed beyond the dynamics of voyeurism and have talked too long. And only in order to say that this "Literature Ability" on the blackboard is perhaps rather sterile.

SIGMA: Well. Are there no reactions?

KAPPA: I must say that, despite a kind of eloquence, doctor, you have brought me closer to the latrines of life than to literature. I could almost stomach Alpha's talk about Jason's bare foot symbolizing a fear of castration, but I now feel that art is reducible to an elegant public lavatory, like the peculiarly smelly Victorian one near the Bank underground station.

PSI: I don't know that one.

KAPPA: I mean to say, you remove a specific content, like Medea's wailing, and substitute the general human smell. Even Alpha's kernel fantasy didn't do that. He only claimed that poor Callirrhoë's erotic chastity must appeal to dreaming maidens down the centuries.

PSI: I have led you into a misunderstanding. I have no philosophy with which to speak of the general and the specific, but consider this case. A woman with a rebellious daughter reads in a novel a scene in which a young man or woman rejects the values of his parents and strikes out into the world to become a communist or an actress. It might seem that this woman would angrily stop reading the novel. But she does not. She is fascinated. Why? Because she is both a mother and a daughter. At one point she too must have been restive about the power her parents held over her. Perhaps she too rebelled, perhaps she invested much energy in not rebelling. Doubtless the latter, because she now has a rebellious daughter. But in either case, she would identify herself with the rejected mother in the novel and at the same time with the daughter. Or, to make Freud's distinction of kinds of identification, which is perhaps too simple, she wants to *be* her mother and to *have* her daughter, just as a small boy wants to *be* his father and *have* his mother. But in this case the woman has within herself the figure of a mother and the figure of a daughter. Perhaps she now sees in the novel a battle she wages daily with herself, to remain a good mother, a good daughter to her own mother, and a desire to free herself from these roles. She finds herself unable to put down the novel; and, when she is finished, she proclaims that it is a very bad novel. This is a very easy example. Perhaps the woman has no rebellious daughter, no child at all. Still, she is moved by the novel. Why? Because, being a human being, she is a daughter, was once young, and carries within herself figures of older women she has admired, hated, emulated. She might also be moved by the dilemmas faced by Callirrhoë or even by the more dreadful psychological paradoxes in Jason and Medea. And it would make no difference whether the novel was set in Bulgaria or China.

KAPPA: Yes it would. We are presently speaking of first-century Hellenic novels written in Greek.

PSI: Perhaps I must be more precise. Alpha too has worried about finding a common ground between the experience of readers in 50 A.D. and readers today, and he has also worried about how we, good people, enjoy the spectacle of pain, implying that we are like our ancestors in this unworthy respect at least. May I offer a few vague comments on these problems? I must assume that the experience of seeing a play or reading a novel has not changed.

KAPPA: You'd better not assume any such thing. Seeing a play out of doors, in the morning, with masks and ritualized gestures, as the Greeks did, is not the same as seeing it in a dark modern theater, is it? And people probably didn't *read* novels silently to themselves but spoke them aloud to themselves and to others.

PSI: Thank you. These are interesting details, but they do not affect my remarks. I speak only of one small but important aspect of the interesting power of art, literary art, to arouse and shape our feelings and thoughts. Let me assume that experiencing a play or novel is not exactly an ordinary experience. It is not exactly the same thing as liking a tree or hating a conversation. It is rather like some other extraordinary experiences. It is something like being under hypnosis, or being in love, or being part of a mob. When caught up, as we say, in reading or observing, we seem to lose ourselves, or part of ourselves.

Sometimes we lose ourselves in elation, sometimes in a sort of drugged passivity. In either case, we experience a loss of reality and of our own conscious judging, and in this state we are willing to feel and believe things and remember things we would not be willing to do if we were not in this hypnotic state, if we had not given part of our selves up to the moment, to the leader of the mob, to the cause, to the author and his book, so to say. Now, what permits this strange captivity in which we are freed from the ordinary? What do we put in abeyance, and what fills its place, within our psyches? We put in abeyance some of our codes, some of the tests by which we distinguish true from false, real from apparent. This permits us to do and feel things we would not ordinarily allow ourselves.

KAPPA: In short, we make a willing suspension of disbelief.

PSI: That is an interesting phrase but a shallow one. We replace some beliefs with others. The psychic functions persist, but their content changes. If we are members of an army or mob, that force or image in us, perhaps derived from our parents, that tells us what we may and may not do is replaced by the officer, the leaders, the whole occasion, which sweeps us up in its own codes and loves and hates. These phenomena of displacement and identification are of course common in everyday life as well, but reading and watching art can be extreme cases. And these, I think, have not changed from 50 A.D. until today. We are caught up—hypnotized, so to speak—by virtue of our souls, not by virtue of our particular society or times. Watching actors, following characters in a book, we give up some of our ego functions and ideals to them, we become them, the bad in a different way from the good, but we especially become a character we can admire. They take the place of vague imagos in our souls, and we are excited.

KAPPA: I have extreme difficulty believing that I become Jason or Pelias or Medea—all of whom I perversely admire—or, much less, woeful Anthia or Callirrhoë—whom I perversely despise.

PSI: Perhaps you unperversely become Heracles. Perhaps you become all the Argonauts, Jason excluded, and identify yourself with their righteousness and invulnerability. The characters and their triumphs make you imagine that you are better than you are—that you can slay giants, fly like a bird, seduce an Amazon. But I speak of the obvious. Why do you perversely associate yourself with the sufferings of Jason and Medea? What in their pain pleases you? This is a complicated question which I do not presume to answer, at least not for you or me personally. But in general, why does all the erotic suffering in these stories please us? How do we identify ourselves with such pain? It is easy to say, as I myself did just a moment ago, that we play the roles of all sorts of characters in a book because we once played these roles, and perhaps continue to play them, in our own psychological lives. But this is not the whole story. It is the spectacle of someone *else* suffering pain that moves us. Medea suffers from her fated shift of allegiance from her father to her father's enemy, and she must in turmoil choose Jason and Hellas over father and home. But we are not female, we have never faced this choice, you say. Well, we have, but I grant it to you. What do we identify ourselves with? Precisely the pain. We do not identify with the disease, which perhaps we have never suffered, but with the symptom, which is universal. We may never have had to choose to marry a second husband to give our unborn child an honest name, but we have suffered the turmoil of choice, of compromising one ideal to preserve another. Or we do not even have had to experience such dilemmas. In short, we identify ourselves with the symptom only, and this is the source of our aesthetic pleasure. Let me cite an example. A friend of ours finds himself in love. At a certain moment he wants to leave his wife, and he breaks down before us, he weeps. *We* are not in love. We do not want to leave our wives. We try to console him. But what can happen? We too can begin to weep. We can become angry at his wife, a very nice lady. We can even become angry at our own wives, who have in fact done us only the usual harm. We call all this sympathy, empathy, but what are we experiencing here? Why should we adopt our friend's feelings and symptoms? First, we too would like to have such a grand passion, perhaps, and to be released from our current attachments. Second, his sufferings arouse our sense of guilt, the guilt he himself, we perceive, must be feeling. We are challenged to feel what our friend feels, and we meet this challenge. We accept the suffering, the punishment, that evidently accompanies his love. But we also enjoy it because we always know that we are not in fact our friend. We have the pleasure, which is aesthetic, of identifying our ego with his on one point only—the suffering that attends freedom and guilt. We identify with his symptoms and imagine that we feel what he feels. Whatever repressed material we think we see being released in him we playfully release in ourselves, and this is what stories can also do for us. But in stories, art makes it all seem meaningful, very bearable. And in stories in which everyone gets his just rewards—which is to say almost all stories—we are especially gratified. We feel as we might if we were part of a mob that in fact did something just—perhaps storm the Bastille. We live, in reading such a story, in a scheme where we can safely suffer and safely be rewarded.

KAPPA: I'm sorry. I really am very sorry, but one really must get one's diagnoses right if one is to explain and cure, and one can't begin to diagnose these old Greeks properly until one understands a little more about their souls. I am appalled to remind you that we have not even mentioned basic feelings and values like *sebas* and *aidōs*, that is, two apparently simple value-feelings like "awe" and "shame." I regret having to bring up such obvious matters, but you've put the fat into the fire. And how can we discuss values without knowing the language, the cultural moment? We cannot. I hardly know where to begin. Even "shame" and "awe" won't do for *aidōs* and *sebas*. And if we understood the special flavor of *sebas* and *aidōs*, we would still face variations of the flavor. All this talk of chastity, guilt, and desire—as though they were felt to be the same everywhere and at all times. Plutarch could not understand the old Roman distaste for nudity, for example. Apparently his Greek voyeurism differed from the Roman variety. To prove your chastity in Argos, you drank bull's blood; in Ionia you walked on live coals. Can we today imagine the extraordinary value they placed on chastity? Apollonius of Tyana restored the organs of a eunuch caught fondling a concubine because the restoration was the worst punishment he could imagine. I'm talking about the Empire period, but also the values of the eastern Mediterranean littoral. Pseudo-Clement exhorted his brother virgins to cast their eyes to heaven and cover their right hand in cloth when shaking hands with a woman and never to sleep where a woman had slept. Saint Paul was an absolute libertine by comparison. Matter itself was unchaste. Gnostics held that matter

was a child of incest, female Sophia having looked too amorously at her Father, the God. And that Christ finally was pro-
ᐧ duced to save men from women.

PSI: These are indeed awesome facts.

KAPPA: These are extreme cases, but can you talk about values in erotic romances without knowing what they reflect? As for *sebas*, awe, the romances are full of it. The feeling that makes you step back from something, what Achilles feels when he imagines the corpse of Patroclus, or when Odysseus sees beauty in Nausicaa. In short, when the invisible becomes visible. This is what Dionysius must feel when he sees Aphrodite in Callirrhoë. It's what readers are supposed to feel when they see that Tyche or Isis is in control of the plot, and Aristotle's dry-as-dust talk of the marvelous and the probable doesn't touch it. And you don't understand Anthia's ideals, or Callirrhoë's, without understanding *aidōs*—the feeling of transgressing against your honor or against *themis*, the proper order of things. If you acted in accordance with *aidōs*, you were acting in accordance with *themis;* and *themis* in fact is a projection of social values.

ALPHA: Isn't *aidōs* derived from *aidoia*, "sexual organs"?

KAPPA: Probably the other way around. But if you want to talk of voyeurism, and art as striptease, you can talk of Aphrodite's drapery slipping down, then off, through the history of Hellenistic sculpture, and this shows how the sense of *aidōs* follows the progress of the sense of *themis*. But you can't take us on an excursion through Soho and pretend you're a tripper in Asia Minor in the first century. A girl or boy preserving chastity through thick and thin in a Greek romance shows their *aidōs*, their sense of *themis*, and these inspire *sebas* in the reader. And this awe makes you feel rather religious, as though virtue triumphant is striking a blow for cosmic justice. Aristotle's talk about marvels and catharses doesn't begin to touch these feelings.

ALPHA: Are you confusing the fourth century B.C. with the first century A.D.?

KAPPA: I am not. My point is, these romances show *new* forms of the old values because they are produced under new cultural conditions. Think of Anthia exposed to customers at the brothel. She doesn't fret about her public humiliation so much as about the *aidōs* of transgressing her private vows to her husband. Think of Callirrhoë worried about her private predicament, all those secret worries she tells only to Aphrodite and us, hiding them in her awe-inspiring public figure. The private has become more awesome than the public. Even Jason's worries are private—so private that only Alpha and Psi can fully understand them. He is not so much the public warrior or king as the man on a private quest. All this means that *aidōs* has become a matter of private individuals.

ALPHA: And the gods have taken to manifesting themselves in bourgeois kids. And this can embarrass the kids, as it would not an old public hero.

KAPPA: More than that. Even the gods now seem to feel that their public glory is not so important as their saving virtuous individuals. But in fact the old heroes were not confused with gods by awed crowds of townspeople. The gods were merely the ancestors of the heroes, and the old heroes did not in themselves inspire *religious* awe, *sebas*. This may seem curious. Here is a genuine paradox for you, Alpha. As characters become more individual, detached from the old legends and given ordinary names and parents, and their *aidōs* is attached more closely to the values of marriage and personal love, they become more like gods and inspire *sebas* in us all. At the same time, they become *less* individual, *less* cunning and innovative and assertive than the old heroes. They all behave and look alike.

ALPHA: I would not say that. It is not a paradox of democracy but of huge polities and a cosmopolitan readership.

PSI: And it is not a paradox of psychology. When Eros comes onto the scene, the other gods must withdraw. There is a sameness in lovers, as some poet has doubtless said. Its symptoms are everywhere the same. And lovers feel like gods. We acknowledge their exhilaration and suffering and would participate in it. They hold us within a religious awe, as perhaps our parents once did. And their only shame would be to break the bond of love which we relied upon and would emulate—the bond that holds together the parents. Even in an epic like the *Odyssey* these familial bonds please us. If our parents become angry, rebellious, individual, we are upset as children. The reader participating in a romance always, I think, plays the role of a child, of a Telemachus.

KAPPA: You missed my point. There was a *change*, a profound change, in feelings of guilt and honor.

PSI: This I must doubt for guilt.

KAPPA: As you will. But it is written large everywhere. Under some conditions, one felt shame when one's public character and therefore honor were tarnished. Under other conditions, one felt shame when one violated private vows and when the only public was the god who had witnessed these vows.

ALPHA: This is not wholly true in the romances.

KAPPA: Granted. But the change is there. The reader is made privy to vows and sufferings unknown to the public in the story, and he feels *sebas* about them. What causes these changes? The psyche doesn't change, you say. Literary forms are deep, inherent structures, and surface structures merely get rearranged. Therefore psychologism and formalism can't explain the new in literature. What *does* change is historical conditions. The way people look after themselves and bugger their neighbors. A folk society grubbing after limited resources, lusting after more land and slaves—in these conditions you get interesting theologies and legends and genealogies to inspire the wretched ingrown folk to keep its own and emulate an invented past. Epic is a luxury of a later society. It indulges in character, wrath, expeditions, all celebrated by bards wandering about with versions of stories from all over. Romance is a luxury of another state of society, when the boundaries of exploitation, and therefore of interesting danger, are almost infinite. In these conditions you have to think you've got a personal god on your side in order to survive. You can't rely on your tribe or city. Your safety lies in the individual soul, in love of one another, in mystery and magic and some divine force that is no longer localized anywhere but can make an appearance in rituals everywhere. But since the promise of eternal salvation is patently false, you conclude your story with a return home, to the *status quo ante*, in the bosom of hearth and home.

PSI: So these are fantasies of fear and not of temptation.

KAPPA: Granted. Temptation too. When life-space expands, you think you can have sex anywhere, whatever dear old dad might say. Sex becomes coin. It's honored everywhere. It's no longer cattle and land exchanged by families. Romance is reactionary, literally a reaction to these conditions. It's set in the past, in days when sex and marriage were inseparable, when even god-like youths were content to go home again. It brings Eros onto the scene so that *themis* can defeat him. And the mystery gods defeat him on his own turf, which is now called Love. This is the underside of so-called bourgeois exuberance. It was a melancholy time. Those tormented faces in the statuary of the second and third centuries after Christ. Those meticulous portraits of individuals, not types. When all you have is money, love, and the fancy that you're immortal like a god, you know your life is a lie. No wonder death seemed attractive. Here we are in an era when almost everybody got himself initiated into a cult that promised him eternal life, and at the same time birth and death dates begin to appear on tombstones. Another paradox. They knew that life began at birth and ended at death, no matter what they believed. We didn't see, in the Ashmolean, any examples of that common tombstone formula. There's room on the blackboard

$$NF \qquad F \qquad NS \qquad NC$$

Meaning, *Non fui, fui, non sum, non curo*—I was not, I was, I am not, I care not.

SIGMA: It's too late for more formulas. Let's go home.

❧8❧
Antonine
Comedy

Not long after the Stoic Marcus Aurelius became emperor in 161, and near the end of that "period in the history of the world during which the human race was most happy and prosperous," there appeared three prose fictions which neither the historian nor the critic can hesitate to applaud. One, perhaps the first comic novel, was written by an Alexandrian named Achilles Tatius. Another, perhaps the first and surely one of the most perfect comic apologues, was written by a Lesbian named Longus. And the third is the famous innovative masterpiece written in Latin by the African rhetor Apuleius—the *Metamorphoses*, or *Golden Ass*. Each of these works differs profoundly from the other two. But all three of them share certain characteristics which make them radically different from the other works I have discussed.

It is easy to understand why critics from Photius on have classified Achilles Tatius' *Clitophon and Leucippe* with romances like the *Babyloniaca* and Heliodorus' *Aethiopica*. They are all stories of erotic suffering and weird adventures by land and sea. But Tatius' hero is a cowardly fool, his heroine is untroubled by the values of chastity, his Amorous Wife is unthreatening and delightful, and so forth. Photius thought that Tatius had an especially dirty mind, and a few others have thought that he was parodying romance. I believe that he used the conventions of prose romance to write a comedy.

Longus' *Daphnis and Chloë* differs more obviously from the romances, with which it is normally classified. Its protagonists are naive foundlings, inferior to us in status and sophistication, who survive perils that are pastoral and emblematic of the growth of erotic knowledge. Having been, like Tatius' *Clitophon*, forced into the mold "romance," its comic characteristics and its generative ideas have seldom received adequate treatment. The comedy of the *Golden Ass*, on the other hand, has long been lovingly acknowledged. But when led to define the genre of what seems to be a sport of literary history, critics have usually argued that the work as a whole is a profound allegory of salvation, a bitter satire on society, a piece of propaganda for Isis, and so on. To classify it—if classified it must be—as a comedy along with *Daphnis* and *Clitophon* seems as unwarranted an act of genre criticism as classifying it as a romance would be.

But these three remarkable works share at least two interesting characteristics. In the first place, all are narrated in the first person (*Daphnis* at least pretends to be). In antiquity this technical device signaled that the story depicted contemporary life as it was shared by author and reader. Paradoxically, this contemporariness in turn signaled that the story was invented; that is, the story was drawn from neither history nor myth and must therefore be a fiction of ordinary life. Being neither serious fable nor serious history, the material was the sort normally treated by comedy.[1] Second, the characters and events of the three works are like those that would in antiquity have been associated with comedy. The principals are foolish, naive, or ridiculous. They are not godlike, and we can neither admire nor emulate them. Their loves are rooted in overtly physical eroticism, and they are not inhibited by the anxieties of chastity. And these characters pass through perils that are so much more serious to them than they are to us that their sufferings are funny. It therefore does not seem ludicrous to call them all—in the face of their profound differences—comedies. In doing this, I do not intend to spring three masterpieces from one genre mold into another. I intend to treat each work in its own terms and to show how the art of prose fiction, near its beginnings in the West, endowed ideas and experience with the various powers of comedy.

COMEDY AS ROMANCE

Nothing certain is known about Achilles Tatius, the author of *Clitophon*, the earliest extant comic epic in prose. Does the *tat* in Tatius derive from the name of an unwholesome Egyptian god? He could certainly write an archly rhetorical Greek; and since he was probably an Alexandrian, some say that he also wrote treatises on etymology and the sphere. But nothing warrants the Byzantine rumor that he became a Christian bishop, save unflagging Byzantine fondness for his *Clitophon*.[2]

The story begins in Sidon in the temple of Astarte, the Mother, who proclaimed, "I am the compassionate prostitute!" to her delighted eunuch-priests. The author, a tourist, is inspecting one of the elaborate paintings that decorated this temple. Europa sits sidesaddle on the back of Zeus, who is a swimming bull abducting her from Sidon. Her left hand grasps a horn, her right gestures pathetically back toward her home shore, her veil is "a painted breeze," and her diaphanous tunic clings to her "deep-set navel, the long slight curve of her belly, the narrow waist broadening down to the loins." Already we enjoy a lasciviousness that has no place in the romances, though Achilles is only describing the tableau stamped on the famous coins of Sidon. He adds, however, a winged boy hovering over the bull—"Eros himself ... turning toward Zeus with a smile on his face, as if he were laughing at him for becoming a bull for his sake." This is not the dreadful, jealous Eros of the romances. The Eros who lords it over this work is an imp. Still, "Look how that imp dominates over sky and land and sea!" exclaims the author, to which a young fellow tourist, standing nearby, responds, "I may term myself a living example of it"—of this ludicrous domination. "Tell me about it," says the author. "You are stirring a whole swarm of stories [*logoi*]," warns the bystander, which "are really like fictions [*mythoi*]." Fictions pretending to be reasoned accounts of fact were the materials of comedy. And when the author remarks that his pleasure will increase with their fictional quality, he signals that the story will deal more with the ridiculous than the sublime.

Gone are the conventions by which romance recruits our serious awe. Clitophon, from neighboring Tyre—the nervous tourist who relates the rest of the book—is a victim, not a hero, of love. He reminds no one of a god,[3] and he looks merely like one who has "suffered many buffets from Eros." This means, as the author remarks, that he is like everyone else. And the girl with whom he once fell in love is no goddess. He tells us that Leucippe is a voluptuous girl with curly golden hair, jet-black eyebrows, and pinked ivory skin, and it was these attributes that "blinded" Clitophon because, as he says with characteristic sententiousness, beauty "wounds deeper than any arrow, and strikes down through the eyes into the soul." This commonplace evokes one of his innumerable rhetorical digressions as he develops the *topos* of lovesickness: he feels admiration (for her tall form), stupefaction (at her beauty), fear (a beating heart), *aidōs* (for staring at her),

shamelessness (he stares anyway). Here the conventions of love at
first sight and of mixed contrary emotions become topics explored
with an obvious pedantry, and we assign this pedantry to the
speaker, Clitophon, more than to the author, who never reappears in the book.[4] Still, given the seriousness of such conventions in serious stories, we hesitate to smile at the exemplary
victim of Eros who has obviously suffered much. Our hesitation
must evaporate, however, when we learn that he is already
affianced, oddly but not unprecedentedly, to his half-sister (his
father's daughter) and that his intentions with regard to Leucippe
are therefore not honorable: he aims to seduce, not to marry, her.
Clitophon is not a romantic hero. His lovesickness produces no
oracles or visions but an ordinary erotic dream ("I sported with
her, ate with her . . . touched her . . . kissed her and it was a real
kiss") which is not interpreted but interrupted by an ordinary
servant ("and I upbraided him for his untimely coming").
Moreover, his love is not reciprocated. Leucippe ignores him,
apparently because he is hardly worth her attention (though he is
the son of her host, she being a houseguest from Byzantium). He
therefore wanders foolishly about the house with a book, "and I
bent over it, and pretended to read; but every time that I came
opposite her door I peeped below the book at her." If we tried to
follow the subsequent adventures of this lovelorn seducer with
the thrilled gravity with which we are supposed to follow those of
Habrocomes and Callirrhoë, we would be making a mistake. We
would do an injustice to the author and miss the power of his
book.

True, the book is, by and large, made up of the conventional
predicaments, passions, and even values that seem "serious"
when suffered by characters worthy of our allegiance. In narrative method it combines the sequence of perils familiar from the
Ephesiaca with the intrigues characteristic of *Callirrhoë*. Its scenes
and speeches are constructed in accordance with the same technical conventions employed by all the ancient novelists, though its
sententiae are more numerous and its descriptions of the decor of·
ordinary life (houses, gardens, closets, decks, apartments, gestures) are much more vivid—differences that are aspects of its
principal technical difference, its first-person narrative method.
Its psychic material, and its play with this material, are also
familiar. For example, Clitophon has a stock "prophetic dream"

before he sees Leucippe. In it he is joined to his sister-fiancée
from the waist down, but an enormous snake-haired woman carrying a torch and a sickle looms out of nowhere and slices his
sister from him. "Providence sometimes foreshadows the future
to men," he says, always prepared with a sentiment; and sure
enough, delicious Leucippe soon arrives to sever his sister from
him. But doesn't the dream express fears of feminization as well
as a longing to be freed from the incestuous project arranged by
his father? Isn't it essentially the dream of the enormous female
imago suffered by Habrocomes? Perhaps so. But such psychic
material must be treated as though it were a material literary
convention. That is, it exists only as part of a particular story, and
the qualitative meaning of its existence is determined by the same
principles that determine the special qualities of the whole work.
To put it most simply, when an inept seducer like Clitophon
dreams of a terrifying imago, we feel one thing; when a paragon
of virtue like Habrocomes dreams of her, we feel another. The
material and technical conventions of romance are here being bent
to comedy.

Consider another instance illustrative of the relationship between conventional material and literary form. Clitophon falls into
a conventional *pensée d'amour*—a tormented debate of the soul like
those fashioned by Euripides, Ovid, Chaucer, Flaubert, and
others. "I am on the horns of a dilemma," he says to himself.
"Love and my father wait on opposite sides of me: my father
stands behind me, holding me back by the respect I owe to him;
Love sits before me, brandishing his torch of fire. I desire to give
my verdict to you, father, but I have a stronger adversary [Eros];
if I do not decide against you, father, I must be utterly consumed
by fire." The historian notes that this speech might have been
delivered verbatim by Medea. The psychocritic notes the pos-
terior position of the father, the penile position of the torch, and
the nice tableau it all makes—the father in his pre-Oedipal role as
desired lover, now being rejected by the boy struggling to grasp
his own phallic destiny. The formalist notes that the turmoil is
suffered by a character who does not know how to accomplish his
mundane erotic desire—to seduce his pretty houseguest. All of
these notes are doubtless correct. And if the formalist goes on to
insist that historical or psychoanalytical analyses commit themselves to half-truths if they do not acknowledge the meaning given

to experience by literary form (in this case, by comedy), he is probably right.

Our miserable hero seeks advice from a homosexual, his cousin Clinias, who will play the role of Homosexual Friend. Clinias' reaction to Clitophon's plight is not unlike our own: he "clapped his hands and burst out laughing.... Then he rose and kissed me—my face bore every sign of a lover's sleeplessness." By convention, the Homosexual Friend loses his beloved boy. This is swiftly accomplished when, first, the boy interrupts the cousinly interview to announce that his father will soon force him to marry and, second, soon returns as a corpse (mutilated in a hunting accident). These events occasion more wit than serious grief. Having learned that his boy must marry, Clinias delivered an oration against women, replete with enthymemes, authorities, and exempla: "If Candaules has a fair wife, his wife murders Candaules.... The fire of Helen's marriage-torches lit another fire at Troy.... If they love, they kill; if they do not love, they kill all the same." Science and philosophy are ransacked for commonplaces: "When the eyes meet one another they receive the impression of the body as in a mirror, and this emanation of beauty, which penetrates down to the soul through the eyes, effects a kind of union however the bodies are sundered." And the commonplaces of romance are of course plundered too: "Your bridal chamber is to be your grave," the mourners tell the corpse; "your wedlock is with death." Many of the ideas are familiar to us from poets like Donne, and the style is that of Lyly's *Euphues*. But the role of ideas, wit, and language itself is what it is in the comedies of Congreve—a source of sophisticated delight.

Though Clinias has assured Clitophon that learning to seduce a girl is as easy as learning to suck your mother's breast, the inept boy soon learns otherwise. A kiss sent to her via a wine cup at table, a pretended bee sting, and an impressive discourse on the loves of peacocks, trees, and rivers, delivered to the air (but in her hearing) in a garden, win him a few inconsequential kisses. But when his sister-fiancée is suddenly abducted by a Byzantine who mistakes her for Leucippe (with whom the Byzantine had fallen in love back home), Clitophon takes action. He studies the arrangement of bedchambers, the location of keys, the suspicions of the porter, and at last manages to steal into bed with a willing Leucippe. But to no avail. Next door, Leucippe's mother is dreaming that "a robber with a naked sword" has thrown Leucippe onto her back and is "ripping her up the middle of the belly with the blade, beginning from below." The mother rushes into Leucippe's room. Clitophon leaps from bed, grabs his clothes, and flees into the darkness. The mother has dreamed of the sort of brigand she's heard of in life and read about in romance, but she, her daughter, and our hero are involved in a bedroom farce. Leucippe is no romantic heroine. She expresses no interest in marriage, she speaks of neither passion nor love, and she flees that night with Clitophon and Clinias primarily because she wants to get out of her "mother's sight," even though she has persuaded this mother that the intruder was unknown to her and that he did not get his prize (about the latter she's correct). Leucippe is a lively, independent girl free of the values that ennoble her romantic sisters. Like Clitophon, she springs from New Comedy.

The first phase of the action is over. In it the paragons, the erotic suffering, the intrigues, and the home-leavings of romance have been reduced—or elevated—to comedy. As the principals set sail for Alexandria, we are prepared to enjoy the transformation of other romance conventions. A tempest, for example, causes the ship to roll so violently that the passengers must run ludicrously "for miles" from rail to rail. The "realism" we associate with comedy marks the behavior of the crew, who shamelessly commandeer the lifeboat, and that of an angry passenger, who slices its lines so that everyone tumbles foolishly into the sea. "Every law of friendship and piety disappeared," laments the sententious Clitophon, ever conscious of *themis* and *aidōs*, as he and Leucippe are washed ashore on the eastern Delta, where of course they are captured by a brigand tribe.

Clitophon is rescued by troops, but Leucippe is left to suffer what Anthia so narrowly escaped—sacrifice by the brigands. As Clitophon and the police watch from one side of a curiously impassable ditch, the robbers drag Leucippe into open view, stretch her on her back, and rip open her belly with a sword. "Bowels gushed out, and these they drew forth in their hands and placed them upon an altar; and when they were roasted, the whole body of them cut them up into small pieces, divided them into shares, and ate them." Here detailed description, which elsewhere gives us a sense of comic realism, contributes to the pleasures of sadism. The very extravagance of the scene makes it especially obviously comic, because it has been mistakenly predicted by the girl's mother. Also, though the first-person method limits our knowledge to that of the onlooking Clitophon, we know—given the comedy (or even the romance convention) that we are enjoying—that this execution is unreal, because Leucippe must survive to the end. Besides, our reaction is superior to that of the pedantic and helpless hero, who inappropriately likens himself to Niobe grieving over the corpses of her children. And the conventional resurrection is also comic. Next day, after quickly crossing the ditch, Clitophon embraces his beloved's coffin, as any romance hero would, though he ludicrously laments the fact that her parts are now buried in the bellies of men. Then some fellow Tyrians rush onto the scene to explain—no, wait, hide your eyes, says one, and knock on the coffin. A faint voice is heard from inside, and Leucippe emerges, scolding the Tyrian for having teased poor Clitophon. It seems they had only slit open a sack of sheep guts tied to Leucippe's belly, using the collapsible dagger of a drowned comedian to do so. Clitophon does not laugh, but they do. So do we, partly in appreciation of a romance resurrection accomplished by a live comedian.

The convention of chastity appears in the third phase of the action. Leucippe announces that Artemis has ordered, in a dream, that "Thou must remain a virgin until I deck thee as a bride." The girl says that she is "disappointed" by this dictum, but she must obey it; and it does intensify the comic frustration of our hero. The Amorous Police Chief who now attempts to seduce Leucippe is put off, not with Anthia's grandiose lie about being dedicated to Isis, but with the lie that she is menstruating. Another amorous rescuer is frustrated when his all too potent love potion drives her berserk. And after a tour through the Delta to Alexandria, adorned with "digressions" on the habits of hippopotami, etc.—digressions which substitute the exotica of contemporary life for the romances' exotica of history—Leucippe is once more abducted by pirates. As hapless Clitophon pursues their vessel in his own, we are treated to a conventional duplication of an earlier event. The abductors bring Leucippe onto deck, "and one of them cried out with a tremendous voice, 'Here is the prize for which you are contending,' cut off her head, and threw the body down into the sea. When I saw this I cried and wept."

Can we take Clitophon seriously as he embraces the retrieved torso? "Now, Leucippe, you are really dead; and a double death, with its share both in land and sea . . . ; though there seems to be left to me the greater part of you, it is really the less. Come, since Fate has grudged me kisses on your face, I will kiss instead your wounded neck." I suppose one might speculate about the aggressions that may underlie repeated dismemberments of a beloved girl; but whatever they are, they are nicely discharged through the absurdity of the lover's speechifying.

In the fourth phase arrives the Seductive Wife/Widow. Here she is no threat to the faithful lovers (one of whom is apparently dead, the other is himself a sentimental seducer); she is instead one of the most delightful characters in ancient fiction. Witty, beautiful, young, recently widowed, she desires only to wed and bed our hero; but he, mourning for months in his little flat in Alexandria, rebuffs her. "I suppose he thinks Leucippe will come back to life again," sighs his slave. We know that she will; but Clitophon cannot think so, and his laboring to remain faithful to a corpse is comic. Finally, after learning that his father will soon arrive in Alexandria, Clitophon agrees to flee with Melitte (the Merry Widow) to her native Ephesus. They marry in Alexandria, but Clitophon will not consummate the marriage "in the city where Leucippe was lost." As Melitte observes to her wedding guests, there is many an empty tomb (*kenotaphion*), but who has heard before of an empty wedding bed (*kenogamion*)? On board ship that night she hopefully snuggles against her "statue-like" husband and delivers delightful encomia of sexual joy. All to no avail. Clitophon fears that they are sailing over Leucippe's head and claims that the bucking ship would throw off their rhythm anyway. Even in her rich house at Ephesus, Clitophon resists his amorous wife for five days. Then, having drawn enough laughter out of his conversion of sublime fidelity into ridiculous fear, Achilles revives Leucippe. Clitophon receives a chastising letter from his fiancée, who has somehow fetched up in the Ephesian countryside as the slave of his wife Melitte. The commonplace emotions of the paradox (he is "astonished and incredulous . . . full of joy and sorrow") and the commonplace of the resurrection ("Do you bring this letter from Hades?") are subsumed in Clitophon's comic guilt: he feels that Leucippe's sufferings "have been *di' eme*"—at once "for my sake" and "by my fault"—and that he has been "caught in the act of adultery." We know that these admirable passions are not warranted by reality. Here again the gap between our knowledge and the sentiments of the hero produces a comic effect.

So too do the intrigues and surprises of the fifth phase. Put to the test again by Melitte, Clitophon feigns palsy. "For what day are we waiting now?" asks the good woman. "How long are we to spend our nights as if we were in church? . . . My bed is like the banquet of Tantalus." She then institutes an excellent intrigue. She asks her new slave, Leucippe (who as a Thessalian is presumably expert with magic philters), to make a love potion for her husband, who behaves like a "eunuch" because "some dead woman seems to be my successful rival." Thus, in a nice comic paradox, Leucippe learns of Clitophon's fidelity as she is commanded to destroy it. But another resurrection now occurs. Melitte's long-drowned husband, Thersander, storms into the dining room and, seeing poor Clitophon in his place, beats him with minutely described blows (teeth, nose, blood, etc.). Since resurrections (and perhaps scourgings) pertain to the cults, Clitophon says, "I knew as little as though I were at the celebration of some secret mystery who the man was or why he was beating me." But even this remark, which we might think has profound thematic resonance in a romance, is part of the reaction of a comic coward: "though suspecting that something was wrong, I was afraid to defend myself, though I could have done so. When he grew tired of pounding me (and I of reasoning), I rose and said, 'Who are you, sir, and why have you assaulted me in this way?'" In answer, Thersander hits him again and throws him into a closet. And in this closet we see the power of that imp Eros, that "fine master of rhetoric," whose triumph paradoxically occurs only after everyone knows that husband and fiancée are indeed alive. Melitte steals into the closet and delivers an oration to our hero, who is manacled to the wall. Will he not pity a wretched woman who has destroyed her marriage but got no pleasure while doing so? or a woman tormented by her desire for "a eunuch, a woman-man, beauty's wet-blanket"? As she bends over and places his hand on her breast to feel her fluttering heart, he at last feels "the claims of humanity." And there on the floor he learns that Eros "is an admirable improviser; he can make any place a proper spot for the celebration of his mysteries."

But Thersander is struck by Leucippe's beauty as by lightning. And of course she will have none of him. "Set out your tortures," she cries, "bring out your wheel"—she will remain a virgin. "You a virgin?" shouts Thersander; "was the pirates' lair a Sunday school?" "I am defenseless, and a woman, but one shield I have, and that is my free soul, which cannot be subdued." Is this a new spirit of feminine individualism, to be heard afresh from heroines of sixteenth-century drama and eighteenth-century novels? And does it not make Leucippe seem morally superior to her seduced fiancé? Perhaps. Her admirable chastity is more likely a consequence of a double standard which dictated that a bride must come to her marriage bed a virgin (and Leucippe must surely come to Clitophon's); and, more likely still, it is an aesthetic consequence of the fact that Thersander is an arrogant slave-driver, while Melitte is an amiable love mistress. That is, we can easily imagine Leucippe submitting to a male version of Melitte, and her noble sentiments must be appreciated in this light.

Intrigues and counterintrigues drive the action to its close. Clitophon is duped into believing that Melitte has murdered Leucippe ("Alas, Leucippe, how often have I seen you die . . . one death coming hot upon the heels of another"), and he offers to be executed for the crime. His irrational guilt provides several comic scenes: Leucippe's father, suddenly arrived from Byzantium, rushes at him, "and I made no resistance . . . but freely offered my face to him." Thersander beats him up again: "Out flowed blood from my nostrils, [but] he accidentally struck his hand on my mouth, right on the teeth, wounding his knuckles badly. . . . Thus my teeth avenged the violence offered my nose." The conventional trials are also comic. Clitophon's advocate is a priest of chaste Artemis who is also, somewhat paradoxically, a student of obscene Aristophanes. Through innuendos that would have made the old comedian blush, he accuses Thersander of a career of sexual perversions that no devotee of Artemis should have been able to imagine. There are chastity tests. Leucippe of course passes hers; and so does Melitte, since she has cleverly and correctly vowed only that she has had no sexual relations while her husband was absent. Thersander flees, and the story ends swiftly with a tying-up of loose ends (for example, we learn that a less valuable female had been substituted for Leucippe in the decapitation scene) but without expressions of love.

I have insisted on the comic character of *Clitophon* to underscore the fact that it demands responses radically different from those we give to novels like *Callirrhoë*. If we tried to take *Clitophon* seriously, we would laugh anyway—but at the author, not with him. However, his characters, style, extravagances, and, above all, his consistent modifications of romance conventions all point to the conclusion that he knew he was writing a comic *pathos erōtikon*, a romantic comedy. I am not surprised that no modern critic, to my knowledge, has treated his work as a comedy: once it was firmly categorized as a Greek romance, or as a parody of Greek romance, it had to be read as such. That it was long read as a well-made work, not as an inept romance, is suggested by the fact that for centuries no prose fiction was more popular among the Byzantines than *Clitophon;* and few of those who commissioned or preserved the twenty-three Greek manuscripts in which it survived in the Latin West could have admired it merely as a parody of an arcane sort of serious tale. Seen as a comedy, *Clitophon* is a historic achievement. It produces the pleasures of New Comedy through adaptation of the conventions of the *pathos erōtikon*. In similar fashion, Menander had, three centuries earlier, blended Old Comedy with some of the materials and methods of tragedy to produce the New Comedy. Though his work did not bear immediate fruit, Achilles Tatius deserves credit for making as profound an innovation.

It might be objected that my use of the term "comedy" for a prose fiction rather than for a stage play is unwarranted by ancient usage. This is not entirely the case. The lame little treatise called the *Tractatus Coislinianus*, written in the first century B.C., suggests that Achilles Tatius and his contemporaries could have called something like *Clitophon* a comedy, if they bothered with such matters at all. Poetry, says the *Tractatus*, is either nonimitative or imitative, the latter genus comprising comedy, tragedy, mime, and satire. "Comedy is an imitation of a laughable action, undivided and complete, each part sweetened by language, through acting and narrative. By means of pleasure and laughter it achieves a catharsis of such emotions."[5] This means that comedies, like the other imitative species, can be treated as both *dramatika kai praktika*—as acted works and as narratives like *Clitophon*. That the *Clitophon* could have been appreciated as being specifically comic is suggested by its exploitation of six of the topics which comedy, according to the *Tractatus*, has at its disposal. Deception, impossibility, and the unexpected are not necessarily comic; but presentation of characters as being worse than we are, as reaching possible ends through illogical means, and as making worse choices when better ones are possible are features *Clitophon* shares with other comedies. It also shares certain affinities with the lowly mime, which may have been more "romantic" than "comic." In a Greek mime surviving from Tatius' lifetime, a lady desires a slave who loves a slave girl; when he rebuffs his mistress, she poisons the lovers, mourns over their corpses, consoles herself with another slave, then poisons her husband, who revives on stage and denounces his wife, and the slave lovers (also only drugged) also revive.⁶ This playlet might have been acted seriously or comically, but it hardly achieves the "tone" of New Comedy, which, according to the *Tractatus*, is not abusive or heavily committed to the ridiculous (as was the Old) but is subtle, arouses laughter moderately, and inclines toward the serious. It was such qualities that moved Plutarch (whose life probably overlapped Tatius') to praise Menander for combining seriousness with fun and for his moral and verbal elegance. Who else, he asks, "fills the theatre with learned men when a comic character takes the stage?"⁷ I suspect that Achilles Tatius would have been delighted to be praised in such terms. In any case, no "romance" before Tatius' mixed fun with seriousness as Menander had mixed them on the stage.

I do not mean that the materials of *Clitophon* are exactly those of New Comedy. Tatius does not use stock *personae* like the Smooth-shaven Bourgeois Lover with Wavy Hair (the waviness indicating ingenuity) or the Smooth-shaven Bourgeois Lover with Curly Hair (the curliness indicating impetuosity). But anyone who had enjoyed in the theater the difficulties of a frantic lover, his voluptuous girl, his ironical friends and slaves, his terrifying rivals, would have recognized those figures in Clitophon, Leucippe, Clinias, Satyrus, and Thersander. He would hardly have mistaken these characters for paragons of virtue like Callirrhoë and Habrocomes. And had he been historically minded, he might have appreciated Achilles' special innovation. The *Tractatus* says that the "mother of comedy is Laughter" and the "mother of tragedy is Sorrow." It seems that Achilles Tatius freshly disguised the youngest child of Laughter (New Comedy) in the clothes of the youngest child of Sorrow (prose romance). Just as Clitophon escaped Melitte's closet dressed, like that other Achilles, as a woman, so it seems to me the work of Achilles Tatius has escaped proper treatment.

IDEA AS COMEDY

Longus, Tatius' contemporary, wrote an entirely different kind of comedy. His *Daphnis and Chloë*, or *Lesbian Pastorals*, is informed, and doubtless generated, by a complex set of ideas. All sorts of ideas, *sententiae*, and arguments adorn *Clitophon* and contribute to its comedy, but none of these ideas cause the work to be what it is. Ideas about love, harmony, and human nature cause the characters, the episodes, the very flora and fauna of the *Lesbian Pastorals* to be what they are. Longus' work is comic, by ancient canons, in that its characters are inferior to us and their difficulties are often ridiculous, but it does not seek the effects achieved by New Comedy or comic romance. It is comic because its generating idea is comic, in the sense that Dante's masterwork is comic for the same reason; and, as its author says, it is designed to heal, to comfort, "to refresh the memory of those who have been in love and educate those who have not."[8] It is, in short, a didactic apologue that combines the materials of pastoral idyll with the methods of prose romance; but its informing concepts are so complex—much more complex than those that govern Aesop's *Fables*, Lucian's *True History*, even Vergil's *Aeneid*—that we can say that it has no real generic antecedents.[9]

Like Tatius, Longus begins with an authorial prologue that centers on an *ekphrasis*—an interpretive description of an object. Once more, the object is a painting, one of the fervid landscapes still popular in the 160s. Hunting one day on the island of Lesbos, the author discovers this painting hung in a grove sacred to local nymphs. It is the most beautiful picture he has ever seen; it is more beautiful than the grove itself. "There were women having babies and other women wrapping them in swaddling clothes, babies were being exposed, sheep and goats suckling them, shepherds adopting them, young people plighting their troth, pirates making a raid, enemies starting an invasion." For some reason, this tableau so affects the hunter-author that he is "seized by a longing to write a verbal equivalent to the picture"—an *eikonos graphē* which is a *historia erōtos*, a written image of a visual image of a scene representing life and love. But apparently he cannot himself grasp the *logos*, the gist or argument of the picture. "So I found someone to explain the picture to me." We are told that this someone is an exegete, a professional interpreter of oracles and dreams. On the basis of the exegesis given him the author writes the story we are reading; that is, *Daphnis and Chloë* is not only an extended *ekphrasis* and an expanded idyll (little picture) but a narrative exegesis, a poeticized idea.[10] The author-exegete writes it "as an offering to Eros and the Nymphs and Pan, and as a source of pleasure to the human race—something to heal the sick and comfort the afflicted, to refresh the memory of those who have been in love and educate those who have not." Here are three intentions, three "final causes," and consequently three formal principles governing one small pastoral fiction. It is to be at once a votive offering, a comforting pleasure, and a didactic instruction. And the author hopes that "the god will allow me to write of other people's experiences while retaining my sanity"— his *sōphrosynē*, his dignified seriousness. It is apparently to be an affecting, serious kind of comedy.

I do not intend to extract the ideas from Longus' little masterpiece, formulate them here, and then show how they are worked out in his poem. In the first place, the ideas without the poem are dead. In the second place, the ideas are as complex as is the state of poetic affairs set up in the prologue. They are not merely themes, nor, on the other hand, do they make the poem an allegory. They are ideas in the Greek sense of the term. That is, the word "idea" might mean "form" in the sense of outward shape and "form" in the sense of an inherent nature that determines outward shape. In literary usage, it might mean an outward form like "drama" or "novel" or an inward form like "comedy." It can refer to the semblances through which reality is perceived as well as to the logical classes by which reality is known. In the mind of an author, for example, an "idea" might be an aesthetic concept or that which the concept grasps in life. Longus in his prologue seems to say that a pictorial semblance (an idea) has grasped a reality (an idea) about life—its fertility and strife. But within this second idea is a third meaningful reality that can be discovered only by interpretation, and this third idea is the reality imitated by the author in his story. The story is itself a verbal icon, a verbal semblance or idea, of the basic idea about life discovered by exegesis of the pictorial icon or idea. This suggests that the verbal semblance, like the pictorial one, demands exegesis; inherent in both, generating and governing them, is a formal idea which the reader ought to grasp. But he must also understand that this formal principle must be inseparable from the outward form, the fable; because together they constitute a single idea, and only together are they comforting, instructive, and sacred.

The specific content of Longus' ideas, his concepts of human nature and cosmic love, may not be entirely his own. They may in large part be drawn from the lore of Orphism.[11] This means that his characters, their names, their adventures, their opinions, the setting of the story, and the pattern of its unfolding may all allude to a system of ideas extrinsic to the story itself. For centuries *Daphnis and Chloë* moved people who knew nothing about Orphism, and one may suspect that this would have pleased its author. Still, a set of signals, a kind of esoteric semantics, seems to be embedded in the work and refers us to meanings whose apprehension must enrich our pleasure.

That Orphism was ever a religion with a fixed ritual and doctrine may be doubted.[12] It probably began as a reform movement, perhaps in the sixth century, that attempted to cleanse the cruder rites of Dionysus; and it may have survived as an esoteric school attractive to small numbers of learned ascetics. It early adopted Orpheus, the legendary priest of Apollo, whose song could raise the dead, as its heroic demigod because he had fallen victim to the Dionysian rites he was attempting to purify with the Apollonian harmonies of his own music; he was either dismembered by orgiastic women maddened by Eros and Bacchus or killed by Dionysus himself. In any event, the Orphics may have attempted to harmonize Dionysian enthusiasm (*ekstasis*) with Apollonian purification (*katharsis*). For example, they embraced the Dionysian belief in human divinity; but for the orgiastic mysteries of Dionysus they substituted their famous puritan ones, and they adopted an ascetic way of life perhaps modeled on that of the primitive Pythagoreans. They developed a body of sacred *logoi*, narrative poems and hymns, which they ascribed to Orpheus himself, and in them expressed a myth that expressed an idea—an idea of creation and human life.

As a verbal icon, the myth, as reconstructed, is simplistic, childish, even ridiculous, as *Daphnis and Chloë* seems to be simplistic and exquisitely naïve. In the *first* beginning, the Primal Egg, which had been formed in *aithēr* by Time, produced Eros, whom the hymns call Phanes—"manifestation," "appearance." Eros is the progenitor of nature and of all the gods. In the *second* beginning, Zeus begot Zagreus upon Persephone. But the Titans, inspired by jealous Hera, murdered and ate Zagreus, whereupon Zeus consumed the Titans in fire. From the ashes of the Titans, and therefore of the eaten Zagreus, sprang mankind. Man is therefore part evil, Titanic, and part good, Zagrean. Zeus also plucked from the ashes the heart of Zagreus, ate it, and spawned Dionysus. Dionysus is therefore all good; he is Zagreus reborn. Man, however, must repudiate the Titan in himself, acknowledge the omnipotence of Eros, the aboriginal god, and accept the promise of eternal life represented by Dionysus. By doing these things he may achieve the fullness of his nature; and just as Zagreus was reborn as Dionysus, so each man may be reborn. After each lifetime he spends one thousand years in Elysium, where he chooses to become either animal or man. After ten choices—or after three sequential choices in which he opts for a pure human life—he is ready to "fly out of the sorrowful weary circle" of reincarnating life, and his soul returns to the *aithēr*, or the Divine Mind. Put another way, he rejoins Persephone, the mother of his divine brother Zagreus-Dionysus, in a uterine bliss in which the discords of body and soul are harmonized as if by Orphic music.

No one could say what form the ideas that underlie this myth may have taken in the minds of learned Orphics in the second century after Christ; but the *Lesbian Pastorals* may represent an idea of these ideas. It is a mythic fable about Eros, Dionysus, music, and the maturation of human love as it repudiates the animal in man. The careful seasonal patterning of the poem suggests an attempt to depict cosmic harmonies in poetic form; and the author's fear that he might lose his sanity may reflect a fear that his Apollonian self-control might be lost in poetic ecstasy. Still, it would do the work an injustice to take it as being "representative" of Orphism or of anything else. It must be understood on its own terms.

One day on Lesbos a rustic slave named Lamon finds an infant boy suckling on a she-goat amidst tangles of ivy in an oak grove. We must remember that on Lesbos were buried the head and lyre of Orpheus and that the island was a haunt of Eros, Pan, and

Dionysus-Bacchus, who invented the vintage for which the island was famous. We may remember this only after we have picked up other Orphic signals in the work, but forememory is demanded here. We also remember that Dionysus sometimes changed his adherents into oak trees to protect them from danger and that the ivy leaf, which is five-pointed like the vine leaf sacred to Dionysus, is an intoxicant of the sort pleasing to the ecstatic god. Two years later, Lamon's neighbor, Dryas, "oak," finds an infant girl suckling on a ewe in a grotto sacred to the nymphs. Like the foundling boy, this girl has been exposed with expensive tokens that suggest a lofty social status. Already we know that their true identities will be revealed at the end of the story; but for now we recognize that the boy's goat-nurse is a totem of Dionysus and the girl's sheep-nurse is a totem of Pan the Pastor, as the nymphs' grove is one of his favorite haunts. Dryas names his foundling girl Chloë, an Attic epithet for Demeter, whose devotees were reborn with Persephone, mother of Zagreus. Lamon names his Dionysian foundling Daphnis, "laurel." But the laurel was a plant sacred not to Dionysus but to Apollo, whose priestesses were inspired by chewing the laurel leaf. In fact, there was already a mythic personage named Daphnis. He had been exposed in a laurel grove, was raised by shepherds, was taught by Pan to play the pipes, became a beloved of Apollo, and invented pastoral poetry. Longus' Daphnis is obviously a blending of Dionysian and Apollonian elements. And when we remember that the legendary Daphnis had to seek his wife through the world after she had been captured by pirates, we recognize a certain affinity between his career and that of the musician Orpheus, who sought his wife even in the underworld. Longus' Daphnis will also learn Pan's music and rescue his beloved Chloë from pirates.

This paradoxical Orphic reconciliation of contraries, of Apollo and Dionysus, is followed by a manifestation of Eros. On the same night, both Lamon and Dryas dream that the nymphs give Daphnis and Chloë to "a very aristocratic boy who had wings growing out of his shoulders and who carried arrows and a tiny bow. This boy hit both of them with a single arrow, and gave orders that Daphnis should in future be a goatherd, and Chloë a shepherdess." The dreaming rustics do not recognize this boy. We do. We are superior to everyone in this sweet, idyllic world. We are sophisticates who can appreciate the allusions to Sappho,

Menander, Theocritus, Vergil, and Ovid that adorn the author's urbane style. Like the author, we are adults, exegetes enjoying the profound naiveties of primitive, childlike, rustic art. We of course understand the literary commonplace that Eros rules all, and in this pastoral world it is appropriate that Eros take the conventional form of the winged boy. But how can this be the Orphic Phanes? Will this Eros be challenged by chaste Artemis or Isis, as in a romance?

At puberty, when Daphnis is fifteen and Chloë is thirteen, Eros "made something serious flare up." This serious matter is human love. It is a matter that involves the animal world, too: the bad as well as the good, all of which Eros rules. Here is what happens. A she-wolf kills many sheep and goats to feed her cubs. She is following the laws of Eros, we are told. The rustics dig pits to trap this wolf, and Daphnis falls into one while chasing one of his goats. Muddied and scratched, he is bathed by Chloë in her nympharium. She sees that he is beautiful. His hair is curly black, and we must recall that goats were black in those days. His flesh is soft and tanned, and Chloë explores it to see whether it is like her own. It is, but different. "Nothing out of the ordinary had happened to Chloë, except that she had set her heart on seeing Daphnis washing again." Her innocence is amusing to us, as is her mistaken belief that Daphnis' beauty "must be the result of washing." But in Longus' story the cosmic is comic. As Eros will explain in book 2, flowers and trees are "so beautiful because they get splashed with water when I'm bathing." These children too are beautified by the love that rules the world.

Love is also painful. "I'm in pain," says Chloë, "yet I've not been injured. I feel sad, and yet none of my sheep have got lost. I'm burning hot, and yet here I am, sitting in the shade. ... Daphnis is beautiful, but so are the flowers." And she wishes that she were a goat so that Daphnis might look after her. This last wish, to be an animal, seems but another turn in a love lament all of whose conventions have been turned to the comic. But it expresses one of the fable's important ideas. In his matching lament, Daphnis cries that Chloë's "lips are softer than roses ... but her kiss hurts more than the sting of a bee. I've often kissed kids ... [and] new-born puppies ... but this kiss is something quite new. ... Oh, what a strange disease!" The disease is love, and its etiology is specifically human. The confused children are discovering joys and pains that surpass those that have been evoked by sheep and goats. Consider Dorcon, a cowherd who desires Chloë. Dorcon, who is as red-haired and white-skinned as one of the beasts he herds, disguises himself as an animal, a wolf, in order to abduct Chloë. But his attempt to satisfy erotic desire by becoming an animal is frustrated when the dogs, following their own natures, nearly chew him to pieces. Human beings may begin their lives exposed, suckled like animals, their identities unknown; and, like the animals, they live as subjects of Eros. But they possess tokens of a higher nature which they deny at their peril.

Our adolescents still do not know the name of Eros. But as spring gives way to summer and they are inflamed by the nakedness they reveal while bathing, it seems that nature must take its course despite their ignorance. For human beings, however, nature takes its proper erotic course only through troubles that develop knowledge and culminate in marriage. In fact, this process of erotic maturation constitutes the action of *Daphnis*. One of the troubles is a certain rivalry between male and female. Daphnis tells Chloë a story about a boy and girl who once contested their abilities to call their herds with panpipes. When the boy won, the girl was so angry that she became a pigeon, and her song continues to lament her loss of humanity. Another trouble is represented by pirates, who raid the pastures and carry off Daphnis himself. They fatally wound poor Dorcon, who dying gives his pipes to Chloë. Chloë creates panic with the panpipes: their music makes the captive cows leap from the pirate ship, the ship is swamped, the pirates drown, and Daphnis is borne to shore by a heifer. This episode corrects an implication of Daphnis' story: the girl's music saves the boy. More importantly, it introduces Pan and the power of music. Pan, an elemental rustic whom the Olympians could never quite assimilate, possesses a crude musical power that links the ectasy of Dionysus with the harmonies of Apollo. He is also a rude manifestation of Eros; after all, his pipes, as Longus reminds us, are made from the reeds into which the nymph Syrinx was transformed when she fled Pan's lust. But his music in Longus' fable always ameliorates the erotic troubles that seem to underlie the harmonic forces of life.

It is vintage time, and the lord of the vintage is Dionysus. This god never appears in the story; but at the end of the work, when it is vintage time once more, Daphnis' true father will arrive, and his name is Dionysophanes—"Manifestation of Dionysus." For now, Daphnis seems to the women to look "just like Dionysus," and they kiss him. When the men see Chloë now, they "jump madly up and down like satyrs before some Bacchante" and wish they were her sheep. They all dance, sing, play the pipes, wrestle rams and he-goats—a chaste and admirable orgy. At this point Longus introduces a sage old cowherd to explain the Love that creates and governs all this and names him Philetas, after the legendary father of Hellenic poetry. Philetas owns a garden of poppies, hyacinths, apples, grapes, figs, and pomegranates. In such a garden it's no wonder that he has that very day seen Eros himself, a boy "with myrtle-berries [emblems of death] and pomegranates [emblems of fertility] in his hands...; and his body glistened as if he had been bathing." Philetas catches him and wants a kiss, but the boy declares that kissing is for the young: each phase of life has its proper erotic activity. Besides, Eros says that he is "not really a boy.... I'm older than time and the universe itself." Well, what *is* he then? ask Daphnis and Chloë. Philetas answers:

> Love, my children... gives wings to the soul. And he can do greater things than Zeus himself. He has power over the elements, he has power over the stars, he has power over his fellow-gods—far more than you have over your goats and sheep. The flowers are all Love's handiwork. These trees are his creatures. He is the reason why rivers run and winds blow.

This definition, though styled for children, gives that imp, that jealous lord, more power than he enjoys in any romance. The idea of Eros here is not unlike the idea of Love grasped by Dante in paradise. But according to Philetas, the love that moves the sun and the other stars is in the young a pain for which there is only one drug—"kissing and embracing and lying down together with naked bodies." Still, for Longus the form of true love, as represented by his emblematic lovers, cannot be consummated, even physically, before marriage and the recognition of the lovers' true identities. They do kiss and embrace and fondle each other's naked bodies, but their innocence makes them ignorant of how to accomplish their confusing desires. Their love must grow through knowledge and through rejection of animal simplicity and the human perversions that are also, as with Dante, manifestations of Love.

One of these perversions is greed. Perverting the celebration of Dionysus' vintage, certain rich young men of Methymna (Mytilene's rival city on Lesbos) sail around the island to poach on their neighbors' lands. They kidnap sheep, goats, and Chloë herself, abducting her from the very cave of the nymphs. These outraged spirits send outraged Daphnis a dream in which he acquires vital new knowledge: he ought to petition Pan, they say; and Pan responds to Daphnis' prayer with a music whose divine power is once more evinced. That night the anchored pirates hear tremendous battle noises and see frightful flashes of fire, and Pan tells their leader in a dream:

> You impious and ungodly wretches!... You've filled the countryside I love with fighting, you've stolen herds of oxen and goats and sheep that are under my care, you've dragged from the altar a girl whom Love has chosen to tell a story about!

Pan here seems to be Love's steward, and he suggests that his master is the true author of the tale we are reading, as he is of life itself. Still, Pan's power is great. At dawn he makes a music that disrupts the order of the nature over which he presides. Ivy trails up the masts of the terrified poachers' ship and around the horns of their stolen goats. The sheep howl like wolves, dolphins ram the poachers' hulls, and in the air Pan's pipes sound like trumpets. Then he restores order by playing the "music used to lead the flocks to pasture," and the dolphins swim away, the herds (with Chloë) swim to shore, and the ships sail back to where they belong. Longus has here adopted an incident from the career of Dionysus himself, who with the aid of Pan's music once prevented his own abduction by entangling a pirate ship in ivy and turning its oars into snakes and its crew into dolphins. Recognizing this, we can reduce Longus' subtle synthesis of cosmic powers to a loose hierarchy: greatest is Eros; then Pan, with his governance of nature through music; then the god-man Dionysus, with his vintage and purified ecstasy; and finally mankind, maturing and perverting himself through forms of love.

Having learned the name and felt the power of love, and having witnessed the force of Pan, Daphnis now learns from Philetas how to play Pan's pipes. He and Chloë mime Pan's chase of Syrinx, recapitulating almost ritualistically the myth of the pipes' origin, just as the preceding episode had shown them recapitulating a myth of Dionysus. And Daphnis plays the call "Come back!" so exquisitely that Philetas gives him the pipes. But Pan, and the innocent reenactment of myth, are not enough. Human lovers feel a need to exchange vows of fidelity. Chloë swears that, if she is not faithful to Daphnis, he may kill her as though she were an animal, a wolf. She insists that Daphnis swear, not by Pan, who is fickle, but by his goats, totems of Dionysus, "for being a shepherd girl she regarded goats and sheep as the proper gods for shepherds and goatherds to swear by." Though we continue to smile down on these lovers, even as we recognize the profundity of the ideas they manifest, we acknowledge the fundamental principle of harmony, of *themis*, that underlies Chloë's argument. And we know, given the direction of the action thus far, that this stage of pastoral love must give way to others, that with deeper knowledge will come deeper sanctions of love.

Winter comes. "Scythian snow" separates the lovers. Daphnis suffers near Chloë's hut, too shy to knock, symbolically catching lovebirds that nest in the symbolic myrtle and ivy near her door. Dryas finally invites him indoors, where he must that night sleep with Dryas. "He thought it very pleasant to go to bed with Chloë's father—with the result that he kept embracing Dryas and kissing him, dreaming that he was doing it all to Chloë." This comic moment might yield a mite to psychocriticism if Daphnis otherwise possessed a "character" or if Longus were as interested in such matters as were the writers of romances; in this book, the amusing scene shows Apollonian laurel (Daphnis) embracing a Dionysian oak (Dryas).

With spring, ignorance becomes more painful and yet more comic. Mating animals excite the lovers; surely they must learn from them how to love. Imitating a ram, Daphnis mounts Chloë from behind, but he cannot manage it and weeps with frustration. It seems that animals cannot instruct human love. So to his aid comes an amorous young matron who has observed his ludicrous attempts from a thicket. Her name, Wolfish (Lycaenium), suggests that she is another example of the perverse who advance the higher purposes of Eros while serving their own lower ends.

She lures Daphnis into the woods, arouses him, and directs him to the proper place. But she warns that, unlike herself, Chloë may cry out and bleed. It is this knowledge that now inhibits Daphnis with Chloë, not Fate or ideals of chastity. Besides, it is summer, the season for marrying, and Daphnis proposes. But now another kind of ignorance, or incomplete knowledge, delays the consummation of their love.

Each set of foster parents forbids the marriage because each rightly believes that the tokens discovered with its foundling bespeak a destiny higher than marriage to a rustic slave. One must know who one is before one can know the fullness of love. Daphnis is desperate, but in a dream the nymphs tell him that "Chloë's marriage is the business of another god." Who can this be? Longus does not tell us explicitly; he characteristically invents episodes and symbols and names that permit us to infer the answer—Dionysus. A yacht carrying a bag containing three thousand drachmas is blown ashore. We have already been told that a vessel like this, belonging to the poachers, had been set adrift when one of Daphnis' Dionysian goats had eaten its anchor line, which was made of a Dionysian vine. Daphnis finds the three thousand drachmas lying on the beach beside another Dionysian totem—a dead dolphin. And with this providential gift Daphnis wins the consent of Chloë's father, Dryas. But Lamon, Daphnis' foster father, pleads for a delay, pending the arrival of the master of them all to celebrate the vintage; and, as we will learn, the name of this prosperous urbanite and landowner is Dionysophanes.

We must not expect a theology from Longus. We expect an aesthetic cogency of plot and symbol that will make us feel the comforting and instructive power of his ideas. That Dionysus plays a vital role in bringing harmony from the strife, ignorance, and perversion that have beset our sweet human beings is poetically suggested, further, by the fact that an ivy-covered shrine of Dionysus stands in the center of the master's huge garden. That Eros governs life is suggested by the fact that the whole garden is his special haunt. That the animal in man must be purified is suggested by the fact that one of Chloë's rejected suitors tramples this garden "like a pig." That man perverts Eros in specifically human ways is suggested by the appearance of Gnathon ("full-mouth"), a homosexual parasite of the master's kindly son, Astylus. Gnathon is like an animal in that he is composed entirely, says the author, of stomach, mouth, and genitals. But we see that that perversion is more human than animal when Gnathon, smitten by uncomprehending Daphnis, asks the boy to present his backside the way a she-goat does to a he-goat, whereupon Daphnis remarks that he never saw a he-goat present his backside to another he-goat and knocks the parasite down. In this slapstick incident we see another expression of Longus' grave ideas: the perverse, like the animal, must be rejected if the fullness of human love is to be achieved.

We must not think that Longus is writing an allegory. The master, Dionysophanes, for example, is not Dionysus or a personification of him. He is tall, gray, handsome—an ideal father; he is also a prosperous landowner who lives in the city. He is devoted to rural Pan and the nymphs and to Dionysus and Demeter (whose nickname Chloë bears)—gods whose festivals, especially in Attica, celebrated the interdependence of city and country. The harmony of discordant forces, like city and country, animal and human, ignorance and knowledge, Apollo and Dionysus, now becomes the principle underlying Longus' invention. That is, the comic resolution of the action expresses a comforting harmony in man's world. But Longus' aesthetic method is not allegorical. When Dionysophanes and his urbane entourage observe that Daphnis looks like Apollo, we remember that he once looked like Dionysus, and we feel that his life harmonizes both gods. When Daphnis displays his prowess with the panpipes, he is rewarded with a nonrural prize—his first taste of urban cookery. Gnathon, still fixed in that discordant state wherein people want to be animals, says that to win Daphnis' love he would "gladly become a goat and eat grass and leaves," and Astylus agrees to give him Daphnis as his slave. But this peril results in an important good: Lamon overhears Astylus' gift of his son, and this prompts him to reveal the boy's tokens. "Lord Zeus!" shouts Dionysophanes; and "Dear Fates!" exclaims his wife, "Daphnis is our son, and he's been grazing his father's goats!" We may recognize in this recognition the convention of the paradox, as we may feel it in the harmonization of contraries throughout the book; but we also must recognize that Apollonian Daphnis is a son of Manifestation of Dionysus (Dionysophanes). We might also ponder why Daphnis flees and prepares to jump into the sea when he learns his true identity: "And perhaps, paradoxically, he might have been lost because he was found," had not a "natural instinct" led him to return to embrace his real parents. Daphnis flees because his true identity will force him to leave his goats, his knapsack, and staff; since he now owns the whole estate and his slave parents as well, he must abandon pastoral childish enslavement for urban adult freedom.

But Chloë has been seized by her rejected suitor, piglike Lampis. Learning this, Daphnis goes to Dionysus' shrine in Eros' garden to lament his separation from Chloë, which has resulted from the "hateful discovery" of his high lineage. And once more Love uses his perverted children to implement the development of his purified ones: Gnathon rescues Chloë from Lampis in order to win favor from the now-powerful Daphnis. Dionysophanes sees that his son loves the slave girl, and Dryas displays her tokens. These do not spark a recognition of her identity; but the good father, having been assured that the girl is a virgin, gives her to his son anyway, and everyone removes to the city, where the last barrier to the maturity of marriage will be removed. Troubled, Dionysophanes dreams that Love puts away his childish bow and quiver and commands him to display Chloë's tokens at a feast. An old guest exclaims, "What is this I see? What has become of you, my little daughter? Are you still alive?" The guest, rich Megacles, had exposed Chloë because he had impoverished himself in urban pursuits—"fitting out warships and producing plays"—and has often dreamed that he would "become a father—by a ewe!" Urban folly has been redeemed by sacred nature; or, as Dionysophanes puts it, the exposed children "were looked after by Pan, the Nymphs, and Love." In fact, Daphnis and Chloë cannot "learn to live in town," so they return to their country estate to make their wedding "a pastoral affair." We are told that they will produce a boy named Philopoemen ("lover of flocks") and a girl named Agelaea ("lover of herds"). But the story concludes with their achieving, at last, the sexual consummation, in marriage, that marks the maturation of their natures: after the harmonious pastoral wedding, "Chloë realized that what had taken place on the edge of the wood had been nothing but childish play."

Exegetes are of course pleased when the clues they have found in a poem whose meaning is not manifest on its surface all lead to one culminating inference, one idea that "solves" the poem. For better or worse, I can offer no such solution to the mysterious simplicities of the *Lesbian Pastorals*, perhaps because Longus, though he pretends to have consulted an exegete, wrote a poem, not a puzzle. Not that a set of ideas cannot be easily excised from his poem: Love makes and governs all, and the All is a harmony and a process; in mankind the process is a painful maturation of erotic knowledge through the discordant evils of aggression, animalism, perversion, infanticide, and urban parasitism; and over this process presides not only Eros but the god-man Dionysus, whose ecstasy of fulfilled knowledge is achieved through, and culminates in, purification or catharsis. These ideas are hardly original with Longus. Nor are they so precisely Orphic that we must interpret the poem as being one of the Orphic *logoi* or as a preachment for that esoteric doctrine. And when formulated baldly they are prosaic commonplaces which offer us neither pleasure nor instruction. Without the poem, the ideas are impotent, just as, without the ideas, the poem is inconceivable. What makes the poem a healing comfort is therefore not so much the ideas themselves as the art which manifests them. How does Longus' art bring his ideas home to the reader?

First, it stimulates and shapes a process of inferring. We are told at the outset that the poem is an act of exegesis, a verbal icon of an idea. We then encounter people named Oak and Laurel, a decor of ivy and dolphins, ancillary tales about Pan and the nymphs, and so on. All this seems to refer us to a set of conventional signs, perhaps Orphic in nature, from which we infer that the poem may be based on an extrinsic system of ideas. This kind of inferring, by which one cracks the code of a poem, is pleasurable enough, but it does not suffice to explain the instructive comforts of the *Lesbian Pastorals* because the poem cannot be translated back into a set of preexistent ideas. In addition to signs and symbols, we encounter emblematic innocents in emblematic predicaments undergoing an emblematic growth in erotic knowledge. Furthermore, the plot is conveyed through pastoral episodes of transparent artificiality, and the episodes are arranged in obviously contrived patterns. All this also invites our question: What is the meaning of all this? But to answer this question about these vital aspects of the poem, we need not infer ideas that lie outside the poem. The episodes themselves, and the unfolding of the episodes, instruct and comfort us with an idea about the maturation of human love. We infer this idea as we feel it, as we smile at and worry about the trials of Daphnis and Chloë. Of course, our pleasure as historians is enhanced when we infer, from the carefully patterned structure of the poem, that Longus is constructing his work like one of those Alexandrian poems whose very shape ("idea") manifests its subject (for example, a poem about wings is shaped like a pair of wings); but it is the kinetic unfolding of the story, more than its emblems and symbols, that leads us to infer its ideas.

The pleasures of inferring make the experience of reading *Daphnis and Chloë* quite different from the experience of reading any of the works I have hitherto discussed. Ideas in these romances play the secondary roles of adorning speeches and substantiating ideals, and we are not invited at every stage to speculate about what it all means. Still, *Daphnis and Chloë* is in many technical ways very much like a romance. Longus depicts emotion through familiar figures and topics of passion. He constructs scenes, devises dialogue, shapes episodes in accordance with the conventions of extended prose narrative. But herein lies a second means by which Longus' art empowers his ideas. The very transparency of his techniques, set in an artificial pastoral world familiar from verse idylls, permits his ideas to shine through. Moreover, the contrived simplicity of his art and setting permits us to enjoy, with him, the pleasures of superior knowledge. The innocence of pastoral Lesbos, displayed through obviously hackneyed narrative patterns, makes sophisticates of us all. We are like the author; and his aloof sympathy, by which he retains his sanity, evokes a similar avuncular pleasure in us. Longus' method of exploiting candidly, in alliance with his reader, the conventions of pastoral and romance, is therefore more than late Alexandrian sophistication: it is a source of poetic power. It also helps make this power comic in character. We are like urbane gods observing the amusing, if painful and emblematic, growth of children. On the strength of this comic attitude we can be brought to a healing memory of our own erotic maturation. If our maturation was somewhat painful, as it assuredly must have been, our participation, from afar, in the comic but profound troubles and recognitions of Daphnis and Chloë can comfort us—or, as Longus hopes, heal our wounds. And if we have not experienced love, our reading can instruct us. Thus the comic art of the *Lesbian Pastorals* underlies all the intentions Longus announced in his prologue—to heal, to comfort, to refresh the memory, and to instruct—because it is this art that makes his book "a source of pleasure to the human race." It is also a fit "offering to Eros and the Nymphs and Pan" because it is a song of the world, one of the sublime transformations of idea into art in Western literature.

MARVEL AS COMEDY

Daphnis and Chloë has not been celebrated for accomplishing this transformation, but Apuleius' *Metamorphoses* has. For over a thousand years the story of the ass-man has been honored as an allegory of man's salvation, as a masterpiece of conversion literature, as an eloquent piece of propaganda for Isis.[13] I think it is better than any of these things. I honor it as a comedy of the marvelous. I do so because all of its parts—its characters, episodes, ancillary tales, fervid style—make a whole designed, as Apuleius himself says, to "charm" us, to make us "marvel," not to move us to adopt an opinion, attitude, or action. Ideas play in it the subsidiary role they play in the comedy of *Clitophon* (though Apuleius needs fewer of them), not the determinate role they play in the comedy of *Daphnis. The Golden Ass* is of course very different from these works in other important ways. It is in Latin. It is a "picaresque" novel. It is "realistic"—though it contains episodes more fantastic than any in Greek romance. It uses none of the vital conventions of romance except in the romantic tales it incorporates.[14] And the story in its main outlines is not original with the author. Still, if I must answer the question of genre which *The Golden Ass* has always demanded of its critics, I must say it is primarily a comedy.

Apuleius adapted, and probably augmented several fold, a comical satire by the witty skeptic, Lucian of Samosata, whose life overlapped Apuleius'. Since only an epitome of this Greek work survives, it is impossible to say exactly what Apuleius added to the original (if he knew it);[15] but the adventures of Lucian's hapless young hero, named Lucius, are essentially those of Apuleius' hapless Lucius. Curious about magic, both Luciuses seduce a servant girl in order to spy on an obscene witch, and both are by mistake transformed into donkeys. Both are taken by robbers to caves, attempt to escape with a captive maiden, are recaptured, and finally are rescued, along with the fair captive, by a posse. Both suffer grievously at the hands of the maiden's slaves and are then sold, first to a band of lascivious eunuch-priests of the Syrian mother goddess, then to a gardener, and finally to a cook, who, observing poor Lucius' unnatural cleverness, panders him to a lady whose erotic ambitions he satisfies. The ass's ability to apply himself like a man wins him a role in the theater (of mounting a condemned woman); but at the crucial moment he escapes, eats some roses, and is transformed back into human shape. Lucian's Lucius now returns to the lady for more fun, but she, eyeing his now merely human equipment, scornfully dismisses him; whereupon he goes home to Patras. Apuleius' Lucius, turning his life toward Isis, the mother goddess whose power has restored his manhood, unhappily struggles toward the top rank of her priesthood in Rome and ends as a shaven celibate whose curiosity about magic is apparently satisfied. By means of his delightful story (one-eighth the size of Apuleius' tale in the epitome), Lucian manages to satirize curiosity, magic, vicious rustics, hypocritical priests, and women. Apuleius retains all these villains and fools but transmutes satire into comedy by developing an action that includes about two hundred characters (of whom thirty-two die) and covers about seven months (in which seventy-three days are mentioned). In addition, his Lucius as man and ass overhears or participates in twenty-seven stories of desperate lovers, witches, feuds, and murders, including the celebrated tale of Cupid and Psyche;[16] and few if any of these marvelous stories were in his source. So described, none of this added material seems particularly comic. Furthermore, the "ancillary" tales often seem even more digressive than those in the works of Apuleius' imitators, Cervantes and Fielding. They trouble any formalist who assumes that extended narratives must follow the rules of plays or lyric poems, and they invite the exegete to find in them a key moral or meaning that would unify an apparently disjointed plot. Still, it is doubtful that Apuleius and his contemporaries could have called any fiction of ordinary life, told in the first person by its protagonist, who is a likable fool, anything but a comedy, unless they adopted the phrase used by Apuleius in his prologue—"a stringing-together of various tales in the Milesian style."

I must postpone discussion of this prologue and of the master-piece itself until I have discussed its author, because Apuleius' life, about which much is known, and the inferences which can be made about his character, have figured importantly in interpretations of his work. Most of what is known about his earlier career derives from an *Apologia* he delivered in court while defending himself against charges of fraud, sorcery, dandyism, and debauchery, so it must be assessed as autobiography of an especially self-aggrandizing character. Knowledge of his later life, during which he doubtless wrote the *Metamorphoses* and became a famous adherent of the mystical neo-Platonist school, as well as an honored rhetorician and priest of Asclepius, derives from legends and rumors about his wizardry. Taken together, these data have long supported the general belief that the *Metamorphoses* is somewhat autobiographical. Not that "Lucius" Apuleius (the name may not in fact have been his) suffered transformation into and out of asshood, like the Lucius of his book (though Saint Augustine did suggest that his fellow African and rhetorician was an ass),[17] but he did enjoy the kind of conversion to Isis that Lucius describes with such apparent gravity in the final book of *The Golden Ass*. If this were true, we would do well to read the whole book as a serious conversion document, a genuine personal statement about the conflict between vulgar curiosity and magic, on the one hand, and true religion and mystical knowledge on the other, and as the heartfelt thanksgiving of a sage to the mother who saved him from human bestiality. I myself do not think that the biographical data support such interpretations of the book.

In or about the year 154 Apuleius married a dowager almost old enough to be his mother. Three years later the lady's family accused Apuleius of having won his bride by magic in order to gain control of her fortune. They based their case on the manifest improbability of a handsome young rhetor (not yet thirty?) loving a lady over fifty; and they cited as evidence of his wizardry his bizarre interest in oracular boys and fish, in mirrors, and in his own beautiful hair. Defending himself, Apuleius declared that he had been well born in Madaura (in Algeria), had been schooled there and in Carthage, had then gone to the university in Athens, where he had shared digs with a boy from Tripoli named Pontianus, who was (he is now deceased) the son of his present wife. After perfecting himself in the art of rhetoric, he settled in Rome, where he quickly acquired a reputation for eloquence in court-room and lecture hall. Somewhere along the line he also acquired a legitimate interest in magic and was initiated into certain mysteries. He does not say whose mysteries these were; but if they were those of Isis, one wonders why he didn't say so, since her cult was most respectable and chaste. In any case, he for some reason abandoned Rome for Carthage, and then, restless still, he decided to try his ailing fortunes in Alexandria but got only as far as Tripoli, where he fell victim to a psychological illness he calls "fatigue." The troubled young man's forensic autobiography now begins to read like one of the romances he never wrote.

In Tripoli lived the wealthy widow Pudentilla, who, after the death of her husband, had been betrothed to her husband's distasteful brother to keep the fortune in the family. But after a while Pudentilla decided (on doctor's advice, says Apuleius) to marry whomever she liked. Alarmed by this news, her son, Pontianus, returned to Tripoli, where, lo and behold, his old roommate lay ill. Apuleius says that Pontianus then conceived a secret intrigue: he would invite his friend to convalesce in his mother's house and persuade him to marry her. This transaction between chums was therefore conceived by the son himself, who, being dead, could hardly confirm the story now. Apuleius says that Pontianus did not pop the question until after Apuleius had roused himself to deliver a smashingly successful public declamation, whereupon Pontianus avowed (curiously) that civic acclaim was a heavenly sign sanctifying such an odd marriage. But Apuleius, though he was the most devout of men, did not leap at the sign or at the lady herself, who was neither well-favored nor young (though she was certainly not sixty, as his accusers allege). No, it was her virtues, he says, that finally won his heart. Then Pontianus had married into a vile family who somehow persuaded him that Apuleius had seduced the widow by sorcery. Yes, even Pontianus had turned against the stepfather he himself had chosen! But what perfidy to suggest that his sudden death had been caused by Apuleius! The charge of murder had been dropped, but now they accuse him of enchanting widows, dissecting fish, playing with mirrors, and primping his hair:

> As to my hair, which they with unblushing mendacity declare I have allowed to grow long as an enhancement to my personal attractions, you can judge of its elegance and

beauty. As you see, it is tangled, twisted, and unkempt like a lump of tow, shaggy and irregular in length, so knotted and matted [*globosus*] that the tangle is past the art of man to unravel. This is due not to mere carelessness in the tiring of my hair, but to the fact that I never so much as comb or part it. I think this is sufficient refutation of the accusations concerning my hair, which they hurl against me as though it were a capital charge.[18]

The judge may have winced at this uncapital pun, but Apuleius' version of the affair apparently won him acquittal. He lived richly ever after in Carthage, honored as a philosopher, poet, orator, and priest of Asclepius (not Isis).[19]

What are the likenesses between this charming African rhetorician and the foolish young Greek who passes through asshood to become a bald, celibate priest of Isis? First, both are interested in magic, the fictional Lucius obsessively so. But this interest was almost universal in the second century, and the fictional Lucius' obsession is not unlike that of his prototype in Lucian's story. Second, though Apuleius makes Lucius a Corinthian, even taking pains to invent his kinship with the famous Plutarch, in the final book he refers to himself as a Madauran, like Apuleius himself. Is this a signal that the fictional Lucius is really Lucius Apuleius? Or is it a slip? Or a scribal insertion? There is no evidence for the third possibility. The weight of evidence is against the normal significance of the first suggestion. But doesn't the second possibility throw some light on the first? Perhaps Lucius embodies some of the personal characteristics of Lucius Apuleius even though his adventures do not allegorize the serious religious experiences of his creator.

First, Apuleius' Lucius, unlike Lucian's, is a hair fetishist. "Hair has always been an obsessive concern of mine," he says. "I observe the hair of beautiful women in public and afterwards delight myself with an image of it privately at home."[20] A slave girl's tress prompts him to make an excursus on this "most important aspect of the body" that runs to six hundred words; and when this delightful girl pins him to his bed like a wrestler, he must ask her to unloose her hair to assure his prowess. And when another potent female (Isis) later appears to him, he begins his depiction with, "First, she had a great abundance of hair blowing and curling on her divine neck." In fact, the odd word *globosus* that Apuleius used in describing his own hair in the *Apologia* Lucius also uses in describing the slave girl's (*conglobatus*) and Cupid's (*globus*) in the *Metamorphoses* (2.9 and 5.22). This eccentricity is perhaps not unconnected with a second experience evidently shared by author and creature: both are vitally involved with older women. Lucius' famous curiosity about magic, which, as Isis later observes, is the primary cause of his suffering, is in fact focused on witches. From the outset he believes wholeheartedly in their erotic ability to enchant, control, debase, mutilate, and transform men. His wild credulity often produces a manic state. The morning after his arrival in Thessaly, haunt of witches, he wakes "stupefied" with desire to see marvels and rushes into the streets to inspect cobblestones, statues, birds, and leaves, hoping that they are men transformed by witches. After learning that his hostess is herself a witch, he rushes to her house, "mad" with desire to see her in action. Most of the stories Apuleius adds to Lucian involve witches or adulterous wives who are more erotic and potent than their husbands. With two exceptions, older women in Apuleius are sex-driven, powerful, and dangerous. One exception is a friend of Lucius' mother who had helped nurse him in his infancy, though her hospitality is in fact tendered with erotic remarks on his good looks—his slender body, blond hair, fair skin, and gray eyes. The other is Mother Isis, the most potent of witches, who demands that he forego both witchcraft and sex.

Perhaps Apuleius put enough of himself into his Lucius to call him at the end, accidentally or not, a Madauran. We may hope that displacement of erotic attention onto hair did not trouble him or his wife; that, unlike Lucius, he never really felt himself to be a ridiculous beast; and that, while living on Pudentilla's fortune, he experienced something better than the mix of dis-ease and redemption felt by Lucius after his adoption by the goddess of good fortune. But such hopes are beside my point. Even though the *Metamorphoses* would yield interesting data to a biographer of Apuleius, the question here concerns the aesthetic consequences of the projection of the author's presumed personal traits into his book. These traits do not permit us to begin reading this book with the hypothesis that it is a serious, even didactic, spiritual autobiography; on the contrary, the fictional Lucius' obsession with witches and hair helps establish him as a comic character, just as Apuleius' odd interests made him seem a dangerous one.

Lucius' eccentricities, because they individualize him, make him more a "realistic" character than a type of foolish curiosity or an emblem of the wandering human soul. Yet his oddities are described with a hyperbole that reduces him to a figure with whom we are most unlikely to make any serious moral identification. Lucius is hardly designed to lead us into the mysteries of Isis, though his erotic queerness helps us to appreciate his difficulties in her celibate priesthood—or does his character explain the particular attractiveness of her demands on him?

We begin the book not with a hypothesis but with a one-sentence prologue:

> I shall string together for you various tales in the Milesian style, and charm your kindly ears with a magical murmur—provided that you do not scorn to peruse an Egyptian papyrus scratched with a sharp reed from the Nile—so that you might marvel at the forms and fortunes of men changing into alien configurations, then duly back again.

The sentence tantalizes us with an accurate but incomplete description of all that we now need to know about this unprecedented book—its narrative method, its matter, and its intended effect. Its method will be a mere "stringing together" (*conserere*) of disparate tales, perhaps something like Ovid's in his old *Metamorphoses;* in fact, however, the tales will be forged together by the single coherent action of Lucius' progress through and beyond asshood. It is intended to charm us with marvels—the primary effect of any contemporary nondidactic work. Its materials, however, are distinctly odd, even paradoxical: they are Milesian tales written on Egyptian papyrus with a Nilotic pen. What does this mean?

Milesian tales were short stories about conjugal betrayal, comic contretemps, and sardonic or cruel trickery resolved in surprising but not supernatural ways.[21] The anthology of such stories compiled in the first century B.C. by Aristides of Miletus (from which the type gets its name) was infamous for its obscenity but has not survived. The *novelle* and *fabliaux* strung together by Boccaccio and Chaucer (e.g., the *Miller's Tale*) include familiar examples of the genre. Whether comic or bitterly cynical, Milesian tales were "realistic" in our sense of the term; they and their characters were much inferior in status to the *erōtika pathēmata*, and they were hardly worthy of a literary man's notice. And these are scratched in another sort of matter, apparently even more to be scorned: Egyptian papyrus. A great many Egyptian stories survive, but no one seems to have observed that Apuleius, in the *Metamorphoses*, is telling one. In Egypt such tales seem to have enjoyed among the scribes a much higher literary status than the Milesian tales did among Hellenic literary men, and there is no reason why Apuleius could not have heard some of them or perceived that Lucian wrote one in the Greek *Ass*. Like the Milesian tales, they were brief; but they were of more diverse character, for they include mythological tales, historical anecdotes, philosophical apologues, and a few elegant autobiographical tales that seem to derive from the lives of real men (these Gustave Lefebvre terms "*romans*"). But one characteristic they have in common: they all involve the marvelous—the deeds of sorcerers, speaking animals, witches. As Lefebvre says, "the marvelous is nearly inseparable from the Egyptian *conte*."[22] The basic stuff of the *Metamorphoses* is indeed marvelous—not only all the witch stories Apuleius adds to Lucian but the fundamental story of a man's transformation into a donkey and back again with the aid of the Egyptian mother goddess. And in this Egyptian material are embedded comic and bitter Milesian tales of "realistic" tone. This seems to be a paradoxical mix of opposites, in itself a marvel. But the Milesian and the Egyptian are similar on one vital score—they both deal in the pleasures of surprise, wonder, astonishing reversals, and recognitions. In this sense, both involve the marvelous, and Apuleius correctly tells us that he welds them together so that we may marvel.

I suggest also that Apuleius may have borrowed his narrative method from some Egyptian literary habits. Egyptian tales were sometimes strung together by being assigned to a single teller who is in some sort of predicament, like Scheherazade in *The Thousand and One Nights*. Poor Lucius does tell all the various fables of *The Golden Ass*, but after his escape. His own story, however, is like those Egyptian autobiographies intended

> to sum up the characteristic features of the individual person in terms of his positive worth and in the face of eternity. His person should live forever, in the transfigured form of the resurrected dead, and his name should last forever in the memory of the people.[23]

In fact, Lucius predicts that his story will have such an effect. In book 2 he boasts that a sorcerer once predicted that he (Lucius) would win great fame and that his life would be a marvelous tale that would provide material for books. The sorcerer was right. But in Apuleius' book, Lucius is not a paragon but a likable fool, and his autobiography is a comedy of marvels.

We first see Lucius riding a white stallion up a hill in Thessaly. He dismounts and joins two pedestrians who are arguing about the powers of witches. Proclaiming that he wants to know everything in the world, Lucius implores one traveler to repeat the tale which the other has found to be ridiculously incredible. After we've heard the wild tale—in which a man named Socrates is erotically enslaved by his obscene witch-mistress, then killed by her magic—we are inclined to agree with the skeptical traveler. But Lucius exclaims, "I think nothing is impossible!" He is more credulous and frantically curious than we would ever permit ourselves to be. On the other hand, he is not wholly unlike us: he is in Thessaly "on business," and one traveler remarks that he has the dress and demeanor of an educated young gentleman. In short, he is like a New Comedy character, eager for experience and capable of surviving it. And is the tale absolutely improbable? After all, its teller claims to have participated in it himself, and in Thessaly anything can happen. Still, the roads, people, and houses of this Thessaly are as mean and dusty as they are in the world we know. Can this Egyptian tale be believed when told in a Milesian setting? Already, in this initial episode, Apuleius is titillating our sense of probability, putting us into pleasurable doubt, preparing us to "believe" Lucius' later transformation into and out of asshood while permitting us to affirm that of course such marvels do not really happen. He also arouses complex sympathies and antipathies for Lucius—a young man inferior to us but so harmless that we know that he must survive his forthcoming predicaments, which, as we can already predict, will involve witchcraft.

The second episode confirms these feelings. Lucius finds that his host in Hypata, principal city of Thessaly, is too mean to give him a decent supper, and he rushes, famished, into the marketplace, where he buys a fish for a fraction of the asking price. The market overseer (an old friend) then announces that Lucius has been duped, throws the fish at the feet of the fishmonger, and marches off proud of his good deed, leaving poor Lucius humiliated and deprived of both money and meal. Lucius is a foolish victim of fools less sympathetic than he; and there is no one else in this world of dupes and dupers with whom we can align our sympathies—not even the author, who seems to be Lucius himself. Though we would never be as credulous or impetuous as he, his good nature, and our aroused desire to spy on shameful witches and to resolve our doubts about their powers, carry us willingly with him. Every episode and incident contributes to the arousal of these sympathies and desires. When Lucius hears that his hostess, Pamphile, can foretell rain from a sputtering lampwick, he is agog; whereas we, along with her hard-bitten husband Milo, would explain her prowess by referring to atmospheric conditions. Lucius hears another incredible Egyptian tale at a dinner party when a guest tells how he was hired one night by a widow to guard her husband's corpse against the women who steal the noses, ears, and other appendages of dead men to work their wills on live ones; the guest believed that he had successfully fended them off (they had entered the room as weasels); but the next day, at the funeral, the corpse, revived by an Egyptian sorcerer, revealed that his widow had murdered him and had stolen the guest's nose and ears and then replaced them with wax replicas. When the other guests laugh, the teller—who should know the truth—is genuinely indignant. Such stories do not raise to independent philosophical status the question whether such marvels actually happen. They arouse and satisfy the desire to hear marvels, and they leave the amused reader in comic doubt.

Up to now the Egyptian tales have been boxed into an ongoing Milesian comedy; in the next episode the two kinds of conventional materials converge. Lucius staggers drunkenly from the party to Milo's house, where he sees three robbers forcing the gate. He slays them. Next morning, which, he has been told, marks the city's Feast of Laughter, he is seized by the magistrates and arraigned before the whole citizenry in the theater. To his horror, the prosecutors accuse him of murder and ask the death penalty. Lamenting widows appear. Lucius stammers a lame defense. But when he is forced to uncover the corpses, he discovers that they are only wineskins. The assembly breaks into mob laughter: Lucius has been the butt of a civic joke offered to Risus, the god of laughter, and he is voted a statue for his pains. But this

Milesian story is "scratched," as its author says, on an Egyptian papyrus. As Fotis (the slave girl whom Lucius is seducing) explains, the wineskins were in fact enchanted. Pamphile, Lucius' witch-hostess, had ordered Fotis to gather hair clippings of a certain handsome young man from the barbershop, but the frightened girl had substituted goat hair. So when Pamphile, using the magic power of the hair, summoned the boy to her bed, goatskins had in fact marched to her door, where Lucius had "slain" them. To enjoy the comedy in both the Milesian and Egyptian elements of this story, we must believe that a whole town could conspire to play a practical joke on a stranger and that goat hair can be transformed into walking wineskins. These are the facts of the case, and we give aesthetic credence to them because we have been prepared to do so and because they are funny. On the strength of this credence we are prepared to accept the comic marvels of Lucius' transformation, which soon follows.

We are also enjoying a special combination of erotic materials. On their first night together, sexy Fotis has decked Lucius with roses (a flower sacred to Mother Isis) and nourished him with a splendid supper in preparation for their romp. Their encounter is described in a military conceit which Apuleius adds to Lucian's athletic one. Even the supper is likened to a breakfast fit for a gladiator—of Venus. The erection Lucius displays to Fotis he oddly compares with the sort of wound soldiers display to win pity from citizens, as though he had been pitiably castrated. But he says with anxious pride, "You see I'm well armed and ready for the merciless battle. I have been standing to arms all day, and now my bow is strung so tight that I'm afraid something will snap if Advance isn't sounded pretty soon. However, if you want my battle-ardor to burn more fiercely still, you darling, let your hair down so that it ripples over your shoulders." This she does; and looking like Venus as she pretends to cover her mount (shaven in the Greek manner) with her palm, she takes up his militant challenge: "Now fight," she says, "and you must fight hard, because I shall not retreat one inch, nor turn my back. Come on face to face if you're a man, strike home, and do your very worst. Take me by storm, kill me, die in the breach. No quarter given or accepted" (Graves trans., pp. 34–35). And she pins him to the bed like a wrestler. The eroticism of this delightful scene is more wholesome, one might boldly say, than that of the preceding witch tales, with their castrations and magical bondage; but it too expresses a form of sadomasochism. The transformation of such passions into comedy is one of the vital powers of the book. Delightful Fotis, who to Lucius is at once vile, threatening, and a good cook, herself represents this transformation because she is both funny and a fit object of Lucius' (and doubtless our) sadomasochistic impulses.

But for Lucius she is primarily a means to another erotic end—the satisfaction of his frantic voyeuristic desire to spy on his truly vile and powerful hostess, Pamphile. Fotis helps him peep at Pamphile as she strips herself naked, smears her body with magic ointment, turns into an owl, and flies out the window to prey on an unfaithful lover. Elated, Lucius persuades Fotis to fetch the same ointment for him. He would join the dreadful woman in her bestiality and peep at her as she peeps at her betraying lover. But Fotis brings the wrong ointment. Or is it really the right one—the one that will aptly punish Lucius for having seen the awful power of the older woman? He anoints himself and turns into an ass, the most lascivious and ignoble of brutes, everywhere enslaved and beaten, the archenemy of chaste Mother Isis. Like a child, entranced by the enormous attractiveness of women, he has believed that they are so powerful that they can control nature and so erotic that they can convert themselves and their lovers into animals—or into immortals. Now his infantile desire to see—but only to see—the marvelous foulness of such women has been punished in a realm beyond mere seeing. Lucius now becomes a masochistically passive victim of the most sadistic torments until he flees a challenge to his own sadism—the task of mounting a condemned murderess in a public arena. To fornicate in public as a beast with a vile, powerful woman is too much for him; he takes refuge in the idealization of woman, the cult of Isis, who demands that he give up sex altogether; and this paradoxical reversal makes a most satisfying resolution of action that turns on his profoundly erotic comic suffering.

That his suffering continues to be comic, for all its sadistic grimness, is suggested by Lucius' immediate reaction to his ridiculous transformation: he is pleased by the enlargement of his member. Moreover, that he will return to manhood is never in doubt. Fotis tells him that the antidote to asshood is the eating of a rose, and this he almost—oh, so nearly!—accomplishes immediately in the stable; but instead he suffers the first of his comic pains: his own slave beats him, and his own white horse kicks him. The absurd consequences of being turned into a donkey are already being worked out. Bandits more effective than enchanted goatskins attack Milo's house and pile their loot onto Lucius' back; and off he is taken into a Milesian world where strange events occur without benefit of magic, where mute Lucius, the ass-man, is himself the only Egyptian marvel. Bruised, debased, tethered in the bandit cave, he hears grim tales of bandit bravery that give us the voyeuristic pleasure of secretly observing what life is like in the underworld. We also learn what it is like to be an animal. Lucius suffers innumerable blows, stumbles on rocks, chews fodder, fears the death that we alone know cannot visit him. The incredible premise of the story—that a man lives inside an ass—is explored in accordance with the strictest laws of probability. In fact, Lucius' sufferings can be extravagantly "realistic" precisely because we know that his predicament is impossible, that his is a comedy of the absurd.

On his string of "realism" Apuleius can bead all sorts of stories.[24] One is the tragic *erōtika pathēmata* of Charity (Grace), a beautiful highborn maiden kidnapped on the eve of her wedding and now being held captive in the brigands' cave. Apuleius weaves this serious tale through his comedy as Xenophon wove Panthea's story through his didactic biography of Cyrus. Another story is the famous fable of Cupid and Psyche, which the bandits' cook—a nameless and cruel crone—tells to console the distracted Charity. The charm and magnitude of this ancillary tale (it occupies one-sixth of the *Metamorphoses*—from 4. 28 to 6. 24) have long made it seem to be a key to the meaning of Apuleius' book, an allegorical simulacrum of the whole: as Psyche (Soul) suffers because of her curiosity about the identity of her lover (Love) but is finally rewarded with immortality, so Lucius suffers because of his curiosity but is rewarded with salvation by Isis. Or, Lucius is the soul of Man, fallen into bestiality but in the end winning, through suffering and surrender, the love of God. The apparent allegorical gravity of the fable and its later sentimentalization in the literature and art of the West make it seem to be an obstacle to any valid argument that the *Metamorphoses* is essentially a comedy.

But the story goes like this: Venus, mother of nature and love, is jealous of Soul because the maiden is so beautiful that people are forsaking Venus' altars to worship her. Venus summons Eros—who here is neither imp nor lord but the wanton marriage-breaker—and commands him to make Soul fall in love with the worst man in the world. Meanwhile, Soul, like Callirrhoë, inveighs against the beauty that has won the admiration of mankind and the enmity of Venus. To diagnose her melancholia, Soul's parents consult the local oracle, which Apuleius says is the Milesian one—a curious detail (4. 32) in such a sweet story. The oracle declares that Soul is destined to marry a winged serpent who is lord of Hell. In stories, oracles are always correct: Soul will marry Eros. How are we to allegorize this? In any case, the girl's parents, vainly attempting to frustrate a fate worse than death, expose her on Execution Rock, from which she falls to a death that leads, as it does not in any other romance, literally to marriage. She falls into the palace garden of Eros, the winged wanton who has himself fallen in love with this image of his mother. Eros visits Soul at night, commanding that she never ask his name or light a lamp to see him. Soul's sisters visit her, turn jealous, and persuade her that her lover is indeed the serpentine lord of Hell. Lifting a lamp one night to see and kill him, Soul discovers that he is a beautiful winged boy. She accidentally pricks a finger on one of his arrows, therefore falls in love with him, and nervously drops hot lamp oil onto his shoulder. He wakes in pain, divorces her (using the ordinary Roman formula for this), and departs. Aggrieved, Soul then murders her sisters: she tells them that her husband wants to waft them down to his garden; and when they leap from Execution Rock, they are killed indeed.

Meanwhile, Venus is enraged because her son has slept with her rival (people will think that she has played the bawd for them!). When Soul visits Venus' temple as a suppliant, the goddess screams, "Have you deigned to visit your mother-in-law? Be assured I will handle you like a daughter." So she does. She orders Sorrow and Sadness to beat her; then, proclaiming that *she* will not suffer the humiliation of being a grandmother, she knocks Soul down herself. As an allegory of one kind of family rivalry, the fable hardly needs exegesis; as an allegory of the soul seeking salvation through divine love, it hardly deserves one; as a story told to cheer up a desperate girl, it seems about right.

Venus sets Soul four seemingly impossible tasks, all but the last of which she survives. The last involves the dangers of female beauty and curiosity: Soul must descend into Hell to fetch Venus a bit of Proserpina's beauty. But when Soul (still rivaling mother Venus's beauty?) peeps into Proserpina's beauty box, she finds Death lying within. But Venus the harridan will not get her way in this romantic fable: Eros revives Soul with a touch of his wing, chastises her curiosity, and persuades father Jove to marry them. Jove cannot resist his beautiful "lord and son" and agrees to make Soul immortal so that the marriage can take place. His motives are quite ordinary: Love's boyish rovings—from which Jove himself once suffered—will now at last be confined by matrimonial bonds, and snobbish Venus will be placated by Soul's new status as an immortal. And the grandchild whom the goddess of erotic pleasure had dreaded turns out to be acceptable too—at least it is named Voluptas.

I find it impossible to discover a cogent allegorical significance in this sardonic little romance. Certainly none is drawn by Lucius, who, overhearing it, merely regrets that he has neither pen, paper, nor fingers with which to write it down. This suggests that he is charmed—as Apuleius wants the reader of his whole book to be—by the crone's "pretty nonsense." He terms the story an *anilis fabula* (4. 27), an old wives' tale; and to denote the teller, who he says is "crazy and drunken," he uses the term *anicula*, a diminutive of *anus*, meaning both "old woman" and "anus." It is hard to believe that a grave Platonist and distinguished rhetor would have chosen this teller and this tale to convey his message about love and salvation. As for the suffering entailed by curiosity, Lucius' own story suffices to tell us something about that. In fact, by reducing an allegorical fable about the old Olympians to an old wives' tale, Apuleius puts it (and the Olympians) on a level below that of his Milesian and Egyptian stories.

The exegete can also find allegorical significance in the subsequent episode. When the bandits leave, Lucius at last decides to make a run for it. He kicks the teller of the famous fable, Charity leaps onto his back, and off they go, dragging the charming crone over the stones. Charity urges him on with childish promises: she will provide him with lush pasture, a statue, and fame as the hero of a new myth wherein an ass saves a virgin. There may be a significance in this last promise. Chaste virgins and lascivious donkeys were opposites reconciled in the rituals of Isis, wherein the goddess rides on an ass's back to portray her triumph over the ass-god Typhon, enemy of her beloved Osiris. But here Charity's remark is plainly a comic paradox; and lest we allegorize their relationship, it is Charity who mistakenly insists that the ass turn right, against his better judgment, onto a road that delivers them back into the hands of the returning bandits, who decide to gut Lucius and sew Charity into his corpse so that she will cook in the sun. This grim idea might in fact suggest the kind of allegory that would seem to appeal to the author of this bitter comedy— Grace broiling inside an Ass.

But Charity's handsome betrothed arrives, dupes the brigands, slaughters them, and leads Lucius off to a lush meadow full of mares, whose stallions kick him brutally. This would seem to end the romance of Charity. But later, after Lucius has been sadistically tormented by her slaves, we learn that Charity's husband has been murdered by his best friend (Charity's disappointed suitor) and that Charity has stabbed out the eyes of the lovelorn murderer, then slain herself. The slave who reports all this remarks, "Such are the results of passion." Indeed, the Milesian tales, the mocking fable of Venus, Eros, and Soul, the ugly pictures of the passionate underworld, and this tragic romance all seem to illustrate the results of passion. They make Lucius' final option for celibacy and profitable priestcraft more satisfying than it might otherwise be.

In the next phase of the action, in which Lucius' fortunes progressively worsen, he complains more and more explicitly against Fortune herself,[25] who for him is a witch, an insatiable tormentor and enslaver of men. Having been released from the care of a sadistic boy who beats his open sores, he laments, "Merciless Fortune, whom I had failed either to shake off or appease, however deeply I suffered, now again loured at me, and, of course, found me a buyer whom she could depend upon to prolong my agonies" (Graves trans., pp. 198–99). His buyers are abominable eunuch-priests, cuckolded tradesmen (whose wives' adulteries make several comic Milesian tales), and a kindly market gardener whom he stupidly and comically betrays to a cruel centurion. He overhears horror stories about a murderous landlord and a woman who poisons her child in order to accuse her stepson, who has rejected her advances, of murder (the child revives and accuses his mother, of course). This last story requires him, he says, to "exchange the sock for the buskin," a remark that confirms the fact that it has been the comic sock, not the tragic boot, that has carried us over so many painful paths. Apuleius' comic string—the absurd story of a fool whose sufferings we cannot liken to our own—can support all sorts of moving stories, and almost all of them turn on the public revelation of the secret wickedness of women. And they all, in a sense, prepare us for the intervention of the good woman, Isis, who is called the goddess of Good Fortune.

For some reason, the marvelous revelation of the guilt of the child-poisoner signals "a sudden change of fortune" for Lucius. It is as though the just humiliation of women aids his career. His new keepers, observing his ability to drink wine, dance, and consume bonbons like a man, pander him to a dowager. He's reluctant; but, after all, he's been continent for seven months, and he is awed by her skill in managing her bestiality. This abomination is played for laughs; the next one is not. His owner arranges to have him mount a condemned adulteress-murderess in the arena prior to her being thrown to wilder beasts. (In the Lucianic *Ass* this woman has no history, but Apuleius makes her another perverse wife: she has killed her husband's sister by thrusting a torch between her legs, and she has then poisoned her husband, daughter, doctor, and the doctor's wife.) Lucius has three motives for fleeing this task. One is shame at fornicating in the theater of his hometown, Corinth, to which the story has brought him (in Lucian's version he is now in Thessalonica): he may be something of a voyeur, but he is no exhibitionist. The second is anger. As he watches the elaborately staged, and lasciviously described, masque of the Judgment of Paris that precedes his entrance into the theater, it occurs to him that all judges, like Paris, are corrupted by Aphrodite: sex corrupts everything. The third motive is fear. Will the beasts that will enter the arena after he has completed his job not devour him as they devour the polluted woman? So, for the second time in seven months, he takes action. He runs the six miles to Cenchreae, at the narrows of the Corinthian isthmus, where he falls exhausted on the beach. Here begins the final phase of the action.

The famous eleventh book is an important document for historians of religion and is often taken as a masterpiece of conversion literature. Moreover, its apparent gravity makes it seem an authentic expression of Apuleius' own religious feelings, and this in turn has made it all but impossible to read the whole story as anything but a didactic or rhetorical work. But a plain reading of the brief book, like a plain reading of the much longer fable of Cupid and Psyche, convinces me that it is primarily a comic resolution of a comic novel that is not governed by any formulatable religious or moral idea.

Lucius dips his head into the sea seven times (because the Pythagoreans had said that this was a suitable number) and prays for help to the rising full moon, calling her Ceres, Venus, Diana, Proserpina: "I beseech you, by whatever name or fashion or aspect, deliver me from the wretched fortune which has so long pursued me." He sleeps, and in sleep sees and learns the true name of the mother he needs. Like another moon, a divine imago rises from the sea in full Egyptian regalia—her luxuriant hair crowned with a crescent moon, her arms entwined with vipers, her hands holding rattles, her feet shod in palm-leaf slippers. The true name, she says, of "the parent of natural things, the mistress of the elements, queen of the dead, the single manifestation of all gods and goddesses" is her own—Isis. She tells him to eat the roses which will be carried in a procession to be held in her honor next morning on this very beach, and she declares that he is now bound to her for life. And, if he keeps "the ordinances of her religion and perfect chastity," he will benefit from her "power to prolong your life beyond the limits set by destiny." No more complete mother could be dreamt of. He wakes.

The procession, so valuable for historians of religion, is for Lucius a "playful masquerade." Here is a tame female bear dressed "as a matron and carried in a sedan chair," "an ape with a bonnet of plaited straw," "an ass with wings glued on his back ambling after an old man, so that you would . . . have laughed at the pair." Funny as it is, the procession includes a rose garland that is the "crown of victory over cruel Fortune"; and when Lucius eats it, he is transformed back into a man. But even this climactic Egyptian marvel is touched with Milesian wit when Lucius, human again, must do his "naked best to hide [his] privates with the sole naturally supplied veil (the hand), while compressing [his] thighs." The chief priest now delivers a sermon which we can, if we wish, take as seriously as its content, if not its context, allows, though the priest himself "labouring hard to breathe under the pressure of inspiration," is rather ridiculous (Lindsay trans., pp. 240–44). Neither birth nor learning, he tells Lucius, has saved you from falling slave to youthful pleasure; your malign curiosity brought you sinister punishment; for the Fortune who has punished you has now, in her blindness, brought you to the blessed religion of all-seeing Fortune, the Providence whose light illuminates the gods, whose true name is Isis. This is taken to be the moral of the book, as doubtless it is. It emerges with aesthetic logic from the action and psychodynamics of the whole. But we would do the book a grave injustice if we removed this message from its context and used it to convert the book into a gravely moral allegory. It functions here as part of the catharsis of moral and physical suffering experienced by our hero, a catharsis neatly expressed by the crowd's joyous shout, "Lucius de sua Fortuna triumphat!" (11. 15). This is a joy shared by the characters and readers of any good comedy or romance.

The work might well have ended here. Even the psychodynamics of Lucius' comic suffering seems resolved when his guilt, curiosity, and voyeurism are cured by his alliance with the good witch of all-seeing Providence. But his sufferings continue during his troubled progress through the priesthood of Isis-Osiris. These pages constitute a treasury of information about the mysteries, and literary critics, regarding them as expressions of genuine religious experience, take them as seriously as they take Lucius' conversion. From me, however, they evoke responses like those evoked by the whole book. Lucius remains inept, ambitious, worried, and curious, and the marvels he experiences remain both Milesian and Egyptian.

After Lucius takes a house in the temple precincts, he learns that "a consecrated life [is] full of snags, that the requisite chastity [is] difficult to observe" (Lindsay trans., p. 246). He cannot be initiated until the goddess tells him in a dream the name of the right priest, "as also the precise sum to be expended on the ceremony." He does dream, but only of the white stallion he was riding at the outset of his adventures. And when the name is finally vouchsafed to him, it is, oddly enough, Mithras, the name of a rival god. He toys with our desire to learn the details of his initiation, which of course no initiate was permitted to tell. "However, I shall not keep you any longer on the cross of your

anxiety, distracted as you doubtless are with religious yearning"
(Lindsay trans., p. 249). This irony leads to the famous passage so
tantalizing to historians of religion:

> I approached the very gates of death and set one foot on
> Proserpina's threshold, yet was permitted to return, rapt,
> through all the elements. At midnight I saw the sun shining
> as it were noon; I entered the presence of the gods of the
> upper world, stood near and worshipped them. [Graves
> trans., p. 252]

This could be an accurate description of Apuleius' own initiation
into "certain mysteries"; in context, however, it is a coy account
of the experience of an ass-man laboring to carry out his religious
vows, without much satisfaction to himself. After he speaks a
magnificent prayer to Isis, the "everlasting comfort of the human
race [who] can mitigate the storms of Fortune and inhibit the stars
in their malicious courses," the goddess admonishes him to go to
Rome, where she "once more interrupted [his] sleep," though, as
he says,

> I had thought myself fully initiated already. . . . After I had
> re-examined all my religious doubts in the privacy of my
> conscience, I consulted a priest. I then learned a new and
> disturbing thing . . . ; I knew nothing of the rites of . . . the
> supreme Father of the Gods, unconquerable Osiris. [Lindsay
> trans., p. 252]

If Apuleius had been writing an allegory of salvation or a piece of
propaganda for Isis, he would have quit by now. But he recapitu-
lates the common difficulties of being adopted by Mother Isis in
describing Lucius' adoption by Father Osiris. This time the necessary dreamed-of priest is Asinus, "Ass," a name "asininely
suggestive of my late plight" (Lindsay trans., p. 252). Furthermore, Lucius' curiosity remains greater than his means of satisfying it. "My poverty . . . kept interfering with my plans; and I
was left stranded (as the saying goes) between the altar and the
block" (Lindsay trans., p. 253). And though he sells the "clothes
off his back" to pay Asinus and is "admitted with shaven head to
the nocturnal orgies" of Osiris, he is "once more molested by
unexpected visionary commands; and a third time I found myself
yearning toward a mystery." The "oppressively shaken and per-
plexed state of mind" that this yearning leads him into makes him

so angry that he is "driven to the verge of distraction" (Lindsay trans., pp. 253–54). This may be serious in itself; but taken as a whole, his religious experience has become ludicrous. The comic strategy that governs the events, characters, and style of this last phase of Lucius' adventures in fact does not differ essentially from those which governed the first, save that now we are due for a happy ending. The "trouble and expense" of his final initiation results in worldly success. Being a higher priest of Osiris makes him "rapidly come to the forefront of the legal profession at Rome"; and our curious, likable hair fetishist ends by protesting that he now joyfully serves Osiris "with a shaven head, not covering or hiding it but showing it openly to everyone" (Lindsay trans., pp. 254 ff.).

This final transformation is itself a comic marvel. It certainly does not seem designed to entice us into the mysteries of Isis-Osiris or to conclude a preachment about curiosity or an allegory of salvation; and if it reflects an experience of the author, he seems to look back on it with amused bitterness. Apuleius has in fact written one of the bitterest of comedies. The sadistic cruelties of men and circumstances, the masochistic enslavement of a hero who suffers more blows than Don Quixote and Sancho Panza combined, the hypocrisy of venal and perverted clergies, the monstrous passions of women—all have charmed our kindly ears because they have been conveyed through the author's incantatory murmur. This murmur is partly a verbal style that is at once idiosyncratic and characteristic of the second century; it is arch, frenetic, extravagant. But when used by a narrator whose perceptions and experiences are themselves extravagant, it also becomes a style appropriate to comedy and in itself a source of comedy. Its unremitting cleverness can absorb the horror of the most hideous events and thereby permit us to enjoy saying, with a kind of cynical confidence, "Yes, this is the world as it is." Furthermore, we can be charmed by horrors when they themselves are as extravagant—as incredible and marvelous—as the ridiculous hero's style. Style, action, and character combine, therefore, to make us marvel; and when the extravagant twists of Milesian fables are entwined with the extravagant wonders of Egyptian ones, our marveling becomes unexpectedly complex: the "realistic" betrayals, blows, dismemberments, and murders of the Milesian materials become as incredible as the marvels of witchcraft, metamorphoses, and salvation of the Egyptian materials; while, contrariwise, the marvels of the Egyptian stories become as credible as the grimly mundane deeds of the Milesian ones. This melding of the credible and incredible, this writing of Milesian stories on Egyptian papyrus, fulfills Apuleius' promise to make us marvel. He makes us marvel at extremes—the worst of life, the most fearsome; and the best, the most desirable. And they are so extreme, they are experienced by such a frantic fool of an ass-man, that the worst and the best both become ludicrous, and this makes the *Metamorphoses* one of the most bitter and profound of comedies.

❧9❧
Discussion
Four

SIGMA: I regret that we have such a short time to discuss such a long essay.

KAPPA: Forgive me for saying that I myself cannot regret it. We shall only be repeating ourselves. Alpha has once more given us some formalist interpretations of individual novels without attempting to say where the novels came from, why they should have been written when they were, or to relate them one with another historically. I must say that I agree with the interpretation of Achilles Tatius. It is indeed very funny. The *Lesbian Pastorals* is mightily overrated, and I cannot see what difference it makes to call it comedy, or an apologue, or a romance, or an idyll, or a glob—it is a saccharine bit of escapist teacake, with ideas dotted on top like raisins. I am awed, privileged to be one of the first to be told, after some two thousand years, that the *Golden Ass* is pure comedy without a serious idea in its brutish head. Aside from these revisionist interpretations, Alpha has only made plain here his basic literary interest. He is interested in genres, not history. Despite his disclaimers, he must find types, categories of things, like an old-fashioned botanist. And these genres seem to be changeless, history-less, ideas laid up in heaven manifested in things here below.

SIGMA: But if genres were true species, they could not produce offspring, as Alpha says New Comedy and romance did when they mated in Achilles Tatius' head.

KAPPA: Just my point. We are now speaking of romance and comedy as beings, as though they existed. As I've said before, I am weary of arguments about literary genres as such. Genre criticism does not illuminate literary works. It adds nothing to my perception of ancient fiction, nothing to my understanding of three works which I acknowledge are most interesting, to be told that they are all three comedies, differing essentially from other not quite so interesting works which are romances. The title of the essay promised at least one link among the three novels, aside from their being comedies, namely, that they are Antonine. But we learn nothing whatever about how they express the era that produced them, particularly the 160s. Therefore, we learn nothing about their specific powers. And I grow weary of saying this. I feel myself turning into an ass.

SIGMA: But only in a comedy, so it hardly matters.

KAPPA: No; Alpha has implied that comedy is a serious business, bitter and profound. But why? He brings to our attention the first prose comic romance, the first prose pastoral, the first picaresque novel, and this in itself is a serious, important business. At least it is to me, especially as each of the three is an accomplished work of art. And lo and behold, all three were probably written within the same decade. What qualities do they share? How do they differ from what has gone before? To both questions Alpha answers, "They are comedies." In earlier works we identified with paragons of virtue; now, along with the authors, we laugh at characters, inferior to us, suffering scrapes we ourselves would get out of. But this antique notion does not answer the questions. The three share a vision of the world.

PSI: What is the world?

KAPPA: The official world of art, power, religion, city, marriage. The civilization that says to our snarling, innocent souls, Thou must. The basic idea, if that is the word, of the *Lesbian Pastorals* is that good, natural human life, the life of Eden, is at war with this world. It is enslaved by this world, in actual fact. It is governed, shaped by property, by poachers, by the city-world that owns it, that says, "I am your possessor and parent; thou shalt not make love until you submit to my version of your gods and get married." Poor Daphnis tries to flee it at the end as though it were another pirate gang, but he can't. He can escape back to the green pastoral world only as an owner himself, where he lives happily ever after; and this is Longus' lie. He says you can have your teacake and eat it too. To make the lie stick, he fabulizes, allegorizes, everything from the start, makes it all make-believe. He sets us a fundamental problem, how to live free in a world, a world owned by city folk, that won't permit freedom, that either enslaves you or gives you specious "freedom" only after you enslave yourself to it. His unwholesome solution is what Alpha says is the noble idea of the work, that nature, Eros, Dionysus, fate, and human nature itself dictate an urbanization, an Apollonization, if you'll forgive these dreadful words, of the Dionysiac human soul. Longus' so-called Orphism is merely the key, the hocus-pocus by which he effects his escape from what he saw in the real world. No wonder he is so troubled at the beginning by a picture of nature as it is. He has to explain it away in a book to keep his sanity. And if there is comedy here, it results from our pleased acceptance of his escapist nonsolution of the problem he sets up. We can tell ourselves that only nits like Daphnis and Chloë, those unreal children in an unreal world, imagine they can live and love freely out in the pastoral hinterland of my city, and even they learn better. That's seriously amusing. And it would be bitter and grim, to use Alpha's words, if Longus didn't sink it all beneath the arts of the old verse idyll. These conventions help him sweeten the sourness he feels but dare not honestly express. The romances at least showed that the world outside home is an absolutely fantastic horror, and their priggish kids stagger out of it to go home again with genuine thanksgiving. But Longus wants his kids to rise in the world, to discover that their birthplace is the city that exploits and enslaves us all, though of course it's run by nice, godlike guys who regret having tried to kill their children; then he gives them their pastoral cake again, although they've already eaten it. A dream come true. And Longus knew very well that the world was totally dominated by the cities, their institutions, armies, religions. He knew cities were machines powered by slaves and designed to exploit the countryside everywhere, all of it bolstered by the empire, a supercity itself. The governance of the world is an issue for him; he is more insightful than the other romancers. But it was beyond him to be honest about this. He transforms the wealth-producing countryside into such an artificial, unreal dreamworld so that we, sophisticated owners and urbanites, can smile down upon it. Things aren't so bad out there after all, are they? Our slaves are happy children, happier than we are. Very funny.

SIGMA: And what of all this is characteristic of the 160s A.D.?

Chapter Nine

KAPPA: Don't you sense a world-weariness, a sardonic expectation of the worst, a haughty preciosity in these three works? The older romances don't have it, and it is a quality that makes Alpha call them comedies. The empire, with all its necessary hypocrisies, is two hundred years old. Everyone is secure and disenchanted. Pirates and witches are funny. Gore and chastity are funny. No wonder Achilles Tatius can make fun with the old romance stuff. I only wish Longus had done the same with pastoral. Lucian of Samosata is a key figure here, satirizing official Greek culture and no holds barred. But Apuleius is good enough. He's very good indeed. He knows that the world is corrupt, and he never hesitates to say so. His bourgeois are leering misers, their wives are murderous megalomaniacs—power, power, power, over all nature and the world of men, is what they desire, and who can blame them? His bandits are rather noble, honorable, and brave, as Lucius learns in their cave. His slaves are miserable wretches, his priests money-grabbing perverts, his landowners mindless or romantic sadists. In this world Lucius is a kind of hero. He seems foolish, of course, because he thinks he can learn things by direct observation and experience; whereas your genuine second-century intellectual knew that true knowledge came through mystical experience, and it was not knowledge of this world that was wanted but knowledge of another, the world of forms, true forces of destiny, where money and sex, of which everyone had all too much anyway, were unimportant. But Lucius' folly is wisdom. He *does* learn the truth about power by direct experimentation. This proves him to be an ass, of course, as we official intellectuals would expect. Everyone like us in Apuleius' time knew that magic was really effective but thought it vulgar and trivial, like the grubby world in which it worked—and we know that it is dangerous folly to dabble in this inferior world. But the ordinary world of magic and bandits and dusty towns is the only true world for Apuleius, and it takes a nice harmless, inquisitive chap like Lucius and converts him into a beast because he cannot help wanting to know it and live in it. As a result, he is enslaved by the world, even enslaved by its miserable slaves. Apuleius makes us feel that being the lowest of the low is rather heroic. He makes us know the suffering of brutalized humanity and its unquenchable aspiration to be fully human. I admire Lucius' capacity to survive the world depicted by Apuleius, and I must say that I even admire his way of triumphing over it. What a good joke for a suffering ass to join the otherworld of official religion in an official capacity, to use the otherworld of mysteries to become a great success in this one. It is of course the classic strategy of all priests. Lucius compromises with both worlds, pays his dues, and wins. This is the sardonic comedy Alpha speaks of, the sly heroism of the victim who gets the last laugh.

Psi: Do you think that Apuleius had all this consciously in mind?

Kappa: Had what in mind?

Alpha: This intention of showing the world of exploited and exploiter for what it is?

Kappa: Is that the question you had in mind, Psi?

Psi: Not quite, but we must let our friend Alpha speak.

Kappa: I was responding to Apuleius as I think a decent reader of the second century might have responded, and I was responding to Longus as a man like Lucian might have responded. The term *comedy* would not have entered their heads, nor would the idea of *idea*. But yet, why not? A man as clever as Apuleius, as he's shown to be in this very book as well as in the *Apologia*, might well have written a funny book deliberately to express his disgust with the world, its ridiculous ugliness, his sense of hopelessness about it. And to make us feel the same.

Alpha: You would agree, then, with those who feel that the book is in fact serious, autobiographical, and rhetorical, except that it's not written to warn us against curiosity and magic and to show us the true powers of Isis-Osiris but is meant to make us praise curiosity and to mock religion?

Kappa: I would agree with you that the religion at the end is part of the comedy, but I do go on to think that the comedy is part of a rhetoric. He wants to show us the moral rottenness of the affluent imperial world, with its phony religions and the systematic brutality of institutions like slavery, public trials, and shows. Why else would an ambitious, philosophical rhetor like Apuleius have written something that falls into no accepted literary genre? If these lowly Milesian-Egyptian materials aren't serving some important end, Apuleius' reputation is ruined.

Alpha: Isn't it very odd that a sophisticated rhetor would have chosen to accomplish such rhetorical tasks with an unprecedented book like the *Metamorphoses?* He had all sorts of other rhetorical means at his disposal that do not require exegesis. If we really thought he was arguing something, we'd judge him to be a lousy rhetorician because we couldn't agree about what he's arguing. Besides, the book established his reputation as a wizard, not as an angry man.

KAPPA: Not until two centuries later—Saint Augustine's time. And you should know that the roles of rhetor and magus were very close. Both were wizards with words, both could make people see and believe extraordinary things. As a magus-writer Apuleius wants to charm us with a magical murmur, as he says, to make us marvel. But he could hardly announce his intentions as a rhetor, to mock society and religion, because he would probably have found himself in deep trouble. He had to be indirect, comic. A satirist.

SIGMA: Now this concept, satire, should reconcile you two about this book, so that we can go on to some more general problems.

ALPHA: Sorry, I could agree that Apuleius' intentions were to attack the world and all its pomps if that's what his book did, as Lucian's probably did. If he had wanted to write satire, he would not have changed Lucian as he did, filling out his book with fables, funny shows, detail. And since he didn't live in Rome, he need not have feared the authorities. His book simply keeps the promises he makes in his prologue, and to charm us he of course becomes a magus-rhetor, that is to say, a poet. He makes us believe that Lucius becomes an ass and that Isis exists.

SIGMA: What is the difference between comedy and satire?

KAPPA: What do you mean, "believe"?

ALPHA: I mean something obvious in our experience. We believe the ideas in a good poem while we're reading the poem. The power of the poem puts our personal beliefs into abeyance. Apuleius makes me believe that Lucius is a donkey and that he sees Isis, though I don't otherwise believe that people can be so transformed or that Isis any longer exists.

KAPPA: You don't believe those things because you don't live in the second century.

ALPHA: Sure, people believed in witchcraft in the second and many other centuries, and witchcraft existed. And people believed in Isis, and she may have existed too. The point is, Apuleius used these beliefs as comic material. Isis is only a character in a story insofar as the writer and reader of the story are concerned. While I'm reading the story, in order to enjoy the story I believe in Isis and in what she says, as I believe in Lucius.

KAPPA: But if you were alive and awake in the second century, you would not have to put certain of your modern disbeliefs into abeyance while reading the *Golden Ass*. You would probably believe in metamorphoses by witchcraft and in the existence of Isis. You would take these things as material for genuine autobiography and rhetoric. You simply cannot ignore contemporary realities. And you take Longus seriously, as having written a most serious argument about humanity and the world; whereas a second-century reader would have seen from the very fabulistic childishness of the whole thing that it was not to be taken as a serious piece of rhetoric. But I suspect that you believe Longus was writing serious rhetoric because you believe his thesis about love; and you don't believe Apuleius was serious because you don't believe that the world is—or was—what he says it is.

ALPHA: My own beliefs—religious and political beliefs—have little to do with it. I temporarily adopt the beliefs working in the poem. Values are another matter. I think we all share Apuleius' values, and the romancers' values, a priori. Or we easily understand them without benefit of art.

SIGMA: On that cue, let me shift our attention to another kind of history. It seems to me, Alpha, that by your account, anyway, these literary forms and techniques don't change or develop much. They don't seem to have a history over the two centuries—or maybe four, from the *Argonautica*—that you've covered. At least you don't mention the influence of one work on another.

ALPHA: Later romancers cite earlier ones, and prose romance was essentially static, probably from the old "Ninus Romance" to Heliodorus' *Aethiopica*, three hundred years later.

SIGMA: But your accounts suggest that two interesting historical processes were at work. First, prose fiction seems to be appropriating forms—comedy and romance—that hitherto were manifested only on the stage. This is of enormous interest. It shows that literary experience, which had been public, at theaters and festivals, could now be private—if long prose novels suggest private reading. Second, the novelists find diverse materials to write comedies with. They don't merely translate New Comedy into prose but, like Longus, use material from the verse pastoral idylls, or, like Apuleius, use vulgar Milesian and Egyptian tales, or, like Achilles Tatius, actually use the materials of earlier novels. This must reflect a law of literary history, that form finds matter in literature more than in life. This history of literature could be called the *Metamorphoses*, and the transformations are of literary materials, not of contemporary feelings or thoughts. A metamorphosis occurs when conditions of literacy or performance change or when some of the materials become dull. You've shown that the novel appears because enough people could enjoy private reading; but what they read were only fresh versions of old stuff and perennial forms. The ridiculous remained the ridiculous, the noble remained the noble.

ALPHA: I'm not sure that "literature" is an autonomous being.

SIGMA: And you've now shown clearly how other factors work. You say that *Clitophon* and *Daphnis and Chloë* have always been categorized as romances, whereas you show that they are radically different—that they are comedies. They seem more or less the same as the romances because they share the same lexical items—lovers, marvelous events, dire perils, ideas about fortune, and so forth. They all share features of the same surface structure—they are long prose fictions made out of episodes that unfold in accordance with the rules of narrative syntax in the West. And they all show good characters, protagonists we can morally approve of, surviving the consequences of erotic passion, broadly defined, with the aid of Fortune and other divine powers, and surviving paradoxically—both surprisingly and believably. OK, so what's the difference between the comedies and the romances? It is in the deep structure, a structure that embodies the intentions of the writer and determines the response of the reader. And the deep structure results from one crucial factor. In a comedy the leading characters are inferior to our standards; in a romance they are our equals or superiors. The writer of a comedy conceives of his materials—the same materials used by a romancer, perhaps—differently, and the sufferings and triumphs of fools, shepherds, and asses generate responses that differ radically from those produced by the similar experiences of paragons.

KAPPA: And I know not whether to laugh or weep, seeing a decent skeptic transformed into a half-formed Aristotelian before my eyes.

SIGMA: I am relying on the simple facts of emotional life. We react absolutely differently to people who do worse than we would do and people who do better. I leave it to Psi to explain why this is so, but it is so.

PSI: I have no explanations not already known to you, but I have questions. What in fact are the feelings we have about fools and paragons? And are these feelings themselves the crucial factors in such literary works? In order to laugh, said Bergson, I think, we must put into abeyance all our emotions, we must think of the fool as being only a machine, not human. Bergson must have meant that we forego what Alpha calls the "serious" emotions—admiration, emulation, hope, fear, et cetera—to make room for others, perhaps scorn and love; he does not say. But we must assert that a sane human without emotions is unimaginable. Freud then says that we laugh in comedy at persons expending too much energy, or not enough, to get their jobs done, and here we can see the folly, the "franticness," as Alpha says, of characters like Clitophon and Lucius. But it seems to me that Daphnis and Chloë are as cool as the paragons of romance who react with appropriate passions to their adversities and act with the appropriate amount of energy, being aristocrats of the psyche. At any rate, we enjoy comic fools also because we have positive feelings about them; they remind us of children and of our own childhood, and we feel a benevolence, a love, even a longing for them, even as we laugh at their errors and pains. But Freud was wrong when he denied that we feel superior to comic characters. When we see them, we enjoy the feeling of being adult, even as the child enjoys feeling grown up. As adults or children we enjoy being superior to ourselves, and both comedy and romance give us this pleasure. Comedy must deflect or soothe the energy in us that judges us, that tells us we are foolish or sinful, by showing us that, after all, folly and vice are not so bad, that the fool and sinner in each of us is, after all, only a child to whom we are superior, a child to be forgiven and, in the end, rewarded with a happy marriage or even salvation. In this way comedy appeases the superego and reconciles it with folly. This is a very serious pleasure indeed, and under its cloak we can vent some of our old rages against the world of adults, the constraints and torments of the real world, and triumph over this world in a fantasy of triumphant childhood. Perhaps, for the moment, we even become superior to our superegos, which always claim to be superior to us, and we laugh. But romance gratifies the superego by giving the ego up to it. The superego knows that the result of erotic passion is what the oracle proclaimed—destined misery; and when the lovers suffer, the superego is normally gratified—especially because the lovers are us, they are for the moment our egos, we "identify" with them, and they suffer in our stead. But once more, as in comedy, the superego is tricked, and we are led to enjoy the gratification of our so-called base desires as we enjoy their denial. This is clear in the Callirrhoë story, but it is present in all. How does it work? The characters of romance are morally flawless and therefore must win the approval of the superego. And our egos join these characters because they are so admirable; and we say to our own superegos, "We are like this, we are in fact *you;* there is at last no gap between what you want and what we want." In short, whle reading the story we become all that our parents and cities wanted us to become, and we look forward to replacing our parents, piously, at the end of the story. But, *but*, we suffer, we suffer. Have pity on us, take care of us, O ye gods, O ye readers! We are in fact helpless as children adrift in this dreadful adult world, the very adult world that you, great Superego, represent in us. The characters of romance are in fact children, good children, passive and victimized, who also enjoy the adoration and the erotic lust of all who meet them. This child in us is indeed the imago recruited by the ego to win over the superego. No, I put it a better way. In a romance, the ego wins all. It allies itself with an erotic child and allies itself with a disapproving superego, and so makes a deep peace between the two. It allays the disapproval of the superego by showing how good the child is in its necessary suffering, and it gratifies the child by showing how it is superior over all other human beings. Romance is therefore also childhood triumphant over the superego, giving us the pleasure of feeling superior to our-selves. But forgive me. I have not thought about this and did not mean to speak about it. There are other factors of vital impor-tance in comedy and romance.

ALPHA: I am surprised that you speak in such general terms.

PSI: Yes, yes, it is a kind of shorthand.

KAPPA: It's what happens when you think in terms of things like Comedy and Romance.

PSI: Yes, yes, and I am surprised, Alpha, that you seem to depre-ciate the importance of psychic materials in the comedies. Do you think that when Oedipal terrors become amusing, as when the drowned husband returns to beat Clitophon and seduce his girl, that they are no longer Oedipal terrors? Or that the shameful spectacle of a young man fondling his father-in-law in bed is drained of its inherent emotional power when the young man is only Laurel and the old man Oak? Or that sadomaso-chism is not important in much comedy, or I should say aggres-sion, as with banana peels and pies in the face and beaten donkeys?

ALPHA: Of course not. I wanted to insist that it is the aesthetic context that gives specific power and meaning to these univer-sal scenes and feelings. For example, you can find the idea, "The world is unstable," in literary works of all ages and kinds; and it's true, the world *is* unstable. But, when spoken by a fool, this idea can be a funny remark; or it can be very moving when spoken by a dying lover.

PSI: But this is not enough. In comedies, threatening material, such as rivalries over girls, intercourse with animals, disem-bowelings of beloveds, is especially important because it is shown to be nonserious. We are relieved of much latent stuff when we are permitted to laugh at these things. We can con-gratulate ourselves, thinking that such are the troubles and sufferings of children, inferior beings, not us. Perhaps you think that psychoanalysis of comedy is also threatening because it might take this pleasure away from you?

ALPHA: No. Maybe. I was trying to emphasize the distinction be-tween the emotional effects of these three works and the others. And I was trying also to emphasize the differences among the three comedies. I want to go back to what Sigma was saying. You were saying that all three novels were the same in their deep structure—were comedies—though they differ in their surface structures or materials, one looking like a romance, another like a prose pastoral idyll, another like a string of dirty or serious stories. But these so-called surface structures have their own meanings and powers. The very fact that *Clitophon* is full of stock romance characters and unfolds like a romantic novel is very important because its readers would have read it while unconsciously comparing it with the romances they'd read and comedies they'd seen and would have taken comic pleasure from the contrasts and likenesses themselves. This is the kind of metamorphosis you must include in your history of literature. And the way Achilles Tatius manipulates tensions and satisfactions is perfectly familiar to any reader of long narratives in the West, then and now, but Longus' method is different and would have surprised a reader then, as it does us now. The action is a pattern imitated from the pattern of the seasons, the year. It progresses in circles, not in a line; and this childish repetitiveness, this transparent naivety, gives its own pleasure, invites us to join the narrator's sophisticated view of the story, and reflects the idea that life is cyclic, rooted in erotic nature. And if you say all surface structures are more or less accidental, you can ignore Apuleius' achievement. He found another way to solve the old question of the storyteller: how to make a good long narrative out of inherited short ones. Most inherited material is short or exists in crude, germinal form in the poet's mind. Homer found a way to do this, almost wholly subordinating separate short stories to one ongoing problem or action. The authors of the Book of Genesis found a theme. Ovid tried stringing stories together by a kind of association within a vague historical frame. Apuleius combines Homer with Ovid and produces a single action with boxed stories inside, even stories boxed within stories. He can at once capitalize on our interest in stories, all sorts of various stories, and capitalize on our interest in one ongoing headlong adventure. No wonder he was venerated by the later early novelists. By anthologizing stories in boxes inside his big frame he can appeal to all tastes, as did Chaucer and Boccaccio, and keep our emotions jumping, so that we don't respond to him exactly as we do to anyone else, even other innovators like Longus and Achilles Tatius. But even to say that all three of these comedies derive from exactly the same formal principle is misleading.

The *Lesbian Pastorals* differs radically from the others, in my opinion, because it is wholly formed by ideas. Its causes are therefore different, its author had a different conception of and use for his romantic and pastoral materials, and we are supposed to respond to it as a poetic argument. Et cetera. As Kappa said, we repeat ourselves.

SIGMA: And you've taught me what to expect when I come in on your side.

ALPHA: I agree with everything you said.

PSI: And you will not object if I do not read my notes on the different kinds of psychic materials used by these three different writers.

ALPHA: Yes, I would object.

KAPPA: We have only until five o'clock.

PSI: Yes indeed; so let me say only that I agree that the *Metamorphoses* is an autobiography of Apuleius in the special but ordinary sense that it must be a fiction of his feelings, a reflection of his personality. Alpha has already suggested the relationships among curiosity, voyeurism, sadomasochism, and misogyny in this funny book. The fear and hatred of women, derived from an exaggerated estimate of their erotic powers, which of course has other roots, can result in sadistic impulses to degrade this power to a level where it can be controlled, punished, and enjoyed, and at the same time it can result in adoration of pure, all-powerful, but sexless womankind. Sex is bestial in this book, coition is a combat, but Lucius is not a sadist. Women may be vile, but they are also nearly omnipotent. How can this be? asks Lucius. This is the question motivating his obsessive curiosity, his voyeurism, which is not ordinary passive scopophilia but carries an active desire to be a witch or goddess himself, to be the all-powerful mother able to control and debase men. His successful curiosity is rewarded as much as it is punished by his becoming an ass. It is true that he becomes less than human, masochistically enslaved by virile men, the bandits, homosexual castrati, and sadistic slave boys, and these are indeed fit punishments. But the punishment by its very fitness is a reward, and nicely so because the donkey is a very able masculine beast. Forgive me if I speak too long, but I see the story as one of gratification of a certain type of ambivalence, present in some men strongly, in all men weakly; and the pains are pleasures, as in all comedy. And his discovery that an all-seeing woman governs the universe is especially gratifying. He can keep the opinion that mortal women are adulterous, murderous, bestial, and magically powerful but also believe that only a woman, divine and chaste, can release him from their terrible thrilling power and from his own curiosity. Mother Isis therefore gives him a second birth as a man, but as a volunteer eunuch able to control men as Isis does, and Father Osiris makes him a success in the world. What could be more satisfying? Such are my notes. But I have been wanting to explore another concept, the concept of "world" introduced by Kappa.

SIGMA: Your exploration must be brief.

PSI: Of course. By "world" I do not mean the world in Kappa's sense, the world as it is or was, but the world or worlds laid down in a novel or play. This world is created by an act of perception by the artist, and it in turn creates in part our perception of the novel; and neither of these worlds, the world sketched by the writer and the world seen by the reader, is of course exactly the same as the so-called real world, nor can the world constructed by the reader as he reads be exactly the same as the world seen by the writer as he wrote. In short, there is an important aspect of narrative art that can be treated by the psychology of perception.

KAPPA: I know my world, but I don't know yours.

PSI: Exactly my point. Our perceptions are functions of our personalities and experiences.

KAPPA: I mean I don't know what you're talking about.

PSI: I mean partly the "setting" of what happens, the sense of where people are, the sense of rooms and doors and where the river is or a ditch, the gestures of people and what they look and sound like. All that strikes our senses from the page makes a world, and all we add, on our own, fills it up. I do not understand how one can describe the effects of a novel without talking about these intimate matters. The feelings, the so-called identifications, the so-called ideas one has while reading are all functions of a perceived world, a world being lived in by the hallucinating reader. And these vital matters have something to do, I think, with literary genres or forms. As I read *Clitophon*, I found myself making pictures of rooms and furniture, of flats in Alexandria, of ships and closets and country roads. Here was enough detail for me to make a world of; and I think my pictures came in large part from illustrations of nineteenth-century novels plus pictures of Pompeian art, and these sources themselves made me feel comfortable, amused by the world of the novel. I then discovered that the pictures I had made while reading the older romances were all very classical—theaters and columns and triremes and short-tunicked young Athenians—whereas to *Clitophon* I could contribute nineteenth-century images. Is this already a difference between romance and comedy? And the pastoral world of Longus is different in content, of course, but not in specificity. I could draw a map—the seacoast here, nympharium here, meadows and pastures here, the main farmhouse over there, with its garden—the thickets too. My map would be somewhat different from yours, but we could all draw maps. And it is peopled by Poussin's noble, romantic figures of academic proportions, plus some by Degas. And I do not move through this world but float above it; it is so comfortably a reverie world that I can take nothing in it seriously. But the world of Apuleius! It is so strongly drawn that we need contribute little of our own, and we would hardly disagree about the shape of the bandits' cave, the feel of dust and rock on the roads, the sound of the citizens of Hypata laughing. It is a hideous world, endurable only by an ass; yet we know that it is a world we would have to endure if we did not protect ourselves from it with comforts—with walls, wealth, and family allies. God help us if we should be lost in it as Lucius is! We can endure it while reading, because Lucius' absurd predicament and all the other marvels we hear of permit us to say, well, it is only an absurd world, not in fact so hideous, because it does not in fact exist. Apuleius creates an ugly world in order to destroy the threat of the ugly world. And this itself is a source of our delight, our comedy: to be shown clearly, more clearly than in any ancient work I know of except the Gospels, a terrible prospect which we recognize as being real and to be persuaded that it is not real. This is the realism of Apuleius and a reason why Alpha calls the comedy grim, sardonic.

KAPPA: Is there time for me to describe *my* private pictures?

PSI: But they would be more than merely private. We would find that we share important feelings about each novel because the novel has shaped our perceptions of its world, coziness, danger, exotica, and so forth; these we would feel, and we could then find the psychological meaning of these worlds and then the philosophical meanings.

SIGMA: Sufficient unto the day are the meanings thereof. Perhaps we'll find it worthwhile to meet again.

KAPPA: And perhaps not.

❧ 10 ❧
Divine
Romance

The conventions of romance seem to invite allegory. Flawless characters easily become, or seem to readers to become, emblems of virtue and embodiments of grace; if their suffering does not sufficiently engage us, their very hollowness can, like a vacuum, draw from us speculations about what the suffering means and what the characters stand for. Repeated dangers and escapes can also seem to manifest some moral or divine principle at work in the world, a beneficent principle that rewards virtue with victory over evil and death. Moreover, characters and the authors themselves often speculate about the meaning of it all, usually in moments of crisis and choice. Malevolent Fortune governs human life, they say. Wanton Eros governs human life. Isis, Artemis, Aphrodite, and the rest can protect their suffering devotees.

When such propositions are expressed repeatedly, a reader might infer that they are theses being argued by the poet through the whole design of his poem. In fact, however, play with profound ideas is itself a convention of the romances, and the ideas are not theses being argued but commonplace maxims introduced to motivate characters, explain marvelous events, ennoble speeches and scenes, and arouse in us the high pleasures of philosophical wonder. A few strong poets have of course responded wholeheartedly to the invitation offered to allegory by romance: Edmund Spenser, the authors of the *Romance of the Rose*, and the composers of the French Vulgate Cycle come to mind. And in the third and fourth centuries of our era we can see how less-adroit writers adapt the various conventions of romance to various rhetorical and didactic ends. In this last phase of Greek romance, where ideas about divinity and divine heroes abound, we must be especially careful in assessing the force of ideas as causes of prose fictions and therefore of our responses to them.

Where ideas clearly determine an author's invention of character and plot, we must define his particular didactic and rhetorical intentions. We must remember that not all "allegorical" fictions work toward the same kinds of goals with the same aesthetic methods; and we shall see how the conventions of romance can be worked into the most eccentric shapes when they do in fact become devices of rhetoric.

A clear example of the conversion of historical romance into divine rhetoric occurs in *The Confession and Prayer of Aseneth*, written in Greek by an Egyptian Jew, probably in the first or second century after Christ.[1] Its survival, not only in ten Greek manuscripts but in Slavic, Armenian, Syriac, Latin, Middle English, and other languages as well, suggests a power that may surprise a reader of my epitome.

In the first of the foreseen fat years, Joseph, friend of the Pharaoh, is traveling through Egypt to gather grain, and he stops with his entourage in Heliopolis at the house of the priest Pentephres. Pentephres' eighteen-year-old daughter Aseneth lives there in a tower of ten chambers. In one chamber are golden and silver idols; in another is rich attire; in a third is treasure; and in the remaining seven are seven attendant virgins. We are told that Aseneth looks like a Hebrew, though some details of her appearance remind modern exegetes of the Egyptian goddess Neith. Like many another heroine, Aseneth disdains men, especially the famous Joseph, who is, after all, only the son of a Canaanite shepherd. But when she actually sees Joseph entering her courtyard in a chariot drawn by four white stallions, wearing a crown resplendent with twelve jewels, she at once falls in love with him. No—"love" is not quite the word: she recognizes him to be a son of God. In this story, the convention of love at first sight and the convention of likening protagonists to deities are made to dramatize a genuine epiphany. And Joseph rejects Aseneth's adoration. He tells her somewhat mysteriously that she must pass from darkness to light, from death into life, before she can become his consort, and she withdraws for eight days. Aseneth melts her idols (giving the proceeds to the poor), burns her rich attire, dresses in black, and showers herself with cinders. On the eighth day she confesses and prays to God in the long poem that gives the romance its title. An angel appears to her, and he looks at once like the morning star and Joseph. He commands her to put on immaculate robes (in which she looks like a young man), and tells her that she will eat the bread of life, drink the cup of immortality, and be anointed with incorruptibility. Her name is no longer Aseneth but "City of Refuge," and she eats of a honeycomb given her by the angel. When Joseph arrives, she washes his feet; and with the Pharaoh's permission the couple are wed, and we are told that they will produce two children.

The writer is making a mythic story to show us how to save our souls. The ten chambers and seven virgins, the four stallions and eight days, the formulas of Joseph and the angel, must all allude to the doctrine and liturgy of a specific cult into which we, like the pagan beauty, must be initiated. To inspire us to emulate Aseneth, the writer borrows some of the basic conventions of erotic romance—disdain, love, parting, suffering, safe marriage; he omits those that do not befit his task, for example, the love of the hero (Joseph seems to be the son of a dispassionate God), and modifies the others, for example, the trials suffered by the parted lovers become the trials of conversion and initiation. The esoteric Jewish cult he is celebrating, and whether it was Essene or proto-Christian, may never be identified; but it is clear that his intention of celebrating it, and of urging us to join it, dictates his choice and modification of conventions.

The second part of the romance is an *exemplum*, a story designed to illustrate a point of doctrine or morals to be held by initiates of the cult celebrated in the first part. In the first of the seven lean years the Pharaoh's son, who had been enamored of Aseneth, pursues the married lovers into Goshen, where Joseph is presenting his bride to Jacob. Playing the stock role of the amorous barbarian or Egyptian official, the Pharaoh's heir plans to abduct the heroine. He tries to persuade Simeon and Levi to help him ambush the lovers. They refuse, but Dan and Gad agree. Alerted by Levi, Benjamin attacks the band of the Pharaoh's son, killing all fifty men and wounding the son himself. The particular Hebraic animosities all this may have reflected are obscure, but the moral point of the "romantic adventure" is clearly made when Aseneth prevents Simeon and Levi from killing their wicked brothers, Dan and Gad. Vengeance is wrong. Forgiveness is right. We pagan readers might rejoice in the moral prowess of the converted pagan Aseneth, while we Hebrews might be satisfied by the death of the Pharaoh's wounded son and especially by the Pharaoh's giving of the crown to Joseph.

Longus seems to have offered his *Pastorals* to all lovers and to the divine forces which they must know; the author of *Joseph and Aseneth* addresses his work specifically to idolatrous Egyptians and divisive Jews. Though Longus may have compounded his poem out of Orphic symbols and ideas, he does not urge us to join any cult; the author of *Aseneth* makes a myth out of the rites and doctrines of an unknown Hebraic cult in order to draw us, Gentile or Jew, into that cult. It is the particularity of this author's materials, audience, and thesis that makes his work "rhetorical" in the strict sense of the word: his romance is an argument addressed to a particular audience at a particular time on a particular issue. Thus, while both narratives are determined by ideas, they are rhetorical in very different ways. The rhetoric of the *Lesbian Pastorals* might loosely be called epideictic, that of *Aseneth* deliberative—designed to lead us to a certain opinion or action. Metaphorical categories aside, such distinctions must be made if we are to understand the bizarre last phase of ancient prose fiction.

It has long been acknowledged that Heliodorus' *Aethiopica*—composed in the 230s A.D.—is the apogee of ancient romance. Pantagruel may have fallen asleep over it, but Sidney and Cervantes emulated it, and Racine claimed that he knew it by heart.[2] These tough poets admired Heliodorus' complex narrative strategy and the moving triumphs of his clever heroine. Must we add that his characters and narrative are shaped by the ideas about divinity and human destiny that abound in the text? Does a religious or moral thesis gather conventions into a poetic argument that persuades us to join a particular cult? Several episodes and many speeches, as well as the narrative method of Heliodorus' masterpiece, tempt us to answer these dismal questions in the affirmative. On the other hand, the whole work seems to derive from another principle of invention—the desire to make an affecting, beautiful story with profound but imprecise implications about wisdom and destiny. Clearly the *Aethiopica* is not wholly caused by its ideas, as *Aseneth* and *Daphnis* are; yet it leads us toward some rather specific opinions about God, religion, and morals.

If the *Aethiopica* is designed to celebrate or augment a particular cult, the cult would be that of Helios; so I must attempt a sketch of that before discussing the romance itself. Heliodorus signs his work "Heliodorus, son of Theodosius, a Phoenician of Emesa, of the line of descendants of the Sun."[3] To claim descent from Helios is no crazy boast when it means that the claimant belongs to the priestly clan serving the Temple of the Sun at Emesa. This Syrio-Phoenician city had recently been refounded by Caracalla (211–17) in honor of his powerful Syrian mother, the dowager Empress Julia Domna; and in 218 a young priest of that temple (reputedly the son of the murdered Caracalla) had suddenly been elevated to the imperial throne. He took the name of his god, becoming Elagabalus (Heliogabalus), focused imperial religion on the Syrian sun cult, married the Moon, and pursued the psychotic debaucheries that led to his murder in 222. The excesses of Elagabalus did no justice to the god served by his sacerdotal kinsman, Heliodorus, and Helios survived them to remain the principal deity of the empire in the third century. Even before the Greeks had tenuously identified him with Apollo, they had sworn by Helios because he witnesses everything that need not be concealed.[4] For Chaldean and Persian magi he had long been (along with the Moon and other planets) a visible manifestation of invisible cosmic harmonies, and Plato of course had used him to symbolize the Chief Form of the Good. Then, through the first two centuries after Christ, he had acquired an important political role. In the first century Nero's Golden House on the Palatine was thought to signify the sunlike power and justice centered in Rome. And wherever later emperors traveled, they might be adored as the Sun, and their consorts as the Moon, as were Antoninus Pius and Faustina at Alexandria in 141. Lest this seem childish folly, we must remember that the empire was thought to be a cosmopolis established to provide mankind with the peace and justice inherent in cosmic nature itself and that the emperor was a figure of the Sun, just as the Sun was the commanding emblem of universal order. In 274 Aurelian named Helios the official guardian of the empire; and well over a century later the learned Macrobius could remark that the Sun is the summation of all the gods.[5] Helios was not, therefore, a god in any ordinary sense. He was for the most part an austere symbol of cosmic order and wisdom. His cults—if that is the proper word for so unitarian a worship—were apparently unenlivened by the rites and passions devoted to such vivid minions of Providence as Isis and Mithras, though this latter god was himself the Spirit of Light and the Soldier of the Sun. Even by Heliodorus' time the particular cults of Helios, even that notorious one at Emesa, would have been absorbed by the universal, official cult of the emperor.

We find no emperor worship and no empire in Heliodorus.

Like other romances, the *Aethiopica* is set in the misty period of Persian hegemony over the East, and it culminates in Ethiopia, the Land of the Sun outside the confines of the later empire, where naked black sages, the purest devotees of Helios, defy their priestly king.[6] The specific cults described in the story—those practiced at Delphi, Memphis, and in Ethiopia itself—are judged to be inferior to a cultless life devoted to the acquisition of wisdom (*sophia*). On the other hand, allusions to Helios and to "the god" abound; and important episodes, especially the final ones, are contrived to direct our thoughts to the idea of destiny and to the pure religion that Helios seems to represent. Still, exactly what Heliodorus means by "Helios" remains vague, and he certainly does not celebrate any specific cult.[7] He wholeheartedly adopts the conventions of romance, refines and disposes them as they had not been before, and artfully enriches the familiar serious emotions with genuine sentiments concerning Providence and the moral life.

Heliodorus is the first novelist to devise a plot compounded of several lines of action and is the first to begin *in medias res*. Epitomizers therefore do him no justice when they straighten out his story by beginning with the birth of the white-skinned heroine to the black-skinned queen of Ethiopia and by then going on to relate how she gives the infant with tokens to a young Ethiopian sage, who in turn gives it to a Greek priest of Delphian Apollo named Charicles, who names the girl Chariclea; how at Delphi Chariclea falls in love with Theagenes and how their elopement is engineered by a witty, self-exiled priest of Isis named Calasiris, who sails with them to Egypt, where the lovers are captured by bandits headed by Calasiris' elder son. In fact the plot begins with this captivity; neither Chariclea nor the reader learns the circumstances of her birth until book 4 (there are ten books in all), and over a third of the whole is narrated as a flashback by the fatherly sage, Calasiris, to a young Greek named Cnemon, whose story is interwoven with those of Calasiris and the lovers. We must conform our discussion to Heliodorus' narrative because his method may in itself stimulate inferences about destiny and knowledge: though we suffer our lives in serial time, we can discover, like Heliodorus' characters, that what has happened in the past and is happening now is the product of a future that has always existed. And even if we make *in Eg.? war for priesthood?*

no such inferences, our emotional response to the story is in large part shaped by its narrative art.

The plot moves through five phases. In the first phase (bks. 1–2. 21) Chariclea and Theagenes are captured by brigands in the Delta, meet Cnemon, and escape. In the second (2. 22–5. 32) their lives up to the moment of their capture are described to Cnemon by Calasiris, whose intrigues, guided by his *sophia*, have brought them to Egypt. We are thus precisely halfway through the whole novel when we fully understand the circumstances that lead up to the initial scene of the book. The third phase (6. 1–7. 11) resolves the stories of Cnemon (who has been pursuing a villainous slave girl named Thisbe) and of Calasiris (who dies after seeing his brigand son reestablished in the priesthood of Isis). In the fourth phase (7. 12–8. 14) the betrothed lovers are embroiled in the intrigues of Arsace, lustful wife of the Persian satrap. And in the last phase (8. 15 ff.) the lovers are captured by the Ethiopians, who take them as human sacrifices to the Land of the Sun, where an elaborate sequence of recognitions and reversals fulfills the destiny enunciated by an oracle at the end of book 2.

Achilles Tatius and Longus had begun with charming paintings. Heliodorus begins with a ghastly *tableau vivant*. On a Delta beach littered with food and corpses sits a magnificent girl holding the wounded body of a magnificent boy. What has happened? Who are they? The girl is dressed as Artemis, so we know that she must be taken seriously, though we recall that it was Isis, Cybele, Astarte, and Aphrodite, not Artemis, who were associated with wounded lovers. But don't we already know that we are reading a scene typical of stories of erotic suffering, somehow displaced from the middle to the beginning of the book, and that in such stories theological precision is not customary? Moreover, we are gazing down on the scene along with the conventional bandits, who do not by convention provide a point of view; and if we expect an authorial *ekphrasis* of the scene, we are disappointed, because here is a poet who dramatizes everything. For example, it is the brigands' shadows falling across her vision that rouse the girl from a reverie which goes unreported. It is through direct discourse—after the awesome pair have been secured in the bandits' island fortress and put under the care of another captive, Cnemon—that we learn that their names are Chariclea (Glorious Grace) and Theagenes (Goddess-begotten), that they are affianced, that their patron is Helios Apollo, and that Chariclea now hopes only to die, "taking with me my chastity as a noble winding-sheet." A predictable development of this stale sentiment and predicament is prevented by the unfolding of Cnemon's story (a version of the Hippolytus-Phaedra tale), which is itself developed in a complex way: part of it Cnemon tells himself, part he reports as it was told to him, part he reserves for a later climax. This thrice-boxed novella is also dramatized with many scenes, dialogue, allusions to Hesiod and Homer, and so on, and it causes events in the main action. Already Heliodorus has shown himself to be a masterful innovator, and his plot is as technically complicated as any hitherto designed by a Western writer, if not more so.

He squeezes critiques of the cults from the old conventions. For example, he converts the stock amorous bandit chief, Thyamis, into an exiled priest of Isis who dreams that the goddess, in a temple strewn with the bleeding carcasses of sacrificed animals, offers him a maiden; and ruled by the "promptings of his passion," Thyamis imagines that she is Chariclea. Next morning he hypocritically tells his followers that, "since we of the family of prophets disdain the popular Aphrodite, it is not for purposes of enjoyment, but to provide offspring for the succession [to the priesthood of Isis at Memphis] that I have resolved to have this woman for myself." What are we to think of a cult whose rites are barbaric and whose chief priest is a brigand, driven from his office by his younger brother? Heliodorus does not say; he makes the conventions lead us to the proper inferences. But our attention is always focused on the story; opinions about religion may emerge from a situation, but they do not seem to determine it.

Heliodorus often seems bemused by his conventions. Note how he handles the episode of death and resurrection, accompanied by the wonderfully paradoxical reversal of fortune. Maddened by his defeat by other brigands, and cursing Isis, Thyamis rushes into the prison cave and kills his fair captive, Chariclea. Theagenes and Cnemon stumble on the female corpse in the darkness, and Theagenes, throwing himself upon it, wails, "O God-sent disaster!" But when Chariclea appears, ghostlike, from the depths of the grotto, and the corpse is discovered to be that of the Greek slave girl whom Cnemon has been pursuing for

shifting identity

months, joyous Theagenes, like the reader, complains, "How was it likely, Cnemon, that a woman from the middle of Greece should be transported into a remote corner of Egypt, as though by a stage-machine?" Cnemon's answer is in fact quite plausible, given what we already know of his story; but the question exemplifies the writer's detachment from the improbabilities inherent in such conventions, signals to us that we too may be self-conscious while enjoying the story, and suggests that the improbabilities of drama exceed those to be found in this narrative. Still, Heliodorus' use of stage drama will become more complicated than this, and he will lead us to infer that the paradoxes of a serious plot are not unlike those of destiny itself. But for now— and as usual—we are interested in the story. Cnemon contrives an escape plan; the lovers disguise themselves as beggars (Chariclea's Artemis regalia being concealed in a wallet slung round her loins) and disappear from view as the present-tense action is suspended.

The second phase of the plot is dominated by an old man whom Cnemon meets "roaming along the bank" of the Nile near Naucratis.

> He was continually running up and down . . . and seemed to be imparting to the river some matters preying upon his mind. His hair hung down in the priestly fashion, and was perfectly white . . . and his gown and other attire tended somewhat to the Grecian style.

No one quite like this eccentric Hellenized Egyptian had yet appeared in fiction, though Achilles Tatius' Aristophanic priest, Petronius' dubious rhetorician, Agamemnon, and the stock figures of buffoon doctor and deflating ironist may all figure in his ancestry. He is a charlatan, a wit, a suffering father, an exemplary possessor of wisdom, and an intriguer for God. He refuses to agree with Cnemon that it is a good day, explaining that "calamities have put me in this brilliant change of costume"— alluding to his name, Calasiris, which denotes the linen robe worn by Egyptian priests, one of whom he was before resigning the bishopric of Isis at Memphis because (as he explains) he could not escape passion for a woman. Now he is seeking his lost children, "born to him motherless" (they will of course turn out to be

Chariclea and Theagenes), whom he had adopted at Delphi, where he had gone to seek wisdom. And so the action begins again.

If the clergy of Isis is bloody and lustful, that of Delphian Apollo is superstitious and obtuse. We may infer this from the foolish Charicles, dean of the academy at Delphi, who believes in magic and cannot understand love.[8] He asks Calasiris' help with his beauteous daughter, Chariclea, whom he had acquired ten years earlier from a black Ethiopian, along with a silken scarf figured with inscrutable hieroglyphics. She refuses to marry Charicles' kinsman, has declared that she intends to remain a virgin of Artemis, and is now the victim of a mysterious malady. Won't Calasiris cast on her one of the famous Egyptian spells so that she may "know her own nature and be conscious of her womanhood"? Calasiris promises to do what he can. Only he understands the oracle (the professional Greeks do not), which volunteers that "Glorious Grace" and "Goddess-begotten" will one day, in the "black-faced country of the Sun," win, as prizes for their virtue, white crowns from black brows. Chariclea and Theagenes (the young Thessalonian paragon who has arrived at Delphi) are of course destined for each other. Calasiris will now become an ally of that destiny, working not through magic, which he despises, but through wisdom; and this wisdom will generate intrigues appropriate to a romantic plot—perhaps because destiny is itself like such a plot.

He works six intrigues. In the first (2. 35–4. 15) he brings Chariclea and Theagenes to recognize that their "malady" is love. Calasiris' definition of their love makes it appropriate to the emerging themes of the romance. When, during a rite, Chariclea handed Theagenes a torch (symbolic of Eros), "the soul of each... recognized its fellow and leapt toward that which deserved to belong to it"; and this conventional recognition illustrates "the divinity of the soul and its kinship with the powers on high." The godlike protagonists, who at first fell into undefined but erotic love, here become souls recognizing a nature which is love. All the same, the flattering Egyptian sage agrees with the stupid Greek priest that the couple must be afflicted by the evil eye. And he dupes the lovers themselves. To make Theagenes confess his love, he decides "to play the mountebank... and appear to divine what I already know... tossing out my hair and imitating some person possessed by a spirit." For Chariclea, "I burnt incense, and, after muttering some pretended prayers with my lips, I shook the laurel over Chariclea . . . ; then, yawning at her in a drowsy, or rather, an old-womanish fashion, at long last I ended my performance, having besmattered both myself and the girl with a fine lot of twaddle."

Destiny is assisted by comic intrigue. Put another way, Heliodorus first wants us to enjoy his story and then draw from it our inferences about destiny. Calasiris translates the message on Chariclea's silken scarf, which announces that she is the daughter of the king and queen of Ethiopia, the "black-faced land of the Sun"; and she is white because at the moment of her conception her mother was gazing at a picture of nude white Andromeda (a princess of Ethiopia) "just as Perseus was taking her down from the rock," and the black queen, fearful of being accused of adultery, had given her infant to a young sage.[9] Moved by Calasiris' ludicrous Egyptian marvels and instructed by his knowledge, Chariclea decides to "convert her malady into marriage," seek her birthplace, and flee with Theagenes and Calasiris.

A commonplace theory of knowledge, expressed in other terms by Apuleius, underlies the comic hypocrisy of Calasiris' intrigues and his role as collaborator with destiny. He explains to Cnemon that there are two kinds of knowledge, one "moving, one might say, along the ground, ministrant to images, and wallowing among corpses, addicted to simples, and relying on incantations." This does mankind no good because it is

> merely the presentation of unrealities as realities, and the disappointment of hopes; a deviser of unlawful actions and the purveyor of licentious pleasures. But the other knowledge . . . the true wisdom . . . looks upward to the heavenly regions: companion of the gods, partaker of the nature of the higher powers, it traces the motions of the stars and gleans foreknowledge of the future. Standing aloof from all our earthly evils, it devotes itself to the pursuit of what is honorable and beneficial to mankind.

Calasiris is clearly not an embodiment of the true wisdom; Heliodorus is not writing allegory but romance; still, it is his *sophia* that enables him to be a successful pander for Providence and to manipulate the powers of old Hellas at its most famous shrine. Other bits of phoney magic mark his other intrigues, which cast him in the interesting roles of Chariclea's father (she adopts him as such) and her pimp (he offers her to various pirates, setting them at loggerheads). Through Calasiris' narrative of past events Heliodorus weaves those of the ongoing present, which end in a "recognition scene, enacted as in a drama," when Chariclea and Calasiris are reunited at Naucratis with shouts of "Father!" "Daughter!"

It is now, halfway through the work, that we learn the causes of the initial tableau; and Heliodorus now adopts the "natural" order of narration. The syntax of the action thus far, which has unfolded like an enormous periodic sentence, with the present-tense action (elapsed time: two days and nights) incorporating long subordinate clauses of past action (elapsed time: eighteen years), has released information to the characters and to us in ways that may be said to imitate the involuted ways through which men discover and enact their destinies. Heliodorus' narrative technique may itself reflect acquisition of the higher wisdom. The lower wisdom is of course quite potent. On a battlefield littered with corpses, Chariclea and Calasiris observe a witch reviving her mutilated son, and, as the boy groans for a return to death, he remarks that Theagenes has been recaptured by Thyamis. Then the woman accidentally transfixes herself through the groin on an upright spear. Apuleius might have applauded the fate of this witch-mother; in Heliodorus the scene dramatizes the horrors of lower knowledge and at the same time shows how even magic can aid the wise, because the corpse's information leads the pair to Memphis, where they discover Thyamis chasing his usurping younger brother across a suburban field. It is not Isis but wise Calasiris that reconciles his warring sons. And his genius (or Heliodorus') for reconciling austere *sophia* with mundane wit and passion is rewarded by the happiness he feels when Thyamis is reestablished in Isis' priesthood. Then the delightful sage dies, his function as ally of destiny ended, leaving his "motherless children" to work out their own fates.

This they do through victories over lustful Eros and religious custom. Arsace, wife of the local Persian satrap, plays the role of Lustful Matron. Her declaration that "love recognizes but one prophecy—possession"—puts her in direct confrontation with the "prophecy" or effective knowledge of true wisdom. Smitten by Theagenes, she and her slave, Cybele (another old goddess), contrive intrigues to bring the boy to bed, raising jealous doubts in Chariclea, who at one point petulantly advises him to give in. But he passes chastely through bedroom to dungeon and out again. When Cybele accidentally poisons herself, Arsace falsely accuses Chariclea of murder; at her trial she stands mute, as though piqued, though earlier she had become vocally hysterical with envy when witnessing a happy marriage. Chariclea, like Calasiris, has too much character to be the emblem of anything, and the precise nature of the power shaping her destiny remains obscure. For example, the execution fire refuses to burn her: is the fire an agent of Helios? If so, we get no hint of it.

Theagenes attributed its cause to the benevolence of the gods,

> but Chariclea seemed to be in some doubt. "The strange manner of my preservation," she said, "points of course to some heavenly, some divine beneficence; but our being subject to so many trying misfortunes in close succession ... may show that we are pursued by divine displeasure ... unless perchance it was some miraculous act of a deity who means, while driving us into utter misery, to deliver us from a desperate plight.

Such speculation makes the miracle a little more plausible. And since the deity that is driving the lovers to misery in order to deliver them has no specific character or name, it makes us wonder whether he, or it, is not the conventional romantic plot itself. Of course, from plots replete with reversals and rescues inevitably emerge ideas about fortune and Providence. But how does Heliodorus in particular lead us to make analogies between plot and destiny, author and god? First, by downgrading the cults of old gods like Isis and Delphian Apollo, he leaves us only with an as yet nameless deity ("true wisdom," "the god") who vaguely governs character and event. But since, second, events and characters are quite familiar, we feel that it is the whole familiar plot that is, as usual, moving all things to a satisfying "destined" conclusion, and so we can identify the plot with the characterless god. Third, Heliodorus' complicated narrative technique draws attention to the mysterious workings of divine powers, as do, fourth, the many speeches about such matters delivered by the characters and by the author himself.

Earlier, in describing Calasiris' intervention between his dueling sons, Heliodorus had said:

> At this point either some divine Power or Fortune in control
> of human affairs appended a new scene to this tragic performance by introducing, as a counter-interest, the opening of
> another drama. On that day, at that moment, it suddenly
> produced Calasiris, as it were, upon the stage.

And Chariclea has remarked that "the *daimōn* diverts himself with
battling against us, as though he had made our fortunes the plot of
a drama on the stage." More frequently and explicitly than any
other novelist, Heliodorus plays on the analogy between plot and
Providence, between art—especially drama—and life. No wonder we infer that god is a romancer; Heliodorus tells us that he is.
His allusions to drama also doubtless serve to palliate some of his
improbabilities and to remind his readers of the thrilling
paradoxes they have seen enacted on the stage.

The final phase of his plot begins with the capture of the lovers
(they have escaped the clutches of Arsace) by the black Ethiopians, who by custom designate them, as the first captives in
battle, to be human sacrifices in the capital, Meroë. "This incident was like the prologue and prelude to a drama," says the
author. "Strangers, captive in chains, ... were being marched
under guard by men who ere long were to be their subjects."
Destiny is paradoxical, and the future exists, as in a well-made
play. But this does not mean that the actors are puppets. On the
contrary, one must collaborate with destiny through wisdom, and
the final phase of the action shows how Chariclea, "in her submission to the guidance of Destiny," engineers the recognitions and
reconciliations that will save her and Theagenes. When
Theagenes wonders why she does not, after their arrival at
Meroë, simply reveal her identity to her royal black parents, she
suggests that we humans are coauthors with god. "Darling," she
says,

> great affairs require great prearrangements. A plot, whose
> beginnings have been laid out by the deity with many complications, must needs be brought to its conclusion through
> detours of some length; and particularly where a great lapse
> of time has blurred the story, it is not clarified to advantage
> at one sharp stroke.

She has become, like her "father" Calasiris, an intriguer for Providence. In fact, she will, I believe, engineer a sequence of recognitions that reflect all those praised and damned by Aristotle, whose *Poetics* (especially chap. 16) she seems to have studied.

To appreciate her intrigues, we must understand her situation. She is captive in what was, with India, the most exotic of lands, on the southern rim of the world, its coasts washed by the equatorial Ocean Stream that separates the Northern Hemisphere from the unknowable antipodes. It is inhabited by barbaric black sun-worshipers whose cult is supervised by the famous Gymnosophists—naked, puritanical black sages. Heliodorus satisfies our appetite to learn about this romantic land. He invents, or adapts, a terrain and a state religion. In Meroë, the sacred capital, are meadows consecrated to the Sun, the Moon, and Dionysus, though the Gymnosophists live in the Temple of Pan. The cults involve animal and human sacrifice. Theagenes and four white stallions are to be killed at the altar of the Sun, Chariclea and four oxen at the altar of the Moon. Only virgins are suitable for these holocausts, and only married persons may officiate at them.

These details establish Chariclea's thrilling problem and depict a religion that we can see cleansed by the higher knowledge. King Hydaspes piously submits to the customs of his nation and orders the usual tests (by fire) to establish the chastity of the intended victims, both of whom pass—Chariclea being once more dressed as Artemis, her regalia now curiously "bespangled with gold-embroidered rays," as though Helios had found a place in a Greek moon goddess. The attendant Gymnosophists proclaim their hatred of all blood sacrifices. Prayer and incense, they say, conform with the spiritual nature of the god. And declaring that "the light that shines about these strangers" shows that they are "aided and protected by some higher power," they withdraw, abandoning abominable cults to the king and populace. Chariclea, swearing an ancient and catholic oath of veracity—"O Sun, founder of my line of ancestors, and ye other gods and demi-gods who are the guiding powers of my family, I call you as witnesses that I shall say nothing that is not true!"—then converts barbaric ritual into a civil trial. A Hellenic Portia, she confounds her good priest-king father by leading him to assert that only foreigners can serve as sacrifices, then by casually remarking, "Enough now, father . . . of vilifying your daughter." Daughter? Chariclea has initiated her scheme of recognitions.

For Aristotle an offhand remark may spark a satisfying recognition provided that it is probable. Chariclea's calculated remark is probable enough, but King Hydaspes only complains that it's bad theater: alluding to a recognition device that Aristotle condemned, he says that the girl has made "an appearance on the scene as by a stage device." Chariclea then tries to work the recognition through a device that Aristotle deplored: she produces tokens from her wallet—the scarf, a necklace, rings. Like good Aristotelians, her parents seem only partly convinced by these, though another deplorable sort of token—the band of black skin on Chariclea's arm—does move the queen. She is finally convinced, however, only by a kind of recognition Aristotle approved of, one by inference: this girl looks like Andromeda, reasons the queen; only my daughter looks like Andromeda; therefore. . . .

Four of Aristotle's five sorts of recognition scenes having been demonstrated, mother and daughter fall, embracing, to the earth. Chariclea has explained that complicated plots are not satisfactorily resolved by a single stroke, and Heliodorus continues to prolong his resolutions to wring last drops of apprehension and wonder from us and to dramatize the cleansing of exotic ritual by true reason. Chariclea says that Theagenes is her beloved but refuses to say outright that he is her husband (he can't be because she's a proved virgin); but she insists that she is married and can therefore officiate at his death. This confuses the poor king, who is striving to maintain barbaric custom, and gives bewildered Theagenes time to prove his prowess by outwrestling a bull and a gigantic black champion. If these deeds symbolize something, we get no hints of it; and the question whether Theagenes gripped the frenzied bull because he was "impelled by the manly spirit that was born in him, or [was] acting on the instigation of some god" goes unanswered because Heliodorus is writing a romance, not an allegory or a treatise. Still, he does ask the question, perhaps to spark in us the higher pleasures of philosophical speculation. Then the fifth—and for Aristotle the best—recognition device occurs, an event that results from the plot itself: Charicles suddenly arrives on the scene.

It is not improbable that Charicles should be searching for his abducted "daughter" and should now be a captive of the victorious Ethiopians. And his dramatic accusation that Theagenes has raped Chariclea (that is, stolen her from Delphi) results, Aristotle might say, in a satisfactory reversal of fortune, because he is acting on information which he believes to be true but which turns out to be mistaken. And this mistaken but probable speech does work the final reversals: if Chariclea and Theagenes are "married," neither is fit to be sacrificed; and Chariclea, the scheme of recognitions complete, falls with remorse at her Greek father's feet, saying that, "even though deeds in the past might be ascribed to the design or ordinance of the gods," she herself deserves punishment.

The remaining speeches, however, confirm our feeling that she deserves nothing of the sort, because they insist that the plot has been designed by Providence. First, the choric populace, though it is ignorant of the Greek language in which all this has transpired, is able to "surmise the truth"—that the lovers' lives have been ordained "by the influence of the same divine power that had designed the whole of this dramatic scene, and by whose means extreme contraries were now composed into a harmony. Joy and grief were intertwined, tears were mingled with laughter." Thus Heliodorus employs the commonplaces of the paradox and the mixed-contrary-emotions *topos* to express his commonplace theme. Second, the Gymnosophist Sisimithres reiterates Heliodorus' more specific theme—the impiety of blood sacrifice. "The gods do not welcome the sacrifice that is being prepared for them," he tells the king,

> and now, to consummate their beneficence and, as it were, bring the drama to a joyous climax, they have produced this foreign youth as the betrothed of the maiden . . . ; come, let us recognize the divine miracle that has been wrought, and become collaborators in the gods' design. Let us proceed to the holier oblations, and exclude human sacrifice for all time.

The sage has also expressed the ethics of destiny that we may infer from the plot: we must collaborate with divine design; or, as the king puts it, "since these events have been thus brought about by the direction of the gods, it would be criminal to run counter to their will." The gods he refers to are the Lord Sun and the Lady Moon, to whom he consecrates the lovers as priest and priestess; but perhaps these deities are only figures of the Providence that also spoke in the Delphic oracle, which, Chariclea now "recognized... was being fulfilled in actual fact."

The questions provoked by the *Aethiopica*—whether it is shaped primarily by a set of ideas or is designed to urge on us a particular cult—must now be answered. Its fundamental "idea" is a commonplace: that a beneficent fortune governs the lives of the virtuous. Heliodorus wholeheartedly accepted this conventional theme, as he did the other conventions of romance: the full cast of stock characters, the values of chastity and suffering love, the perils and wonderful reversals. To all these conventions he gave an unprecedented fullness. Details of setting, dress, speech, motive, all drawn from familiar life, attract us to the story itself, as does his fresh weaving of past with present action; and some of these vivifying details lead us to formulate opinions. When the Amorous Bandit Chief is the chief priest of Isis, and the Obtuse Father is the dean of Delphi, we cannot think well of their cults; but when austere sages express notions about the spiritual nature of the gods and the impiety of blood sacrifice, we must approve of them because they help to save the lovers. Is there not, however, a set of systematic references in the novel by which Heliodorus means to lead us to one god—Helios—and one set of religious and moral principles? I think there is not. Heliodorus refers to the divine by many commonplace names—*daimōn*, *to theon*, *oi theoi*, *tychē*, and so forth.[10] It is true that people swear by the Sun with remarkable frequency in the *Aethiopica* (4. 13; 8. 1, 26; 10. 11; etc.) but usually in association with other powers, as when Chariclea, on the execution pyre, "raising her hands to the quarter of the heavens where the sun sent forth his beams... cried, 'Sun and Earth and Powers that above and beneath our earth are beholders and avengers of wrongdoing in mankind, ye are witnesses to clear me of the charges brought against me.'" Still, it is Helios alone who is associated with fire that then refuses to burn her. But are the fires that had earlier destroyed Thyamis' camp, which Theagenes called "the unspeakable malignity of the divine will," and the fire from which Calasiris with chicanery had plucked a palmed amethyst, also agents of Helios? I do not think that Heliodorus works with symbols as systematically as Longus. On the other hand, he has the Ethiopians providentially capture Chariclea on the day of the summer solstice at Syene (Aswan), when "the rays of the sun stand directly overhead." Helios may indeed be the best, the chief, emblem of cosmic harmony; but it is the harmony itself that manifests the destiny which mankind seeks to know and collaborate with.

Does Heliodorus celebrate a particular moral code? We are told by the most authoritative speakers in the novel—Calasiris and the chief Gymnosophist—that we must collaborate with destiny, and the whole plot is evidence supporting this dictum. But the relationship between destiny and particular moral choice is as imprecise as the theology of the book. For example, Heliodorus says that either Fate brought Thisbe to her death, or her wickedness did it; either Chariclea's purity saved her from the pyre, or "the god" did it. Heliodorus speculates but does not decide. His code is really no more specific than the rule inscribed on the temple of Helios at Rhodes: "The first and greatest rule is to be pure and unblemished in hand and heart and to be free of an evil conscience." On the other hand, there is one human power essential for collaboration with destiny—*sophia*. Wisdom is what is possessed by Calasiris and the Gymnosophists and acquired by Chariclea. With "higher knowledge" they perceive the just destiny that governs them.

In a romance, however, this perception does not become a matter for philosophical speculation. It becomes a recognition, and it is described in the conventional terms of the paradox. For example, when Calasiris read Chariclea's hieroglyphic scarf, he "recognized and admired the wise dispensation of the gods. Filled with mingled feelings of pleasure and pain, I went through the singular experience of weeping and rejoicing at the same moment. My soul felt relaxed by the discovery of unknown facts and the conclusive explanation of the oracle" (4. 9). No tidier application of certain Aristotelian concepts of aesthetic pleasure could be found: the "relaxation" of tense appetite for knowledge brought on by surprising but probable recognition that evokes an inference about destiny. Heliodorus' readers, however, would doubtless have recognized in his references to *sophia* a concept broader than the aesthetic recognition. Particularly in the third century, one relied on wisdom to resolve the problems of life. The fundamental problem presented to anyone who can perceive that there is a cosmos is, simply, to know the cosmos. Knowing it, he might understand the past and the future, judge both, and act in the present. By this means he could control what demanded control in life—ignorance, misfortune, passion—and harmonize himself with the cosmos, which is Wisdom itself. Nobody in Heliodorus' book fully exemplifies the virtues of a third-century sage. The wise work comic intrigues and Aristotelian schemes of recognition; they suffer through ignorance and passion and misfortune, and only the gods—or the plot—bring them to happiness.

In fact, Heliodorus' most persistent emblem, or concept, of god and destiny is not Helios or wisdom but the plot of a stage play. He seems, on the one hand, to emulate the vividness and economy of drama; on the other hand, he scorns its extravagances and improbabilities and uses these to argue his own relative credibility.[11] In any case, drama provides a kind of middle term in his analogies between plot and destiny, poet and god, recognition and wisdom; and, as a middle term, it serves nicely to express the relationship between ideas and poetry in the *Aethiopica*. The idea is that destiny saves the pure, who collaborate with it through wisdom; but destiny is a plot in which we are all characters, and therefore the plot itself, the poetry, so to speak, demonstrates the truth of the idea. By being well-plotted, the novel becomes of itself an emblem of the idea. No extrinsic idea or argument need be found to explain what happens in the masterpiece; the meaning of the plot emerges from the intrinsic plot. Art can of itself express the meaning of life because life is the product of a divine art. Such notions are doubtless symptomatic of a certain preciosity, of an age where art reflects heavily on itself and poetry becomes a prime subject of poetry. In any case, here, in the last of the Greek romances, god becomes a divine comedian who works with the materials of tragedy; he is, in short, a romancer. Here, near the end of our history, as the Gymnosophist observes, the god has brought "the drama to a climactic point"—to a *lampadion dramatis*, "*lampadion*" being the "point" on the coiffure of one of the stock female masks used in comedies. Then Heliodorus, the god's collaborator, signs his work with the boast that he is a descendant of the Sun, though there is no real reason to doubt the legend that he had become a Christian bishop of witch-ridden Thessaly, where he introduced clerical celibacy.

But there is a remarkable final phase of ancient prose fiction too interesting to ignore. In it the material and technical conventions of romance, along with the psychological factors they expressed, undergo surprising transformations. This fiction is primarily oriented to the male. Its mode is biographical, and its manner is scientistic. In it the divine manifests itself in the heroic and the heroic in the divine.

This body of fiction may be introduced by a work, often called a romance, which emerged from the same temple circle at Emesa with which Heliodorus aligned himself. However, *In Honour of Apollonius of Tyana*—"the life story of a man who enjoyed divine favor"—is not a romance; it is a piece of hagiography.[12] Apollonius was a wonder-working sage who died in 97 A.D., and before her suicide in 217, the dowager empress Julia Domna commissioned the sophist Philostratus to write his biography.

Philostratus says that he is merely editing documents collected by his patroness, though at times he signals to us that he's writing fiction. In any case, he produced a kind of gospel or *praxeis*, the "acts of an apostle," celebrating the shadowy neo-Pythagorean revivalist, a son of the god Proteus, a condemner of wine, sex, fancy food and raiment, and blood sacrifice, a god-man who passed many miracles in many exotic lands and raised the dead, including himself. Philostratus insists that Apollonius' powers derived from *sophia*, the higher knowledge, not from wizardry, the lower, and that he did not manipulate destiny.

Apollonius of Tyana shares many values with the *Aethiopica*, and some have therefore suggested that both works carry forward a program of publicizing the Emesan sun cult initiated by Julia Domna some twenty years before Heliodorus wrote. And indeed Heliodorus' Calasiris can be compared with Philostratus' Apollonius. Both sages are vegetarians and teetotalers, both despise blood sacrifice, and both tolerate all sects that worship divinity with prayer and incense; both, moreover, have a sense of humor: Calasiris wittily reflects on his own chicanery, and Apollonius sardonically tells a superstitious king that he will vouch for the medicinal powers of ground rhino horn when he can truly vouch for the king's immortality. On the other hand, while both profess to despise magic yet practice it, Calasiris' practice is blatantly phoney, while Apollonius' is for real. Calasiris works, not miracles, but the intrigues demanded by the plot—because he is a character in a plot; Apollonius incessantly performs miracles and delivers opinions from the time he sets out, as a teenager, "to live the life of Pythagoras" (1. 7)—because he is the hero of a saint's life, every incident of which is designed to make us acknowledge his power and wisdom.

The differences between a romance constructed on aesthetic principles and a biography designed to honor a saint may be observed in the way each work handles an identical episode. In book 2 of the *Aethiopica* Calasiris meets Cnemon on the bank of the Nile near Naucratis. In book 4 of the *Apollonius* the wonder-worker meets a young man at the very same place. As Cnemon had played Hippolytus to his amorous stepmother, so has the young man in *Apollonius*. But Cnemon's story is a line of action woven through the first half of the romance, whereas the boy in *Apollonius* appears only in order to provoke the awesome powers of Apollonius: before the boy can tell his story, it is divined by the sage. The crowd and we are duly awestruck, and the boy is dismissed. Heliodorus may well have known the *Apollonius*; but he must have scorned many of its assumptions, and he certainly composed an entirely different kind of fiction. By submitting himself to the conventions and powers of prose romance, then developing and innovating on them, he made the most sophisticated and potent of romances. He also made a text that is meaningful without being an apologue, like *Joseph and Aseneth*, or a didactic biography, like *Apollonius*.

"Aretalogy" would be a more accurate term than "biography." All of our remaining prose narratives are "aretalogies"—honorific accounts of the marvelous deeds and opinions of extraordinary men. Two of them—those celebrating Saint Paul and Saint Peter—are didactic and divine; two others—about Apollonius of Tyre and Alexander the Great—are secular and nondidactic. The biographical mode is characteristic of the era (late second century into the fourth), which was fascinated with the wonderful "lives" or "souls" through which Wisdom manifests itself in the world —or through which, as Plutarch suggests, history conducts itself and yields its lessons.[13] All of them are, or pretend to be, compilations of eyewitness reports, letters, and speeches of great men known to history. This scientistic manner may reflect an old or a new Alexandrian concern for historiographic accuracy; it is also one of the means by which fiction, especially the fiction of marvels, lays a claim to veracity. All aretalogies are rhetorical in that they are encomia, but each of the didactic ones is shaped by a particular thesis or argument.[14] They are, in a way, documentary novels centered on males and their psychological and doctrinal problems. In this sense, and in their handling of old romance conventions, they are new.

It has long been recognized that the conventions of romance appear in many of the Greek, Latin, Coptic, and Syrian stories which, taken together, are sometimes called the Apocrypha. The writers of these uncanonized gospels, *acta*, and aretalogies could hardly have escaped, or conceived of escaping, the techniques by which characters and episodes were depicted or values and scenes made emotionally powerful. But these stories are not romances; nor are they romantic apologues like *Joseph and Aseneth*. They are histories. More exactly, they are designed to supplement, to fill out and support, the histories canonized in 327 A.D., though they were written before that event. For example, the apocryphal *acta* of John, Peter, Paul, Thomas, and others augment and ornament the marvelous deeds and recount the whole missionary careers to death of men whose lives are, after all, told but meagerly in Luke's Acts of the Apostles. The authors in effect respond to our wondering questions: What did Jesus do when he was a child? What exactly did Paul *do* in Iconium or Antioch? What was Peter's opinion of Gnosticism? Just how did Nicodemus and Joseph of Arimathea deal with the Sanhedrin after the Crucifixion? By answering such questions, the apocryphal writings provide the faithful with historical information. At the same time, these stories often argue one side of a definable doctrinal issue and, in general, console and inspire us with truths about the faith we have accepted. In short, they are rhetorical in the strict sense of the term because they argue specific issues for a specific audience of Christian believers and those willing to believe. In this way, the Apocrypha differs radically from the other "cycles" that have developed in the West. The "matters" of Troy, Thebes, Arthurian Britain, and Carolingian France all proliferated into stories that also responded to questions: How did Odysseus return home? Where was Lancelot when Arthur fought Modred? But the matter of Christ had by the fourth century generated a cycle devoted exclusively to sacred history and rhetoric. The paradoxical survival of lovers, the cults of unbelievers, the miracles of fortune, all are shown to be subject to the power of Christ, who is at once Wisdom and Wisdom's True Prophet, working through his saints. His plain truths and saving marvels may be recounted in swift, plain narrative that may seem crude to sophisticated readers of Heliodorus and Longus, whose gods are faceless riddles. His history need not be couched in Milesian tales, pastoral myths, or intricate plots.

The stories do involve, however, the conventional predicaments and passions of Hellenistic romance. The Acts of Paul, composed in Asia Minor probably between the death of Apuleius and the birth of Heliodorus, includes the story of Thecla, a comely virgin of Iconium. Paul visits Iconium in the Lucan Acts, chapter 14, but Thecla is not mentioned. In the apocryphal *acta*, Paul preaches for three days in Thecla's father's house, and Thecla listens the whole time from behind a window, which prevents her from seeing or being seen by Paul. We have been told that Paul is "a man small of stature, with a bald head and crooked legs, in a good state of body, with eyebrows meeting and nose somewhat hooked, full of friendliness; for now he appeared like a man, and now he had the face of an angel."[15] Here already are the features of the traditional icon of Paul, drawn in a "realistic" detail more characteristic of comedy and history than of romance. But despite these features, which would hardly attract an ordinary girl, a romance convention now applies: Thecla falls in love with him at first sight (rather, at first hearing, since she cannot see him); and her love reflects another modification of the conventions: it is attached not to his person or even his soul but to his ideas, especially his augmentation of the Beatitudes—"Blessed are they who have kept the flesh pure, for they shall become a temple of God; blessed are the continent, for to them will God speak; blessed are they who have wives as if they had them not. . . . Blessed are the bodies of virgins, for they shall be pleasing to God." In short, she falls in love with the very ideals of Artemis which romance heroines were obliged to modify in the face of their erotic love for a godlike young man. Still, the power of her love is familiar from the romances. It will utterly change her life, which will henceforth be centered on Paul and his preachments.

To fulfill her love, she must renounce the fiancé chosen by her family and suffer many perils to her life and values, the principal value being chastity—not the marital chastity of the romances but chastity absolute. Her mother, seeing that Thecla "is dominated by a new desire and fearful passion," warns the fiancé that he has a rival, and the young man causes Paul to be cast into prison.

Thecla visits him there by night to hear him "proclaim the mighty acts of God," and "she kissed his fetters." She is discovered, "bound with him in affection," and Paul is brought to judgment, while "Thecla rolled herself upon the place where Paul taught as he sat in prison." Thecla's passion for Paul is more vivid than that of any romance heroine for her beloved, but this can be so precisely because we know that her erotic suffering is divinely inspired and is rooted in sacred chastity. When Paul is exiled from Iconium as a sorcerer, we have that conventional phase of the action in which the "lovers" are separated. Still, Thecla's execution pyre (demanded by her outraged mother) is quenched by rain summoned by the absent Paul's prayers; and Thecla praises the Father and the Son for having saved her, "that I might see Paul." Here is no conventional speculation about the causes of these conventional miracles: the writer is adapting romance conventions precisely to teach us where true miracles come from. Thecla reencounters Paul in a grotto and accompanies him to Antioch, where a Syrian falls in love with her. When Paul refuses to protect her, she publicly rebuffs her wooer and is condemned to the arena. A local woman prays to the "God of Thecla," and Thecla survives several attacks by wild beasts, including some ravenous seals in a pool in which she baptizes herself. Everyone rejoices at this, but "Thecla yearned for Paul." She finds him in Myra. Astonished by her reappearance, Paul fears that "another temptation" is upon her. What exactly this temptation might be remains obscure, and Thecla leaves Paul to preach the word of God to her mother, to Iconium, and to many in Seleucia. In some versions of the story she finally disappears, at age ninety, miraculously sealed in a cave, to which she had fled while being pursued by young rapists.

Once more, the material conventions of romance have become devices of rhetoric. The inexplicable sudden passion for a godlike and unhistorical young man becomes adoring devotion to a historical apostle, who looks not like a god but—sometimes—like an angel. The passion challenges the codes of ordinary life, displaces suitors or fiancé, and causes flight into a world of erotic danger, against which one is protected by chastity, paradoxical good fortune, and providential miracles. But in the Acts of Paul chastity is not reserved for a husband but for God, who counts it "blessed" and a means to salvation; paradoxical reversals and miraculous escapes are worked by prayer and the power of only one God, a God who is more than a mere commanding emblem of other gods. Stock episodes like the trial and the execution, and stock characters like the rebuffed lover and choric crowd, are all molded to reflect the power of God in his saints; and suffering is consummated, not only by a return home, but by conversions, by the happiness of righteousness, and by the death that opens eternal life.[16] The story of Thecla, like those in the enormous hagiographical literature that followed it, is wholly informed by rhetorical and didactic principles. It is devised to illustrate the validity of the beatitudes about chastity preached by Paul at the outset, and the writer naturally borrowed the materials of erotic romance to make his poetic argument. His style and techniques he borrowed from the Lucan *acta* and other narratives already canonized, changing them too in ways that it would be impertinent to analyze here.

It must be remembered that the story of Thecla is only an extended episode in a narrative devoted to celebrating the powers of God in Paul. Though I chose it because of its affinities with Hellenistic romance, it shows that there are no romances in the Apocrypha—unless we also put *Joseph and Aseneth* into that category. The conversion of neutral romance conventions into divine rhetoric is at once more simple and more subtle in the so-called Romance of Clement, perhaps the most famous item in the great cycle that developed from the Matter of Christ. There are in fact two surviving versions of the text, the Clementine *Recognitions* and the Clementine *Homilies*. Both derive from a lost "basic" story, probably written by a Syrian shortly before 250, when Heliodorus was perhaps still alive. The evolution of the basic text into the surviving versions illustrates how a story can be shaped and augmented by various rhetorical and didactic intentions. In the first version, Clement, an orphaned young Roman patrician troubled by metaphysical *Angst* and repelled by the shallow doctrines of the philosophical schools, finds true wisdom in Saint Peter. Like that other true prophet, Calasiris, Peter presides over certain moving "recognitions": Clement finds and recognizes his mother, who had fled Rome on the advice of a dream, and his father, who had pursued her. This early version was apparently shaped by the writer's preference for a mystical concept of wisdom (perhaps not unlike Heliodorus') over particularistic theological doctrines. About a century later, a Christian of perhaps heretical leanings augmented this story enormously with "homilies," in which Peter instructs Clement in the author's Gnostic doctrines, and Peter's higher wisdom is dramatized by confronting it with the magic of the magus Simon, who is mentioned in Acts 8:9–24. The pro-Petrine, anti-Pauline didactic tract that survives in Greek as the Clementine *Homilies* is a rewriting of this Gnostic text. Meanwhile, sometime before 360, the *Homilies* and the basic story were transformed by a writer who eliminated some obviously heretical matters and emphasized others; and this adaptation generated the version known as the *Recognitions*, which was translated into Latin in the early fifth century by Rufinus, who eliminated the heresies of his predecessors. It was Rufinus' cleansed *Recognitions* that was widely disseminated in the West, and it is this version that I will deal with here.[17]

The basic story is subsumed, almost buried, under huge amounts of didactic material—Peter's homilies, instructions, and disputations. The homilies and discourses of the Apostles likewise surmount the narratives of their travels and deeds in the Lucan and apocryphal *acta*. But here a single action, not the Apostle's, ties up the whole mass; and it is focused on that feature of a well-made plot—the recognition and its accompanying reversal—that had long been held to be the most affecting part of a narrative. The authors of the *Recognitions* play on the double power of discovery remarked by Aristotle—the discovery of identities or hidden causes that effect a change of fortune and a catharsis of emotion and the inference that can be drawn from such discoveries about the workings of fate in human affairs. In the *Recognitions* the latter power results, not from inference, but from "proof," and it refers us, not to fate, but to the ways of Wisdom and God. The protagonist does not suffer from love but from a need to know wisdom and his parents, and this double need, rather than marriage or martyrdom, is satisfied by Peter and God. It is a new kind of romance—an active male quest for knowledge and power, not a fated suffering focused on an active female. As such, it prefigures certain medieval romances, especially those associated with the Grail material, which itself derives from the apocryphal Cycle of Christ.

Stimulated by a sermon of Barnabas in Rome, the despondent young Clement seeks out Peter in Palestine and finds him on the eve of his great confrontation with Simon Magus, a potent sorcerer and shape-shifter who claims to be a god. Peter explains Christian solutions of the ancient problems adumbrated by Heliodorus. For example, the Wisdom men seek is Christ, who is also the one True Prophet. And to explain Christ, Peter must expound Creation and the history of revelation—an exposition that consumes seven times the number of words consumed by Clement's description of his predicament and search. Peter's subsequent debate with Simon dramatizes the conflicts between wisdom and magic, between higher and lower knowledge, that obsessed the age. Already we can understand that the theory, so to speak, of this text justifies the inclusion of so much didactic material: knowledge itself, as the title suggests, is the primary way to salvation. Like Heliodorus, even like Longus, the writer of the *Recognitions* is more than a little touched by Gnosticism. But Simon's false knowledge, which he has learned in Egypt, is as powerful and perhaps more beguiling than Peter's. Why should this be? Because the two knowledges, and the two prophets, represent one of the syzygies—those pairs of opposites (hot/cold, same/different)—whose conflict moves the universe. This means that Simon must triumph before Peter can defeat him. After lengthy instruction, and after witnessing the wonderful moot debate between the prophets, Clement recognizes Peter's truths. He puts his recognition in these terms:

> For I have you [Peter] alone as the object of all my affections, instead of father and mother and brethren; but above all this, is the fact that you alone are the cause of my salvation and knowledge of the truth ... and I am afraid to be without you, by whose solid presence all effeminacy, however irrational it be, is put to shame. [7. 5]

Clement has given Peter the love of a very young son; and through love for this father come salvation, wisdom, and masculinity. As it had in the *Argonautica*, the psyche of the male here becomes material for "romance."

But Clement must also recognize his true parents if he is to know and possess all that the story promises him. The mother is easy. A beggar woman tells Peter that she had once fled Rome because her husband's brother was enamored of her, though she had invented a dream as an excuse for her flight. Peter's questions reveal her identity; and Clement, "immediately bathed in tears, fell upon [his] mother, who had fallen down, and began to kiss her" (7. 23). Having escaped incest by such drastic means, the mother had maintained her chastity throughout her wanderings, and she is now rewarded with baptism. This incident, like almost all the others, is made to redound to the credit of Peter, whom all adore. We must remember that the *Recognitions* is a curious kind of *acta* of Peter fused with a kind of autobiographical aretalogy of Saint Clement of Rome.

The recognition of Clement's father, as we might expect, is much more complicated, both psychologically and aesthetically. It informs the last third of the whole work, and it turns on a fascinating identification of Clement's father with evil Simon. The father, Faustinianus, first appears on the scene as an "old workman" and soon engages Peter in a debate not unlike that of Simon. Faustinianus believes that all things happen either through chance or through "genesis" or "nativity"—that is, fate, as determined by birth and the stars. It is appropriate that a natural father adopt such views and that a spiritual father like Peter should argue the power of God and free will against the old gods and destiny. But the old man stands firm, finally, on one piece of personal evidence: his own wife, he says, had fled with one of her slaves because her horoscope had determined her to be a whore and to die by water. This of course leads to the culminating recognitions—mother is not a whore and dad can become (like Clement and his lost twin brothers) a disciple of the spiritual father. But we are not done with the old father. He needs further cleansing. Astonishingly, he one day appears to the group wearing the face of Simon. That is, the magician has cast his own face onto Faustinianus because, we learn, he wishes to punish him for defecting to Peter (he had been a follower of the sorcerer) and to trick the authorities into arresting him in lieu of himself. Peter works a counterintrigue. He sends Faustinianus to Antioch, where he stands before the populace as Simon and confesses to his (Simon's) wickedness. Thus Peter deceives the deceiver and reconciles the male generations: "As God has restored your sons to you, their father," he tells Faustinianus, "so also your sons restore their father to God." Faustinianus is then baptized and achieves a status not unlike that of Peter: "the whole city received him as an angel, and paid him no less honour than they did to the apostle."

The aesthetic powers of the recognition are here put into the service of rhetorical and didactic intentions: to distinguish true Christian wisdom from its mighty Egyptian opposite, to teach Christian views of most of the religious, metaphysical, and ethical issues of the era, to offer an "Acts of Peter"—perhaps to counterbalance the Lucan Acts, which is so much devoted (after chap. 7) to the wrath of Paul, and to celebrate the gentle prowess of the first bishop of Rome. For erotic love between boy and girl, authors substitute the love of filial disciple for fatherly master. These fundamental changes rule out most of the material conventions of Greek romance; the stock scenes of the trial and the recognition remain, but the typical scene of the Lucan and apocryphal *acta*—the scene built upon the delivery of a homily, consequent confrontation with authorities, and banishment— dominates the narrative. For the female psychology of erotic temptation and moral triumph they substitute the male psychology of confrontation and reconciliation with the father. Chariclea, seeking her home, found three fathers—a Greek, an Egyptian, and her natural black Ethiopian one—among whom there was no serious conflict. Clement, seeking wisdom, also found three fathers—Peter, his own inferior Faustinianus, and the evil power associated with Simon and Faustinianus; the conflicts among these fathers are reconciled by one of them, Peter, through the power of the one true Father. And it is to the vicarage of this Father that Clement succeeds his spiritual father, Peter, as Papa of Rome.

Clement's experience seems to reflect that of boys who early in life believe that their fathers are wonder-workers or gods, discover that they are disappointingly human "old workmen" or wicked power-seekers who imagine that mother is erotic; they find surrogate fathers who conform to their earlier ideals and then successfully reestablish a single father image whom they can emulate, serve, and replace. It is an experience common enough to give the basic story of the *Recognitions* a certain power; and through such power our doctrines are generated and take on emotional life. But the father can also be a hero who makes his discoveries and writes his autobiography. The anonymous author of the famous *Apollonius of Tyre*, for example, claims that he has worked from a copy of Apollonius' autobiography in his own library, the other copy being in the library at Ephesus. He is thus like many a medieval author who claims that his source is a "book." The origins of the story are in fact obscure; it was perhaps first composed in Greek, but its earliest versions are Latin, of the late fourth century, and it survived in Danish, Dutch, Hungarian, Old French, Old English, Spanish, and Slavic versions, through to Shakespeare's *Pericles* and Eliot's *Marina*. [18] In any case, if Apollonius described his early life, his romancer does not. The story begins with Antiochus, king of Antioch, who is in love with and sleeps with his own daughter. To discourage suitors, Antiochus has devised a riddle: "I am borne along by crime; I devour my mother's flesh; I seek my brother, my mother's husband, and the son of my wife, and I do not find them." The answer to this riddle is Antiochus himself, and it suggests that the roots of his incest are complicated. The suitor who fails to solve it is decapitated. Apollonius, prince of neighboring Tyre, immediately finds the answer, as though he naturally knew about fathers being like privileged brothers who marry and devour mothers. Still, he is apparently confused when the obviously correct answer causes Antiochus—who after all must have composed the riddle in order to be found out—to send him back to Tyre to think of a better one. Back home, Apollonius correctly realizes that Antiochus will try to kill him. He flees to Tarsus, where famine reigns.

Apollonius relieves this famine by a munificent gift of grain, which demonstrates one of the most admirable kingly or fatherly virtues—generosity. He is also told that Antiochus has put a price on his head because he, Apollonius, "wanted to take the place of a father." A conventional tempest, described in Vergilian terms, blows him to Cyrenaica, where he comes ashore a ruined stranger. His beauty, his defeat of the local king in a ball game in the baths, and his skill with the harp—like Tristan's in Cornwall—soon win the heart of the king, then that of the king's daughter, who persuades her father to appoint him her tutor. Wiser than Antiochus, the king at length recognizes, helped by a riddling letter from his daughter, that the girl loves her tutor, and he consents to their marriage. When the bride is six months pregnant, news arrives that Antiochus and his daughter have been struck dead, in bed, by lightning and that for some reason (because he solved the riddle?) Apollonius is the heir to Antioch. The couple take ship for Antioch or Tyre, but at sea the bride apparently dies (the afterbirth won't come). Apollonius grieves, we are told, because the girl's father will grieve. He secures her corpse in a coffin, with money for the journey, and sets it adrift. It comes ashore on a beach near Ephesus, where a strolling doctor (like the Ephesian doctor in Xenophon) and his apt student revive her, whereupon she becomes a chaste priestess of Ephesian Artemis. Apollonius sails on to Tarsus, where he leaves his infant daughter with friends, and goes on to Egypt, vowing not to cut his hair or nails until he can give away the girl in marriage.

The story now becomes, for a while, the daughter's, whose name is Tarsia. But her adventures are reduced primarily to one of the trials suffered by romance heroines: she is incarcerated in a brothel. She had become so beautiful that her stepmother tried to kill her; but pirates sold her to a brothel-keeper in Mytilene. Her story, set within that of her father, will come to an end when her father recognizes her; and given her situation, and the earlier story of Antiochus, we will not be entirely surprised when her father becomes her final customer. Her first customer is the noble Athenagoras, prince of Mytilene. He is so moved by the story of her life that he dissolves into tears, gives her gold, and leaves her untouched. When the next man in line asks how it was, Athenagoras replies ironically that "it couldn't have been better. I was actually moved to tears." So is the next man. Tarsia remains a virgin and makes a fortune with her affecting tale. When Apollonius is blown by a storm to Mytilene, we know that Tarsia's ploy will be worked on him. And this recognition will be especially moving, because Apollonius now believes that his daughter is dead, and he is in despair. But the whole romance, though it is so different from any we have encountered, relies as heavily as the others on the factor of "recognition," from Apollonius' recognition of Antiochus' secret crime to those, involving the same powerful material, that we will now enjoy.

First, Athenagoras recognizes that Tarsia is Apollonius' daughter after conversing with the melancholy Tyrian's slaves. He then engineers a recognition scene that would have made Chariclea blush with envy. He descends into the ship's hold, where Apollonius, hairy and mute, has buried himself, and offers to comfort him with a girl whose sad story will cure any depression. Tarsia goes down into the bilge, sings her story of loss and betrayal.

Apollonius is too despondent to understand it, though the story, which has been so profitably seductive, is father's too. She returns and entertains him with eleven riddles, all of which he solves, but none of them trigger the recognition that other riddles have triggered in this story. Finally, Tarsia tries to drag him away bodily. He shoves her down and bloodies her nose. Meanwhile, Athenagoras, like us, paces the quay, awaiting the recognition. Will the daughter be driven to use sex to comfort her father? Will he be driven to the sin of his putative father-in-law, Antiochus, from whom he inherited Antioch? When the relationship between man and whore coincides with that between father and daughter, the tensions always sought by romances to vivify the paradoxical recognition and reversal become especially pleasing. The recognition finally comes when Tarsia abandons art and weeps out her story in such prosaic detail that even her father cannot avoid seeing that this beautiful prostitute is his daughter. "You are my only hope!" he cries. "You are the light of my eyes! Now may this city perish!" Recognitions always enlighten; but we may understand Apollonius' uncharacteristic and unconventional curse on the city as expressing an anger against the place where he and his daughter have suffered such dreadful temptations. In fact, the brothel-keeper does perish. But Apollonius gives Tarsia as a bride to her first customer, Athenagoras. And on the advice of a dream he sails to Ephesus, recognizes his wife in the person of the chief priestess of Artemis, and presides over the execution of the wicked stepmother at Tarsus. He rules over both Tyre and Antioch until he is seventy-four, when, having written his autobiography, he dies.

With *Apollonius* we have sailed into a new era. True, like some earlier romances, it seems to be generated by a kernel fantasy. That is, we cannot avoid noticing, when we ask questions about its unifying principles, that all of its principal episodes touch upon a single basic experience—the desire older men feel for younger women and vice versa. Even my crude epitome of the work shows that this formulation of the kernel fantasy is simplistic; and an analysis of the art of the story could show how we admire Apollonius and Tarsia in contrast with the Antiochan couple and how the potent tensions inherent in the material of incest are aroused and relieved. It is also true that this art in part derives from some conventions of the ancient heroic fiction whose best monuments are the *Odyssey* and the *Aeneid*, combined with some exploited by older Hellenistic romance.

Still, the basic predicaments and the protagonist of *Apollonius* signal a new era. A handsome (but ungodlike) prince, generous, wise, and adroit, is ruined by his perception of a dreadful secret; after his marriage, he loses both wife and daughter, only to recognize them again, "revived" from the dead, and all live happily. Erotic love gives way to one of its perverse forms. And the lover becomes a parent; the "point of view" is that of the father and his predicaments. The lover-father's aretalogy offers us no moral lessons, no recognition of the true nature of wisdom or the divine. In fact, the gods are now absent, save the one god whom Apollonius very occasionally solicits. They make nothing happen, and they are not subjects of speculation. This secularism, and many of the other features of *Apollonius*, are characteristic of the strongest line of fiction in the medieval period, whether the fiction be tragedy, comedy, or romance. Divine rhetoric, as represented by the Clementine *Recognitions* and the saints' lives, could only rarely transform inherited materials into masterworks like the thirteenth-century Vulgate Cycle and its satellite narratives, and it did so with the aid of material drawn from the Apocrypha.

Our final work also adumbrates later fiction. The *Life of Alexander* is the aretalogical *acta* of the first world king, compiled by a Hellene nearly six hundred years after Alexander died at Babylon. For centuries the work was attributed to Callisthenes, nephew of Alexander's tutor, Aristotle. Whoever he was, his hero's cunning, wisdom, prowess, and ambition, as well as his "tragic fall," brought on by fortune and betrayal, provided conventions with which regal heroes could be celebrated and lamented in later periods. His intention is not, like Xenophon with his *Cyropaedia*, to teach but to arouse sublime awe for a cosmic yet historical man. To do this he does not eschew the fabulous or avoid the psychological materials that make his semidivine hero like one of us.[19]

Alexander's father was not, Pseudo-Callisthenes tells us, Philip of Macedon but Nectanebus II, the last pre-Ptolemaic king of Egypt, that country where Wisdom measured the earth and empowered man's reason with the art of magic. Nectanebus could repel armies with his magic but finally abandoned his throne in the face of destiny, put on a priestly *calasirus*, set up shop in Macedonian Pella, and seduced Queen Olympias (Philip being away at war) by changing his shape into that of the god Ammon. Nectanebus' motives are wholly erotic; but in a way he *is* Ammon, and when he tells the queen that their son is destined to be a godlike king of the world, he prophesies truly. Thus Callisthenes claims Alexander for the Egyptians and attributes parentage to a man more potent than the father (as in many "myths of the birth of a hero"). Throughout his *Life*, Alexander will in fact feel himself to be the son of a god, of a royal Egyptian wizard, and of Philip, and he will act accordingly.

In his first sentence Callisthenes had said that magic is "the power, the might of reason," collapsing the distinction between higher and lower knowledge. Alexander's birth illustrates this shocking doctrine: Nectanebus rationally persuades the laboring Olympias to stay off the birthing stool until the best hour—as divined by astrology—arrives, whereupon Alexander arrives with it. Alexander himself says (3. 1) that it is Reason that permits the Greeks to overcome the barbarians, but his own career is a marvel caused by the divinity in him. Even as a child he thinks of rulership, because he is "taught by some god," though he excels in martial exercises through personal strength. At about age thirteen he kills his father, Nectanebus: as the astrologer is teaching the lad his arts (at the boy's request), Alexander suddenly throws him against a rock, because, "not understanding the matters of earth, you seek to know heaven." After the dying Nectanebus explains that he is his father, Alexander grieves but feels blameless, because even the astrologer has said that these matters are fated. His *enfances* end when he "reconciled his parents"—angry Philip with Olympias—"so that all the Macedonians marvelled at him." Or perhaps they end when Alexander allows his dying father, Philip, to kill the man who had fatally wounded him and attempted to rape Olympias. At any rate, once his two human fathers are dead, Alexander may set out to conquer the world.

Callisthenes is selecting and shaping his materials—anecdotes, legends, sayings—in accordance with an idea about the collaboration of reason and divinity in a destined man. The inspired founding and reasoned planning of Alexandria conform with this theme, as does Alexander's conquest of Tyre and his protracted struggle with Darius the Persian, which occupies the middle portion of the biography. Letters, battles, feats of cunning, oracles and dreams, and descriptions of exotic natural phenomena carry us through Alexander's return, after conquering Hellas, to Asia, where his divine wrath is mixed with reasoned mercy as he embraces his dying enemy, Darius, whose treacherous assassins he ultimately tricks into surrendering by swearing a false oath on his mother's safety. In India, whose bizarre wonders he describes in letters to Aristotle, he learns from an oracular Sun-tree that he too must die by the hands of his friends. He immediately asks the adjacent Moon-tree whether he will ever again embrace his mother. No, says the Moon, he must die in Babylon. But it is through his mother that he dies. Olympias writes that she is beset by one Antipater back home in Hellas; and when Alexander summons the man to Babylon, Antipater contrives to poison him. After describing his excruciating death quite vividly, Callisthenes gives a rather confused account of his politically potent last will. As he dies, Alexander prays that he may become the third mortal—after Heracles and Dionysus—to become immortal. This prayer is apparently answered when Zeus's eagle is seen to carry a newly fallen star back into the heavens. But the aretalogy concludes with a statistical account of the facts of mortality: "He was born in the month of Tybi [Capricorn] at the rising of the new moon, and he died in Pharmouthion [Ares] the fourth day at sunset."

Pseudo-Callisthenes has brought us back to Alexandria. Here again are the Alexandrian yearning for historical authenticity, the yearning for "Egyptian" marvels, the yearning for "Greek" reason. Here too, and still, are the universal human constants of the Oedipal project, in which a hero succeeds through killing, saving, reconciling, or adopting various fathers. Jason had only barely succeeded; Apollonius, Clement, and Alexander have less trouble in an era of world gods and world kings; while heroes like Roland, Arthur, and Percival will have more trouble in theirs. The era also provides commonplace notions about destiny, magic, and divinity, with which the hero is seen to accomplish his identity; and the authors always, of course, have at their disposal a great fund of conventions—technical and material—of great antiquity to rouse us to wonder, tears, and the passions that we can enjoy. I need not list these conventions or retrace the almost innumerable ways ancient novelists brought their readers to various kinds of satisfaction. The reader himself can calculate the constants and the variables, the art and the ideas, that have come to light, I hope, in this inquiry into the novels written before the rise of the novel.

Notes

CHAPTER ONE

1. I accept the dates accepted by Ben E. Perry, *The Ancient Romances* (Berkeley: University of California Press, 1967), p. 350.

2. Latin *novellus*, a diminutive of *novus* ("new" or "extraordinary"), yielded the late Latin substantive *novella*, an "addition to a legal code." This in turn yielded the French *nouvelle* and Italian *novella*—a diminutive story whose material is fresh, untraditional, and whose resolution is extraordinarily surprising. The English noun *novel*, which could denote any sort of novelty, became in the eighteenth century our specifically literary term, though the language had, since the mid-sixteenth century, possessed the Continental terms which survived in Milton's "a mere amatorious novel" and Dryden's "the trifling novels which Ariosto and others have inserted into their poems." *Romanz*, appearing as a noun before 1140, denotes a long story whose materials are traditional, being drawn specifically from the historical matter of Rome (i.e., from Vergil, Statius, et al.) and told in French octosyllabic couplets or monorhymed stanzas. Very soon the term could signify any long story versified in any vernacular; but the story's matter was always purportedly inherited, not "novel," and therefore "true." This claim to authoritative historicity did not of course protect romances from being castigated on moral or aesthetic grounds in every age and language, but the term "novel" offered even less support to the fictionalist's inveterate claim to veracity. Thus the eighteenth-century English novelists called their fictions "histories"—accurate accounts of hitherto unrecorded events—until, by the end of the century, "novel" made its own claim to realism, and "romance" was banished to the title pages of novels like *The Monk*, to fantasy, or to the moonlit historicism of Hawthorne. One of the periodic shifts in the Western sense of realism is reflected in the fact that, whereas romances had been aesthetically credible because they were traditional, novels were credible because they were not.

3. From the preface to *The Loves of Chaereas and Callirrhoë* (London, 1764), the first English translation of Chariton's first-century romance. The anonymous "editor" suggests that the tale should be called a history

because it has "much the appearance of a true story . . . containing a great variety of incidents, all well prepared; and very artfully interwoven; with scarce any thing improbable and improper; and the whole drawn up with a gravity of stile becoming an historian." This is accurate praise of Chariton, and only a few years later the "editor" might have called him a novelist too, though not precisely in the sense suggested by Clara Reeve in 1785:

> The Novel is a picture of real life and manners, and of the times in which it is written. . . . The Novel gives a familiar relation of such things, as pass every day before our eyes, such as may happen to our friend, or to ourselves; and the perfection of it, is to represent every scene, in so easy and natural a manner, and to make them appear so probable, as to deceive us into a persuasion (at least while we are reading) that all is real, until we are affected by the joys or distresses of the persons in the story, as if they were our own.

The novel's power over our fantasies is therefore stronger than that of the romance, "which treats of fabulous persons and things" and "in lofty and elevated language, describes what never happened nor is likely to happen" (Clara Reeve, *The Progress of Romance through Times, Countries, and Manners*).

4. Longus, "The Love Romances of Parthenius," in *Daphnis and Chloe*, trans. Samuel Gaselee (Loeb Classical Library, 1916), p. 257.

5. Northrop Frye, *Anatomy of Criticism: Four Essays* (Princeton, N.J.: Princeton University Press, 1957) p. 383. In this influential book, "romance" also reflects the ideals of the ruling social or intellectual class; it is a human and historical *mythos* whose essential plot element is adventure, "which means that romance is naturally a sequential or processional form," though a major adventure (a quest) "gives literary form to romance." The quest entails a struggle between a hero and his enemy (in which one or both die), the disappearance of the hero, and his return, discovery, or recognition. This definition of romance does not fit the Greek romances. According to another influential book, an entity called "romance" appeared after the epic synthesis of myth and history broke down; it represents the allegiance to *mythos* which is nondidactic, and it aims at beauty, not truth: "The world of romance is the ideal world, in which poetic justice prevails and all the arts and adornments of language are used to embellish the narrative" (Robert Scholes and Robert Kellogg, *The Nature of Narrative* [New York, 1966], pp. 13–14). This definition does not fit the "world," and the rather plain style, of the Greek romances.

6. Cicero, *Letters to His Friends*, trans. W. Glyn Williams (Loeb Classical Library, 1927), 1:373.

7. Xenophon, *Cyropaedia*, trans. Walter Miller (Loeb Classical Library, 1914), 1. 1. 3.

8. Friedrich Nietzsche, *The Birth of Tragedy*, trans. Francis Golffing (New York: Doubleday-Anchor, 1956), pp. 109–10.

CHAPTER TWO

1. W. W. Tarn, *Hellenistic Civilization*, 3d ed. (London: Methuen, 1966), p. 278.

2. Callimachus may also have been Apollonius' mentor. In a hymn honoring Apollo and his native Cyrene, he seems to accuse Apollonius of envy as well as copiousness. (See Callim. 2. 95 ff.) For Apollonius' epigram, see the *Palatine Anthology* 9. 275.

3. R. C. Seaton, introduction to Apollonius Rhodius, *The Argonautica* (Loeb Classical Library, 1912), pp. x–xi.

4. These are the assessments of Marshall M. Gilles, *The Argonautika of Apollonius Rhodius, Book III* (Cambridge: At the University Press, 1928), p. xlii; Gilbert Lawall, "Apollonius' *Argonautika:* Jason as Anti-Hero," *Yale Classical Studies*, vol. 19 (1966); and E. V. Rieu, *Apollonius of Rhodes: The Voyage of the Argo* (Penguin Classics, 1959), p. 15.

5. Hesiod, *Theogony*, trans. H. G. Evelyn-White (Loeb Classical Library, 1936), ll. 956–62. See also Hesiod, "The Catalogues of Women," pars. 13, 37–42, 45.

6. *Fourth Pythian*, ll. 105 ff., in *The Odes of Pindar*, trans. C. M. Bowra (Penguin Books, 1969).

7. Apollonius of Rhodes *Argonautica* 1. 1–17. I use E. V. Rieu's lively if loose translation throughout (Penguin Classics, 1959). Hermann Fränkel's Oxford Classical Texts edition (1961) has been supplemented by his *Noten zu den Argonautika des Apollonius* (Munich, 1969). A new edition of *Le Argonautiche* is appearing from Bari, edited with commentary and Italian translation by Anthos Ardizzoni. The *Argonautica* was adapted into Latin by Valerius Flaccus (c. 70 A.D.). Greek manuscripts survive from the early eleventh century (e.g., Laurentian XXXI. 8, which Apollonius shares with Aeschylus and Sophocles and which contains a set of famous scholia). The *editio princeps* is dated 1496; the Aldine appeared in 1521.

8. In book 2 the Argonauts had rescued Argus from the Black Sea, in which he had been shipwrecked while returning from Colchis to reclaim the kingdom of his father, Phrixus, who had ridden the golden ram to Colchis to escape *his* father, who had been persuaded to sacrifice young Phrixus by Phrixus' stepmother. Phrixus had given the Golden Fleece to Aeëtes in exchange for one of Aeëtes' daughters, and later he died. Since the outlandish Colchians did not bury males, return of the Fleece would lay Phrixus' ghost. Apollonius alludes to this story several times but gives it no real importance in his poem.

9. Euripides' Medea spoke in a tormented debate of the soul that helped set the style. For example: "Alas, what shall I do? My heart fails me, my friends, at the sight of my children's shining eyes. I cannot do it: goodbye to my old plans. . . . But what is the matter with me? Am I to be mocked? Ah! Not this, my spirit, do not do this! Let them alone, wretched woman,

spare your children!" (*The Medea of Euripides*, trans. D. W. Lucas [London, 1949], ll. 1040 ff.). Aside from Vergil (*Aeneid* 4), Ovid also drew on Apollonius (especially for his Medea, *Metamorphoses* 3), as did apparently James Joyce in planning *Ulysses*. See Richard Ellmann, *Ulysses on the Liffey* (Oxford: Oxford University Press, 1972).

10. Zeus may be angry because Apsyrtus-Phaethon is murdered in an island sanctuary of Artemis, though the lady herself doesn't seem to mind; or maybe he is angry simply because he "heartily abhors the killing of a man." In any case, he decrees that the Argonauts will suffer until the crime is absolved by Circe, Medea's aunt; and she does absolve them, though their fortunes are not much improved by this. The name "Apsyrtus" suggests "swept away," which alludes to the older story in which his dismembered body was thrown overboard by the Argonauts, piece by piece, to delay his pursuing father, Aeëtes, who stopped to pick the pieces from the water. This in turn suggests that in older versions Apsyrtus had accompanied the Argonauts in their flight; but Apollonius makes him the pursuer and has Aeëtes stay at home.

CHAPTER FOUR

1. For references and discussion, see chapter 6, below.

2. See *Daphnis and Chloe*, ed. S. Gaselee (Loeb Classical Library, 1914), pp. 377 ff.

3. The first two are edited and translated by S. Gaselee, ibid., pp. 386 ff. The third is in *Papiri della Società Italiana* 13, no. 1305 (1953): 82 ff.

4. The first-century-A.D. "Harpyllades Fragment" also describes a tempest in such a way that it is assigned to a lost prose romance. See Bruno Lavagnini, *Eroticorum Fragmenta Papyrica* (Teubner, 1922).

5. Ibid. It is called the "Metiochu • and Parthenope Fragment."

6. Translated and discussed by E. R. Dodds, "A Fragment of a Greek Novel," in *Studies in Honour of Gilbert Norwood* (Toronto: University of Toronto Press, 1952), pp. 133 ff.

7. In a story of the late thirteenth century a man is propositioned by his older brother's wife and complains, "You are just as it were a mother to me, and your husband like a father." The wife then accuses the man of this "abominable thing," and he is executed, then revived to tell all. In another Egyptian tale, a prince exiled by his stepmother must leap to the window of the king's daughter in order to win her, does so, and is still denied by the king; whereupon the daughter, displaying the strength of "romantic" love, declares, "If he is taken away from me, I won't eat, I won't drink, I will die this very hour." The king relents, and the couple live happily ever after. Such stories prompt J. W. R. Barnes to argue that the Greek romances are Egyptian in origin and character ("Egypt and the Greek Romances,"

Mitteilungen aus der Papyrussammlung n.s. 5 [1956]: 29 ff.). He also asserts that the "first romance in the Greek language is a translation from Egyptian," referring to the early-second-century "Dream of Nectanebus" (ed. Lavagnini, pp. 37 ff.), in which a king hears Onuris (Gk. Ares) complain that he is excluded from his new temple because words aren't yet inscribed on it. The king dispatches Petesis to do this, but Petesis sees in the temple precincts the most beautiful girl he's ever encountered . . . and the fragment breaks off. But all these stories seem to be novellas of limited magnitude.

8. Quoted by Eric G. Turner, "Scribes and Scholars at Oxyrhynchus," *Akten des VIII Internationalen Kongresses für Papyrologie* (Vienna, 1955), in *Mitteilungen aus der Papyrussammlung der Österreichischen Nationalen Bibliothek,* n.s. 5 (1956): 143.

9. The standard edition is that edited by G. Dalmeyda, *Xénophon d'Ephèse: Les Ephésiaques* (Paris, 1926), but I quote from the Moses Hadas translation in *Three Greek Romances* (Indianapolis, 1964), pp. 71–126. The story's compactness, plus Suidas' mention of such a work in ten books (the surviving text is divided into five) prompted Rohde and Dalmeyda to believe that the *Ephesiaca* is an epitome. And Lavagnini (*Studi sul Romanzo Greco* [Messina, 1950], pp. 145–56) points out that the author was probably not an Ephesian or a special advocate of Ephesian Artemis, seeming to prefer Isis and/or Helios—unless the epitomizer converted an older Ephesian epic to Isis. Still, an image of Isis dwelt in the Temple of Artemis/Diana at Ephesus, and the goddesses had no quarrel.

10. Hadas (*Three Greek Romances*, pp. ix–x) says that it is: "If *An Ephesian Tale* is an absorbing tale of love and improbable adventure, it is also a tract to prove that Diana of the Ephesians (who was equated with Isis) cares for her loyal devotees . . . ; in part, at least, it aims to justify the cult of Artemis-Isis." R. Merkelbach (*Roman und Mysterium in der Antike* [Munich, 1962], pp. 91–92) argues that the original *Ephesiaca* was, like most other romances, an Isis romance, that Habrocomes is Eros, and that Anthia, representing Artemis-Isis, is Psyche. Dalmeyda observed (*Xénophon*, p. xviii) that the story might be read as a vengeance-of-Eros tale, with the two goddesses collaborating to preserve Anthia's virtue.

11. From a description of Heliodorus' romance made, in the ninth century, by Photius. See *The Library of Photius*, trans. H. J. Freese (New York, 1920), epitome 73.

12. Among recent critics, E. Courtney, in "Parody and Literary Allusion in Menippean Satire," *Philologus*, vol. 106 (1962), makes the strongest case for the *Satyricon*'s being "in frame and many of its episodes a parody of the novel" (p. 86).

13. Photius, *Bibliothèque*, ed. René Henry (Paris, 1960), vol. 2, no. 94.

Photius comments on Heliodorus and Achilles Tatius in epitomes 73 and 67. Suidas also treats a work called *Babyloniaca*, which he says contained thirty-nine books.

CHAPTER SIX

1. The standard edition is W. E. Blake's (Oxford Classical Texts, 1938), whose translation (*Chariton's Chaereas and Callirrhoë* [Ann Arbor, 1939]) I use throughout. Chariton's work did not see print until 1750, so it did not enjoy the vogue enjoyed by the other Greek romances (Heliodorus' *Aethiopica*, Longus' *Daphnis and Chloë*, etc.) in the Renaissance.

2. Diodorus Siculus *Library of History* 13. 75, 91, 112; Plutarch *Dionysius* 3.

3. One's "daimon" was one's spiritual ego or genius, and the link between one's inner being and one's god. It was apparently a person's daimon that was adopted by or married to the god through initiation into a cult; so one's god was also one's daimon. That the daimon was a person's "character" is suggested by Menander's use of the term in this sense.

4. Only Samuel L. Wolff, in *The Greek Romances in Elizabethan Prose Fiction* (New York, 1912) sufficiently emphasizes the importance of paradox as "a principle of the genre." He notes the frequency with which the romances speak of situations being "new and strange" (*kainos*), "against reason" (*paralogos*), "unthought of" (*adokētos*), etc., though for Wolff all this reflects "a base view of life" (p. 235) and "a puerile delight in 'hearing or telling new things'" (p. 167).

5. Cicero, *Paradoxa Stoicorum*, ed. H. Rackham (Loeb Classical Library, 1942).

6. R. Reitzenstein, in his *Hellenistische Wundererzählungen* (Leipzig, 1906), divided *Callirrhoë* into five "acts"; and Ben E. Perry (*The Ancient Romances* [Berkeley, 1967]), in emphasizing his view that romance is "fundamentally drama in substance and historiography in its outward form" (p. 140), analyzes the novel as a drama.

7. It should be pointed out that Callirrhoë is seen by the adoring crowd as an attendant of Artemis (1. 1. 12) and as being like both Aphrodite and Artemis (4. 7. 5). These paradoxical identifications nicely express the paradox of her character, but her true patroness is Aphrodite.

8. Johannes Helms, *Character Portrayal in the Romance of Chariton* (The Hague: Mouton, 1966), p. 13.

9. Frye's definition of the *mythos* of romance, in *Anatomy of Criticism: Four Essays* (Princeton, N.J.: Princeton University Press, 1957), as being also "a sequential or processional form" (p. 186) centering on a quest and an agon, has little to do with the Greek romances.

10. Norman Holland, *Dynamics of Literary Response* (Oxford, 1967).

11. I gather remarks from the *Rhetoric*, especially 1371a31–1371b12.

12. Letter no. 66, written in the late second century.

13. Perry, *The Ancient Romances*, pp. 44–45.

14. Sophie Trenkner, *The Greek Novella in the Classical Period* (Cambridge: At the University Press, 1958), esp. pp. xiii–xv, 57–61, 77, 112 ff., 179–86. She conjectures that lost Attic novellas, derived from legends and realistic Dorian fables, converted *logoi* of purported facts into *plasmata* (fictions) that became the lost "Milesian Tales" of Aristides. Popular stories of all sorts, "historical, marvelous and realistic," first got into epics: Euripides exploited the idealistic sort, and from such dramas as his derive the Greek novel.

15. R. Merkelbach, *Roman und Mysterium in der Antike* (Munich, 1962), following but modifying K. Kerényi, *Die griechisch-orientalische Romanliteratur in religionsgeschichtlicher Beleuchtung* (Tübingen, 1927). Cf. also Remy Petri, *Über den Roman des Chariton* (Meissenheim am Glan, 1963).

16. Bruno Lavagnini, *Le Origini del Romanzo Greco* (Pisa, 1921) and *Studi sul Romanzo Greco* (Messina, 1950); Martin Braun, *History and Romance in Graeco-Oriental Literature* (Oxford: Basil Blackwell, 1938). See J. Ludvíkovsky, *Řecký Roman Dobrodružny* (Prague, 1925), and R. M. Rattenbury, *New Chapters in the History of Greek Literature*, 3d ser., ed. J. A. Powell (Oxford, 1933), for somewhat different views of the development of romance from historiography. Pierre Grimal, in his introduction to *Romans Grecs et Latins* (Paris, 1958), adds the "spirit of Platonism" to epic, tragedy, history, comedy, adventure, and folktales as a source of romance to explain the predominance of Love in the stories. Elizabeth Haight, in *Essays on Ancient Fiction* (1936), *Essays on the Greek Romances* (1943), and *More Essays on the Greek Romances* (1945), takes an equally eclectic view.

17. See especially those in Seneca the Elder *Contraversiae* 1. 2, 4, 6. Henri Bornecque, ed., *Sénèque le Rhéteur: Contraverses et Suasoires*, 2d ed. (Paris, 1932). Cicero *De Inventione* 1. 27 and *Auctor ad Herennium* 1. 12–13 give other hints about the relation between rhetoric and romance. See also S. F. Bonner, *Roman Declamation in the Late Republic* (Liverpool, 1949), and M. L. Clarke, *Rhetoric at Rome* (London, 1953).

CHAPTER EIGHT

1. Ben E. Perry (*The Ancient Romances* [Berkeley: University of California Press, 1967], pp. 111–12) remarks that these are devices of comedy and observes that Achilles Tatius is unique among the writers of Greek prose romances in using them.

2. Suidas (tenth century) says that Achilles Tatius was a native Alexandrian and became a bishop. The wide dispersal of papyri suggests the early popularity of *Clitophon*, and its Byzantine popularity is suggested by the fact that a ninth-century hagiographer gave the parents of Saint Galaction the names Clitophon and Leucippe. But the twenty-three sur-

viving manuscripts (dating from the ninth through the seventeenth centuries) are mostly of Western, not Eastern, provenance. *Clitophon* was first printed in a Latin version (1544), with new editions in 1551 and 1554. It was not printed in Greek until 1601. Italian (1547, 1551), French (1573, 1575, 1586, 1635), English (1597, 1638), and German (1644) translations antedate the one I use, by Stephen Gaselee (Loeb Classical Library, 1917). The modern critical text is by E. Volborg, *Studia Graeca et Latina Gothoburgensia*, vol. 1 (Stockholm, 1955), with a commentary in vol. 15 (1962) of the same series. Among modern critics, Perry sees in it a "sickening of Eros" (*Ancient Romances*, p. 106); and though he likens it to Joseph Andrews (pp. 111–17), he believes that it belongs to the "idealistic" strain in romance. D. B. Durham argued that *Clitophon* is a parody of romance (especially of Heliodorus' *Aethiopica*), pointing out that its protagonists are *not* chaste, that rhetoric, gore, chastity tests, etc., are all ludicrously exaggerated ("Parody in Achilles Tatius," *Classical Philology* 33 [1938]: 1–19). This interpretation has not been accepted, especially since the discovery of a second-century papyrus showing that *Clitophon* antedates the *Aethiopica*. But verbal relationships between Achilles and Heliodorus are so close, and *Clitophon* seems so "realistic," that Pierre Grimal (*Romans Grecs et Latins* [Paris, 1958], pp. 871 ff.) suggests that the early fragment represents a lost version of the story which Achilles Tatius adapted in the third century under the influence of Heliodorus.

3. When Clitophon hears the story of Apollo and Daphne, he wants to *imitate* the god (1. 4), but this only measures the distance between these characters and those in the romances who look and behave like gods.

4. *Clitophon* was famous for its euphuistic style, including "learned digressions." The style is "redolent of the rhetorician," says Gaselee justly (p. vii), but it is archly so. The loves of trees and rivers (1. 7), kisses (a mingling of souls, 2. 8), swords separating lovers (2. 29), flora, fauna, etc., etc.—almost everything becomes a "topic" for the narrator, making his style that of a frantic young pedant, a comic character.

5. See Lane Cooper, *An Aristotelian Theory of Comedy* (Oxford, 1922), pp. 224–26. It is hardly likely that the *Tractatus* is a crude version of Aristotle's famous "lost book on comedy." See G. M. A. Grube, *The Greek and Roman Critics* (London, 1965), pp. 141–42, 144–49.

6. See W. Beare, *The Roman Stage*, 3d ed. (London, 1964), pp. 314–19.

7. Plutarch *Moralia* 711f–712d, 853a.

8. I use Paul Turner's translation, *Daphnis and Chloë* (Penguin Classics, 1956), which contains hitherto suppressed depictions of erotic activity. The manuscript tradition is rich but complicated, a "great lacuna" in the text not being filled until the nineteenth century. It was first printed in Greek in 1598, but Amyot's famous French version had already appeared in 1559 and Angell Daye's English one in 1587. Daye's characterization of

what he calls "The Shepheards Holidaie" conveys a sixteenth-century explanation of its great vogue: it is a work "excellently describing the weight of affection, the simplicity of love, the purport of honest meaning, the resolution of men, and disposition of Fate, finished in a Pastoral and interlaced with praises of an almost peerless princess."

9. Though Longus of course owed much to bucolic poetry as well as to prose romance, he also alludes frequently to Homer, Sappho, Ovid, Vergil, Menander, and others.

10. Perry (*Ancient Romances*, pp. 110–11) justly observes that the *Lesbian Pastorals* is itself an *ekphrasis*. But Achilles Tatius (5. 4) expresses a conception of the power of paintings that perhaps underlies Longus' preface: "Those [exegetes] who profess to interpret signs," says Clitophon, "bid us pay attention to the stories of pictures, if such happen to meet our eye as we set forth on our business, and to conclude that what is likely to happen to us will be of the same character as the event of the painted story." Longus makes his invented painting prophesy his invented story. The painting is also a kind of *logos*. Before a performance of his play, the poet could mount a platform and disclaim its *logos*—its subject or plot. Aristophanes (*Wasps* 54 and *Peace* 50) and Aristotle use the term in this way.

11. The Orphic dimensions of *Daphnis and Chloë* are explored in a remarkable article by H. H. O. Chalk, "Eros and the *Lesbian Pastorals*," *Journal of Hellenic Studies* 80 (1960): 32–51. Though he rightly hesitates to claim that *Daphnis* is an Orphic document, his suggestion that it is has not found much favor among critics. My own debt to his article is very heavy, and I rely on it throughout. But I cannot agree, for example, that Daphnis and Chloë "are the Year-God, and their experiences are his annual ravishing, death or imprisonment, and rebirth" (p. 38), or that several episodes represent cult initiations, or that Eros becomes Dionysus in the end, or that the poem is based on the well-known syncretic principle whereby everything becomes a symbol of everything else.

12. The nature of "Orphism" is a matter of dispute. Compare, for example, Chalk with W. K. C. Guthrie, *The Greeks and Their Gods* (London, 1950) and *Orpheus and Greek Religion*, rev. ed. (New York, 1967). Its doctrines must be reconstructed from the famous Orphic hymns, fragmentary *logoi*, and from references in Plato, Euripides, and others. Still, Guthrie can say that the Orphics "worked out an elaborate and consistent scheme of purgatory, paradise and apotheosis" (p. 312).

13. William Adlington's preface to his English translation (1566) expresses the Renaissance (and earlier and later) view: though it seems "a mere jest and fable," the *Metamorphoses* is "a figure of man's life . . . a pattern to regiment [men's] minds from brutal and beastly custom," showing how "under the wrap of this transformation is taxed the life of mortal man, when as we suffer our minds so to be drowned in sensual lusts of the flesh

and the beastly pleasures thereof . . . that we lose wholly the use of reason and virtue," and how meditation and prayer can restore us "to the right figure of ourselves" (Loeb Library *Apuleius*, ed. Samuel Gaselee, pp. xvi–xvii). Elizabeth Haight is more succinct: it is "a sort of Pilgrim's Progress of the Ass-man . . . in search for the spiritual meaning of life" (*Essays on the Greek Romances* [New York, 1943], p. 192). Almost all critics agree that it is a religious autobiography with comic elements, but R. Merkelbach (*Roman und Mysterium in der Antike* [Munich, 1962]) asserts that Lucius is Psyche, that Isis is Eros (or Venus), that Lucius-as-ass represents life without Isis, and that all the story's episodes allegorize salvation by Isis (e.g., Charity freed by her fiancé is Soul freed by Isis-Eros-Venus).

14. For Perry (*Ancient Romances*, chap. 7) it is basically a romance of the nonidealistic sort composed rather ineptly of preexistent tales onto which Apuleius "tacked" the eleventh book to make it all seem worthy of a literary man. For P. G. Walsh (*The Roman Novel* [Cambridge, 1970]) it is a "romance rather than a novel" because "at no point apparently does it come to grips with the author's real world" (p. 142). Apuleius, he says, tried "to reunite the two hitherto disparate streams of Greek fiction into a new pattern of romance, in which he simultaneously seeks to achieve the ironical comedy of a Lucian and the edification of a Chariton" (p. 176). The book "lacks the homogeneity of a closely articulated work of art" (p. 143), being composed of a "comic exterior" masking "an artful but serious evangelism" (p. 189), its moral being "that full knowledge of reality is gained not by magic but by contemplation of divinity in the other, more real world, and that true happiness is to be sought not in sensuality but in the gratuitous love of the godhead" (p. 142).

15. M. D. Macleod (in *Lucius, or The Ass*, Loeb Library *Lucian*, vol. 3, [1967], pp. 47 ff.) decides that the surviving *Ass* is an anonymous epitome of a lost longer work by Lucian of Samosata (117–80 A.D.) and that Apuleius used Lucian's original. Others say that the *Ass* is Lucian's work itself (or his own epitome of it) or that one Lucian of Patras wrote either the original or the epitome of Lucian. Macleod's is the dominant view (see Perry, *Ancient Romances*, pp. 211–27). P. G. Walsh (*The Roman Novel*, pp. 144 ff.) makes a nice assessment of the relationships between Apuleius and "Lucian."

16. Sallie S. Rust, "The Composition of Apuleius' *Metamorphoses*" (unpublished Master's thesis, University of Chicago, 1919), makes those counts, not I.

17. Augustine *City of God* 18. 18.

18. See *The Apologia and Florida of Apuleius*, trans. H. E. Butler (Oxford, 1909), p. 25.

19. Saint Augustine warns (Epistles 136 and 138) against those who

claim that Apuleius was a wonder-worker more powerful than Christ. For a fascinating comparison of the rhetor and the magus, see Peter Brown, *Religion and Society in the Age of St. Augustine* (London, 1972).

20. For translations I use Jack Lindsay, *The Golden Ass* (Indiana University Press, 1962) and Robert Graves, *The Golden Ass of Apuleius* (Pocket Books, 1954). The reader is warned to treat the Graves translation, and the introduction to it, with caution, despite their vigor and charm. The text is edited by D. S. Robertson, *Les Métamorphoses* (Paris, 1940). The forty manuscripts and the date of the *editio princeps* (1464) testify to its perennial popularity. See Elizabeth Haight, *Apuleius and His Influence* (New York, 1927) and P. G. Walsh, *The Roman Novel*, chap. 8.

21. The exact character of the "Milesian Tales" is disputable, though they were certainly thought to be obscene. Antonio Mazzarino (*La Milesia e Apuleio* [Turin, 1950]) claims that the genre could include even a "bella fabula" like that of Cupid and Psyche and proposes a subgenre—the "Milesia Punica," or Milesian tales of religious faith—to explain the paradoxical mixture of seriousness and fun in the *Metamorphoses*. But the only real evidence for the existence of such a subgenre is the *Metamorphoses* itself.

22. Gustave Lefebvre, *Romans et Contes Egyptiens de l'Epoque Pharaonique* (Paris, 1949), p. ix.

23. Miriam Lichtheim, *Ancient Egyptian Literature* (Berkeley, 1973), 1:4.

24. For Perry (*Ancient Romances*, chap. 7), Apuleius—though he is often desultory and negligent—is the first author to combine prose tales drawn from history, philosophy, elegy, idyll, etc., and to suffuse comic novellas with humane sentiment.

25. See esp. *Met.* 7. 2–3 and 8. 24.

CHAPTER TEN

1. *Joseph et Aséneth*, edited and translated into French by Marc Philonenko, *Studia Post-Biblica*, vol. 40 (Leiden, 1968). This is the shorter version.

2. The *Aethiopica* never lost its popularity. Twenty-two manuscripts survive (two from the eleventh century, twelve from the fifteenth and sixteenth). The Greek text was printed in 1534, Amyot's French translation in 1547, a Latin one in 1552; Underdowne's English one (completed in 1587—followed by Nahum Tate's in 1686) much influenced Sidney's *Arcadia*. For Rabelais, see *Pantagruel* 4. 63. Other allusions or imitations are in Guarini's *Pastor Fido* 5, Tasso's *Gerusalemme Liberata* 12, Cervantes' *Persiles and Sigismunda*, *Twelfth Night* 5. 1, and Montaigne's *The Affection of Fathers to Their Children*. Racine began a play based on it. The editors of the standard edition, R. M. Rattenbury and T. W. Lumb (*Héliodore: Les Ethiopiques*, 3 vols. [Paris, 1935], 1:xiv) date it in the 230s

A.D. Pierre Grimal (*Romans Grecs et Latins* [Paris, 1958], pp. 517 ff.) would put it in the reign of Aurelian (270–75), when the sun cult reached its zenith; and E. Feuillâtre (*Etudes sur les Ethiopiques d'Hélidore* [Paris, 1966], pp. 145–47) would put it in the earlier second century.

3. I use W. R. M. Lamb's translation, *Heliodorus: Ethiopian Story* (Everyman Library, 1961).

4. As in *Iliad* 3. 277. Apollo was not clearly associated with Helios until the fifth century.

5. Macrobius *Saturnalia* 1. 17 ff.

6. Ethiopia was for the earlier Greeks a semilegendary land on the southern rim of the world (washed by the Ocean Stream), occupying all of Africa south of Egypt and Libya. The exact dwelling of the sun might be on the lower borders of the Red Sea and Indian Ocean. In the *Odyssey* Homer calls its black inhabitants "the most remote of men," and in the *Iliad* Zeus dines with the "blameless Ethiopians." Being exotic, the Ethiopians were thought to be pure, especially in their religion, which was thought to be heliocentric. Diodorus Siculus (*History* 3. 1) says they were the first people to practice religion, making them even more ancient (and perhaps wiser) than the inhabitants of Mother Egypt. See Donald Levine, *Greater Ethiopia* (Chicago, 1974), chap. 1.

7. Franz Cumont (*The Oriental Religions in Roman Paganism*, trans. Grant Showerman, 1911 [Dover Reprint, 1956], pp. 127, 134) summed up the development of the sun cult:

> When it transformed the ideas on the destiny of man, astrology also modified those relating to the nature of divinity.... Solar panthe-ism, which grew up among the Syrians of the Hellenistic period as a result of the influence of Chaldean astrology, imposed itself on the whole Roman world under the empire.... The last formula reached by the religion of pagan Semites and in consequence by that of the Romans, was a divinity unique, almighty, eternal, universal and ineffable, that revealed itself throughout nature, but whose most splendid and most energetic manifestation was the Sun.

8. In my view, this makes it extremely unlikely that the aim of Heliodorus' novel is "to illustrate in an edifying fiction the veracity of the oracle, the prestige of Delphi as a religious or intellectual center, the civilizing mission of Apollo's city" (F. Feuillâtre, *Etudes sur les Ethiopiques*, p. 147).

9. Andromeda boasted that she was more beautiful than the Nereids, who complained to Poseidon, who flooded Ethiopia and sent a monster, to whom Andromeda was offered, naked, on a rock. But Perseus, passing by with Medusa's head, saved her; and their son, Perses, became the progenitor of the Persians.

10. Heliodorus also uses the odd neo-Pythagorean name for the gods,

hoi kreittones. For a view of Heliodorus' "theology," see Franz Altheim, *Helios und Heliodor von Emesa* (Amsterdam, 1942).

11. But Jacob Burckhardt long ago (1852) remarked that "when epic and drama lost their popular and living force, romance became the appropriate substitute form" (*The Age of Constantine the Great,* trans. Moses Hadas [Anchor Books, 1956], p. 225).

12. I use the translation by J. S. Phillimore, *Philostratus: In Honour of Apollonius of Tyana* (Oxford, 1912).

13. Burckhardt observed (*Age of Constantine the Great,* chap. 6) that biography was a most important genre for "neo-Platonists," especially in the third and fourth centuries, because the human soul was an emanation of the Absolute One, though many types of spiritual beings—gods, angels, daimons, etc.—stood between the One and individual souls.

14. For example, an apocryphal Greek Passion gospel, told by Joseph of Arimathea, is focused on Saint Dismas (the good thief), whose crime, we are told, was stealing the Law of Moses from the tabernacle and whose reward is Christ's saying that he would that day sup in paradise. Dismas appears with Jesus to Joseph and John after the Resurrection to describe the passing of the guardian cherubim into glory, where he *alone* will live until the Last Judgment. The writer invents his story (using canonical and apocryphal materials) to make two doctrinal points: (1) it was not Jesus who "stole the law"—it was Dismas, who robbed the rich to benefit the poor; (2) contrary to some opinion, the saints will enter paradise only after the Second Coming. See M. R. James, *The Apocryphal New Testament* (Oxford 1924), pp. 161–65.

15. I use the translation of R. McL. Wilson in Edgar Hennecke, ed., *New Testament Apocrypha,* 2 vols. (Philadelphia, 1965), 2:354.

16. "The Acts of Xanthippe and Polyxena" (c. 250 A.D.) shows through the adventures of two sisters how chastity leads to salvation. It adds shipwreck, the conversion of a husband, and a friendly lioness to the "romance" conventions of escapes from rapists and love for Paul (Polyxena stays with Paul to her death, "in her fear of temptations"). Perhaps such episodes were added to support the conclusion: "Seest thou by how many devices God saves many?" In *The Ante-Nicene Fathers,* edited by Alexander Roberts and James Donaldson (New York, 1912), vol. 9.

17. The very complicated textual history of the Clementine writings is epitomized by J. Irmscher in *New Testament Apocrypha,* pp. 532–35. English translations by Thomas Smith of the complete *Homilies* and *Recognitions* may be found in Roberts and Donaldson, *The Ante-Nicene Fathers,* vol. 8.

18. Verbal and perhaps material likenesses with the *Ephesiaca* have prompted speculation that Xenophon of Ephesus wrote the Greek *Apol-*

lonius of Tyre. In the Latin versions, only the Christian god of charity and chastity is evident, and some say that several incidents seem designed to celebrate forgiveness and almsgiving. I follow the translation of Paul Turner, *Apollonius of Tyre* (London, 1956), whose texts are ninth- and fourteenth-century Latin versions of the version called *Historia Apollonii Regis Tyri*.

19. I use the translation by Elizabeth H. Haight of Pseudo-Callisthenes, *The Life of Alexander of Macedon* (New York, 1955). This is the alpha version (as edited by W. Kroll, *Historia Alexandri Magni* [Berlin, 1926]), thought to be the oldest of five recensions, dating from about 300 A.D. It was probably compiled from a fanciful history of Alexander, from a first-century-B.C. collection of imaginary letters by and to Alexander, a set of Alexander-Aristotle-Olympias epistles about India, and a political account of Alexander's last days, written soon after his death in 323. (The other recensions date from two to four centuries after the alpha version.) Reinhold Merkelbach reconstructs this complicated textual history in "Die Quellen des griechischen Alexanderromans," *Zetamata*, vol. 9 (Munich, 1954). For an account of the enormous medieval Alexander literature, see George Cary, *The Medieval Alexander* (Cambridge, 1956).

Index

Index

idea as, 130–45; marvel as, 145–66; as romance, 118–30

Comedy, New. *See* New Comedy

Comedy, Old. *See* Old Comedy

Confession and Prayer of Aseneth, The, 184–86; compared with *Daphnis and Chloë,* 185–86

Conventions. *See* Romance, conventions of

Cosmopolis, 12

Cults, 68–70

Cyropaedia (Xenophon), 7–9

Cyrene, 14

Daimon, 74, 77, 226

Daphnis and Chloë (Longus), 3, 117–18, 130–45, 167, 168–69, 228–29; compared with *The Confession and Prayer of Aseneth,* 185–86; compared with *Metamorphoses* and *Clitophon and Leucippe,* 117–18, 170–82

Debate of the soul, 121–22

Delphian Apollo, cult of, 192

Diaskeuē, 59

Dionysius the Elder, 75–76

Domna, Julia, empress, 203

Dramatikon, 59

Dream, prophetic, 120–21

Duplication, principle of, 58

Egyptian tales, 152, 154–55

Eikonos graphē, 130–31

Ekphrasis, 130, 131

Ekstasis, 132

Emesa, 187

Emotive powers, of *Argonautica,* 16–19, 24–29, 40

Enthusiasm, Dionysian, 132

Ephesiaca, (Xenophon of Ephesus), 3, 44–58, 66–74, 225–26; compared with *Argonautica,* 55

Epic Cycle, 14

Eros, in *Daphnis and Chloë,* 133–39

Erotas hypokrinomenon, 59

Erotic sufferings. See *Erōtika pathēmata*

Erōtika pathēmata, 4–10, 26, 157; in *Argonautica,* 20

Ethiopia, 188, 232

Euripides, 24; *Medea,* 14–15, 223–24

Exegesis, narrative, 131

Exemplum, 185

Explanation, definition of term, 32

Fantasy, 73–74

Faustinianus, father of Saint Clement, 211–12

Feminine individualism, 127

Founders' Company of London, 9

Fourth Pythian (Pindar), 14–15

Gallus, Cornelius, 4–5, 6

Genres, literary, 167–68; development of, 100–109

Gods, likeness of characters to, 46–47

Golden Ass. See *Metamorphoses* (Apuleius)

Golden Fleece. See *Argonautica* (Apollonius)

Greek romances, 3–4. See also *Erōtika pathēmata*

Hair, in *Metamorphoses,* 149–50

Heliodorus: narrative method, 195–96; *Aethiopica,* 3, 59, 186, 188–202, 231–33

Helios, cult of, 186–87, 188, 200

Hellenistic era, 11–12

Historia erōtos, 130–31

Homer, 94–95

Homilies, Clementine, 208–9

Homosexual: friend, role of, 122; temptation, 48–49

Iamblichus, *Babyloniaca,* 3, 58–63

Idea as comedy, 130–45

Inferring, 143–44

In Honour of Apollonius of Tyana (Philostratus), 203–4; compared with *Aethiopica,* 203–4

In medias res, 188